Gu Shutang Academic Fund of Economics

For further volumes:
http://www.springer.com/series/10787

Yunbo Zhou • Yan Qin

Empirical Analysis on Income Inequality of Chinese Residents

Translated by Dr. Cui'e Hu

Springer

Yunbo Zhou
Nankai University
Tibet University
China, People's Republic

Yan Qin
New York University
USA

ISSN 2195-0059 ISSN 2195-0067 (electronic)
ISBN 978-3-642-24951-8 ISBN 978-3-642-24952-5 (eBook)
DOI 10.1007/978-3-642-24952-5
Springer Heidelberg New York Dordrecht London

Library of Congress Control Number: 2012932062

Printed on acid-free paper

Springer is part of Springer Science+Business Media (www.springer.com)

Preface

Since the system reform and open-door policy, the income inequality of Chinese residents has continuously grown, and as a result income distribution has remained one of the most heated issues in both the academic community and government departments concerned. Small wonder that it has also become an important and challenging topic in the field of economic studies. I myself have been in this field for a long time, and fortunately made some contribution, if I may say so. Dr. Zhou Yunbo, when he was a PhD candidate under my supervision, assisted me greatly with my research. He graduated as an associate professor of Economics in Nankai University. His book *Empirical Analysis of Income Inequality among Chinese Residents*, coauthored by Qin Yan and Ruhul Salim, is built on his research report of the Youth Project of National Social Sciences Foundation, which he took charge of. As his supervisor, I am glad to provide the preface for this book in order to congratulate the three scholars and warmly recommend it to readers as well.

This book provides a detailed measurement and precise analysis of income inequality among China's urban, rural, and total residents, including their status quo, drivers, and dynamics, using large sets of the most upgraded statistical data and household survey data. As a monograph specialized in Chinese income inequality, the book investigates the requisite properties of indices for measuring income inequality, some new indices, new methods for estimating the Gini Coefficient, and methods of judging polarization. One of the values of the study is that, after giving a detailed introduction of several income inequality decomposition methods, it applies them to analyze the household survey data of Shandong Province and Tianjin, and to examine the main factors that impact the income inequality of urban and rural residents. I am glad to say the book is a novel study with new conclusions and using new data. Furthermore, the new methods of analyzing income inequality introduced here may serve as a valuable reference work for other scholars in this field.

In regard to theory, the book once again reinforces some significant claims in my previous studies on income inequality. In the late 1980s, I proposed the inverted-U hypothesis on the relation between economic growth and income inequality under public ownership economy (Chen Zongsheng 1991). My premise of public ownership is quite at odds with the inverted-U hypothesis under private ownership economy put forward by Kutznets and was therefore named Chen's Inverted Theory by my peers at home and abroad. In the follow-up research, by looking into the impact of system reform on income inequality, I developed the echelon inverted-U curve and put it into empirical tests using data on Chinese urban and rural income inequality (Chen Zongsheng 1994; Chen Zongsheng and Zhou Yunbo 2001c, 2002). This monograph, focusing on new economic data from recent years, again proves that at present, the income inequality of Chinese urban, rural, and total residents is steadily increasing, as demonstrated in the first half of the inverted-U curve of the public ownership economy.

In other aspects, the book also continues and improves my previous studies. To cite but one example, I made systematic measurements of the impact of the abnormal and illegal rent-seeking income on Chinese residents' income inequality, such as tax dodging and avoidance on the part of self-employed and private business, corruption income of the Party and government officials, personal income transferred from group spending, and smuggling and fraud (Chen Zongsheng 1991). Due to scarce data and methods, presenting an exact description of how much the abnormal and illegal rent-seeking income has influenced Chinese residents' income inequality poses a great challenge. What I did in the 1980s was a tentative quantitative measurement and based on much guess and assumption, including estimating the size of various abnormal incomes, and their impact on residents' income inequality. In the beginning of the new century, in a book I coauthored with Dr. Zhou Yunbo, we measured in great detail various abnormal and illegal rent-seeking incomes from 1988 to 1999, and their impact on the income inequality of urban, rural, and total residents. Now, the three scholars continue my study by measuring their impact on residents' income inequality since the new century. Their study proves that, by and large, the impact of rent-seeking incomes on income inequality is being weakened. This is in accordance with the trend of Chinese economic system reform.

In certain regards, the book is a good supplement to previous studies on income distribution. For one, with respect to the theoretical analysis of the inverted-U hypothesis, many studies borrowed the dual-economic theory to construct the urban–rural two-sector model and prove this hypothesis with regard to urbanization. However, given the urban–rural gap, the impact of population transfer from rural areas to urban areas on income inequality is an inverted-U trajectory of increasing followed by decreasing, an opinion held by quite a few scholars including me (Anand 1983; Chen Zongsheng 1991, 1999). And for this purpose I even offered detailed mathematical proof, which of course needs improvement. I am glad to see that the three scholars of the book do so by giving stricter mathematical proof and simulation tests using projected data. Take another example. Concerning the factors behind the birth and development of rent-seeking income in the transitional economy, Dr. Zhou and I once assumed that the fundamental factor was the institutional defects (Chen Zongsheng and Zhou Yunbo 2000, 2002), but this book offers more explanations, suggesting that institutional defects are the objective factor and the increasing motive for speculation of economic individuals because of the imbalance and instability in the transitional economy is the subjective factor. They believe the boom of contemporary rent-seeking activities is a result of many factors combined. Perhaps, their explanations sound more complete.

Of course there are some conclusions I do not quite agree with. For one, the authors, after examining the impact of urbanization, conclude that income inequality of the total residents is on the decline. I feel uneasy about the exactness and completeness of the data they used, though the conclusion supports my inverted-U hypothesis of public economy. Even if the data are acceptable, whether the dynamics are sustainable or not still remains questionable. Chinese economic growth as a whole is at the stage of mid-level income and below, a stage which sees constantly widening income inequality as proved across countries. Moreover, conclusive empirical data show that the urban and rural income inequality throughout the country is steadily growing. So we have every reason to believe that the emergence of the inverted-U phenomenon is local and temporary. No doubt, whether they are right or not needs to be tested by the practice of Chinese economic reform and development.

After reading the book, I am glad to find that the three authors have devoted much time and energy to the study and filled in some gaps in this field. Though there remains space for improvement and further tests, the book promotes a rigorous scholarly attitude and persistence in economic studies. I highly recommend it to readers, as it is a scholarly reading of high quality about Chinese income inequality.

Nankai University, Zhou Yunbo
Tianjin, China

Acknowledgments

This book is an improvement to the research report in National Social Sciences Foundation (NSSF) Project (Project No. 05CJL005) headed by Professor Zhou Yunbo and also part of the NSSF Important Project (Project No. 07 and ZD045) led by Professor Chen Zongsheng. Some of the contents and viewpoints in the book were either published in domestic and international journals, or listed and read at international conferences at which a few of them had been awarded as "best article". In fact, one of the authors once coauthored a book with Professor Chen Zongsheng in 2002 entitled *More Remarks on Income Distribution during China's Reform and Development*, from which this book may be deemed as the next step in that it retains the old contents and methods, but also makes new contribution.

At the time of publication, we would like to show our special thanks to Professor Chen Zongsheng, who, as a vice secretary general in Tianjin People's government as well as a Professor and Doctoral supervisor in the Economic Studies Institute of Nankai University, has contributed valuable opinions and advice in the formulation of the final statements as well as the selection of analytical perspective of the book. His scrupulous attitude toward scholarship, his way of doing research that combines theory with practice, and his notion of academic freedom and tolerance have set up a model for our young scholars. It is true that without his instruction, the book would not have been finished at present level within such short time.

Moreover, Professor Gu Shutang, the venerable economist of old generation, was deeply concerned with this book. Generous advice was also given by such well-known professors in the Economic Studies Institute of Nankai University like Zhou Liquan, Liu Xin, Xie Siquan, Zhou Bing, Zhong Maochao, He Jingtong, Luo Rundong, and Liu Gang, as well as Prof. Steven Lim, Prof. Frank Scrimgeour, and Dr. Michael Cameron from the Economic Department of Waikato University in New Zealand. My sincere thanks go to Prof. Zhang Xiaodong in International Economic Institute and Prof. Zhao Hongmei in Economics Institute of Nankai University, as well as Prof. Mark Holmes in Waikato University in New Zealand for their valuable advice on the selection and use of empirical models of the book. Prof. Fan Hongkang and Wang Zhaojun in Statistics Department of Nankai

University have been very helpful with the deduction of math models. Some postgraduates under Zhou Yunbo's supervision wrote drafts for parts of the book; they are Wei Zhanzhong, Wei Liangliang, and Gao Yan. Laborious compilation was done by Gao Yuwei, Wu Peng, Shen Yangyang, and Fu Yeting. For their devotion and labor, I could not thank more. Meanwhile, my heartfelt thanks also go to my family who has given me lots of encouragement and support, both mentally and physically. Finally, I would like to express my thanks to Chai Ning from Springer, without whose efficient work this book would not have come out so soon.

Zhou Yunbo

Contents

Chapter 1
Introduction

As the first chapter, this chapter introduces the background of the study and offers a literature review both at home and abroad, and then it gives a bird's-eye view of the methods and structure of the book.

1.1 Background and Literature Review

1.1.1 Background of the Study

Since the system reform and opening door, China's economy has seen a rapid and steady growth for almost 30 years thanks to the continuing economic reform, increased degree of marketization, and improved productivity. In 1978, the early stage of the system reform, China's per capita GDP was only 381 yuan, but in 2009 it jumped by more than 14.6 times at comparable prices to 29,678 yuan. Rapid economic growth results in an improvement of urban and rural income as well as living standard. In 1978, the per capita disposable income of urban resident in China was 343.4 yuan, and the per capita net income of rural resident was 133.6 yuan, but in 2009 they rose to 17,175 yuan and 5,153 yuan respectively, 9 times and 8.6 times that in 1978 at comparable prices. Meanwhile, Chinese residents' living standard has been profoundly improved. All these achievements since the system reform prove the choice for market-oriented economic system correct and required.

With the transformation from plan economy to market economy, the income distribution system, as a vital part of economic system reform, has also undergone great change. The single and egalitarian mode of distribution based on work in plan economy gave way to incentive and competitive mechanism under market economy. After around 30 years of practice of reform, a new income distribution system has come into being, with distribution based on work as the major body, and other distribution modes based on contribution, factors, and techniques as the supplement. The new income distribution system, however, has given rise to continuous

Y. Zhou and Y. Qin, *Empirical Analysis on Income Inequality of Chinese Residents*,
Gu Shutang Acad Fund Econ, DOI 10.1007/978-3-642-24952-5_1,

enlargement of income inequality in urban and rural areas. In 1978, the Gini coefficient of urban income inequality was only 0.16, the Gini coefficient of rural income inequality was about 0.22, and the Gini coefficient of total income inequality (including the urban–rural gap) was 0.3 or so (Zhao and Griffin 1994). In 2008, they rose to 0.3801, 0.42616, and 0.46809.[1] It is internationally acknowledged that the Gini coefficient below 0.2 suggests absolute equality, the Gini coefficient between 0.2 and 0.3 suggests relative equality, that between 0.3 and 0.4 suggests proper inequality, that between 0.4 and 0.5 suggests too large inequality, and the Gini coefficient above 0.5 indicates polarization. Accordingly, income inequality of China's urban resident in 2006 approximated too large, rural income inequality reached too large, and the total income inequality was approaching polarization. True as it is that this international standard has certain limit and may not reflect China's scenario, the fact of continuous enlargement of income inequality of residents since the system reform is out of question and has attracted much attention from both government and academia.

Proper income inequality serves as incentive for economic bodies and promotes economic efficiency. However, too large inequality will stir social unrest and therefore affect economic growth. In this regard, it is worth learning of the experience of economic development of Latin American countries since World War. From 1950-1980, economic growth rates of these countries are 5.3% on average and the total GDP rose almost threefold and the per capita GDP doubled, despite the record growth of population. Nevertheless, governments in these counties, strongly convinced of the economic development theory popular of the moment, make point of economic growth to the most important factor of concerted development of society and economy. They believed that economic growth is the first thing in the morning, and with rapid economic growth, all social problems including unemployment and poverty will be readily solved, a wrong belief which led to continuingly widened gap between the rich and the poor. Even after 1973 of the petroleum crisis, the governments did not change course, but adhered to the pursuit of economic growth, and as a result, these countries all found themselves on the road of debt growth.

[1] For the Gini coefficient of urban and rural income from 1978 to 1999, see Chen Zongsheng and Zhou Yunbo (2002). That from 2000 to 2008 is based on our calculation from data in *China Yearbook of Statistics* after proper adjustment. The reason for adjustment is if the Gini should be calculated by the seven-grouping data provided in *China Yearbook of Statistics*, it would be too low relative to other measurements in representative regions. On inquiry from experts in the State Bureau of Statistics, we learn that the various data from over the country go to the Bureau has been flattened, and regional inequality has been smoothed. To see the real impact of regional inequality, we must readjust the data. For concrete steps of adjustment, see Chen Zongsheng and Zhou Yunbo (2002: 32–34). Besides, the data about rural income in China Yearbook of Statistics are not normalized, a far distance from direct calculation of Gini Coefficient, and need adjustment and estimation, the methods of which are seen in Chen Zongsheng and Zhou Yunbo (2002: 37–40). The Gini coefficient of total income inequality is calculated by means of Urban/Rural Weighted Method, the concrete calculating method of which can be seen in Chen Zongshegn and Zhou Yunbo (2002: 28).

The breakout of debt crisis resulted in economic recession, high inflation rate, and unprecedented social conflicts. Economic growth in the region broke down and the degree of income inequality stands the highest throughout the world.

Other's fault is our lesson. Though the widening income inequality in urban and rural area has not incurred serious social riot, it does not mean everything is going fine. First, the overall income distribution is pyramid like. To cite the city as one example, if the urban middle class is defined between 60,000 yuan and 500,000 yuan of family yearly income, then, calculated by the income data of urban household survey in 2004, the middle class households take 5% of the total urban households, and the rich families take only 0.3%. The overall urban income distribution pattern is like a pyramid (Urban Social Economic Survey Division of NBS 2006) and that in rural areas is even worse. Second, urban–rural income gap and regional inequality are still over large, and the ascending trend has not been effectively curbed. In 1978, the ratio between China's urban per capita disposable income and its rural per capita net income was 2.57, and in 2010 it rose to 3.10. Some studies show that China has the largest urban–rural gap over the world (Li 2006). The same is regional inequality. In 1978, the urban per capita disposable income in east China was 366.97 yuan, that in middle China 307.94 yuan, and in west China 329.94 yuan, the ratio between them was 1.11:0.93:1. Likewise, the rural per capita net income in the east, middle, and west of China was 172.33 yuan, 133.12 yuan, and 119.57 yuan, and the ratio between them was 1.44:1.11:1. However, by 2009, the urban per capita income in the east, middle, and west of China rose to 20,481 yuan, 14,097 yuan, and 14,213 yuan, respectively, and the ratio between them was 1.44:0.99:1, while the rural per capita net income in the three parts of China rose to 7,047 yuan, 4,904 yuan, and 3816 yuan, and the ratio between them was 1.85:1.29:1. Third, income inequality between sectors keeps going up. Statistical data show that in 1978 the highest average wage was found in architecture, with per capita 714 yuan, and the lowest was found in social services, with per capita 392 yuan, the former being 1.82 times of the latter. In 2010, the highest average wage went to financial industry, with per capita 60,398 yuan, and the lowest went to forestry, with per capita 14,350 yuan, the former being 4.2 times of the latter. (For details see Table 1.1.1). Fourth, some abnormal and even illegal income is still cropping up, such as corruption income of some Party and government officials, income from tax-dodging and avoidance of private businesses, group spending on public funds in state-owned organs and enterprises. All told, the income inequality caused by these factors has aroused strong public protest.

In the context of constantly widening of income inequality of urban, rural, and total resident, we need to launch detailed analysis on its status quo, driving factors and problems, and put forward principles and tangible policies for adjusting and regulating China's income distribution pattern, which, we hope, should guarantee a sustainable, healthy, and steady economic growth.

Table 1.1.1 Urban–rural inequality, sector inequality, and regional inequality in 1978 and 2010

Item	1978	2010
Per capita dispoable income of urban residents / Per capita net income of rural residents	2.57	3.10
Per capita wage of the higest wage industry / Per capita wage of the lowest wage industry	1.82	4.2
Ratio of urban per capita disposable incomes between the east, middle and west	1.11:0.93:1	1.44:0.99:1 (2009)
Ratio of rural per capita net incomes between the east, middle and west	1.44:1.11:1	1.58:1.29:1 (2009)

Source: *China Statistics Yearbooks* and *Collected Statistics of 50 Years of the New China*
Notes: (1) The east China includes 12 provinces and municipalities, viz., Liaoning, Hebei, Tianjin, Beijing, Shandong, Jiangsu, Shanghai, Zhejiang, Fujian, Guangdong, Hainan and Guangxi; the middle China includes nine provinces of Heilongjiang, Jilin, Shanxi, Inner Mongolia, Henan, Hubei, Anhui, Hunan and Jiangxi; the west China includes ten provinces and municipalities, viz., Shaanxi, Gansu, Ningxia Hui Autonomous Region, Qinghai, Xinjiang, Sichuan, Chongqing, Guizhou, Yunnan and Tibet. (2) Since the data of a few years and some provinces are unavailable, the ratio between urban per capita disposable income and rural per capita net income is an average. (3) The figures for calculation in the table are the ratios between urban per capita disposable income and rural per capita net income in their nominal values, not adjusted by prices index

1.1.2 Literature Review

1.1.2.1 Present Research on Income Inequality of Urban Resident

Chen Zongsheng and Zhou Yunbo (2002), one of the authors of the book, once examined the dynamics of China's urban income inequality and the factors that impact it since the system reform. Measurement of urban income inequality using published data showed that the urban income inequality, though smaller than rural one,[2] is much more accelerated, especially after the 1990s (Chen and Zhou 2002).[3] Based on 1988–1998 Tianjin's urban household survey data and 2004 large sample survey data of Tianjin urban residents, Chen Zongsheng and Zhou Yunbo (2002) investigated the main factors that impact urban income inequality in the context of system reform and economic growth. Decomposition analysis from income components indicated that due to market-oriented reform, income from state-

[2] The most commonly used explanation for the lower urban income inequality than rural one is that most urban residents are employed in state-owned sectors which have relatively lower income inequality, while rural income, dependent on a variety of factors like distance to cities, quality of land, non-agricultural development and climate, demonstrates higher inequality.

[3] Research by Ximing Wu and Jeffrey (2005) substantiated this conclusion. Investigating the change of urban total income inequality using published data from 1985 to 2001, they found that in the years under review, enlargement of urban income inequality, which is less than rural one, was more accelerated and would end up surpassing rural income inequality.

owned sector is making less contribution to inequality of total income, whereas property income and income from non-state-owned sector are making increasing contribution. Analysis on the increased inequality of total income from 1988 to 1998 revealed that distribution effect should mainly answer for the widening inequality of total income, that is, the distribution change of each income components should take the leading responsibility for the increasing of urban income inequality (Chen Zongsheng and Zhou Yunbo 2001c, 2002). Decomposition by population features of urban residents proved that industry, education, occupation and duty, and unit ownership attributed much to urban income inequality and its change (Chen and Zhou 2001c, 2002; Xue and Zhou 2005). Besides, the impact of abnormal and illegal income on urban income inequality from 1988 to 1999, such as tax-dodging of self-employed and private businesses, corruption of Party and government officials, transfer of group spending to personal income, and smuggling, was measured. By and large, all these abnormal and illegal income increased income inequality of urban residents by more than 30% on average. In occasional years the Gini coefficient of urban resident's income came next to the benchmark of polarization for public economy, that is, 0.4262 (Chen and Zhou 2002).

Li Shi and Zhao Renwei (1999) used data of sample survey data of urban residents to make an overall analysis on the main factors that enlarged the urban income inequality since the system reform. According to their research, the development of non-state-owned sectors and the accumulative effect of properties were largely responsible for the constant enlargement of urban income inequality. Since the internal distribution mechanism of non-state-owned sectors was centered on efficiency and more flexible, it was natural for them to have a higher income inequality than their state-owned counterparts. Even if the income inequality within non-state-owned sectors remained the same, the rise of their employment alone would push up total income inequality of urban resident. The magnitude of unequal distribution of financial assets among urban households was much more than that of income distribution, and their contribution to total income inequality was much more than their share in total income. Corporate reform impacted income distribution at least from two aspects. First, the change of distribution pattern within enterprises resulted in increased income inequality among employees. Next, modern enterprise institution reform speeded up bankruptcy, breakdown, and laid-offs, and affected some employees' income level and ultimately triggered higher urban income inequality. This conclusion is supported by some follow-up research. Decomposition analysis of urban income component by Shujie Yao (1999) showed that premium in state-owned sectors and non-wage revenue in self-employed and private businesses was more unevenly distributed than wage income. Hence, the main factors that impact urban income inequality came from the wage system reform and plural property right systems. Gustafsson and Li Shi (2000) examined the main factors that impact urban wage inequality using survey data in 1988 and 1995 by Economic Research Institute of China Academe of Social Science (CASS). Their research indicated that it was the emergence of self-employed, private, and foreign capital businesses, and the wage reform aimed at higher efficiency in state-owned sectors that mainly drove the enlargement of urban wage inequality. In addition, their research showed that because of shortage of labor migration, regional inequality played an important role in widening urban income inequality.

Xin Meng (2004) did a research on the relation between the system reform and income inequality of urban residents using urban and rural household survey data in 1988, 1995, and 1999 by Economic Research Institute of CASS. He found that in soft stages of system reform from 1988 to 1995, the major reason for enlargement of income inequality was that some groups seized the more revenue from economic reform and growth, and the enlarged regional inequality took the main responsibility. In the radical reform stage from 1995 to 1999, the increased income inequality was mainly attributed to the shrinking of the income of low-income group caused by large-scaled unemployment in state-owned sectors.

How economic growth affects income inequality urban and its change is also one of the heated topics. In his research on the Gini coefficient of urban resident's income and per capita GDP from 1978 to 1995, Zhou Wenxing (2002) constructed an error correction model, by which he found that urban economic growth was double-edged in relation to income inequality and in the long run, there was a positive correlation between the two. Luo Chuliang (2004) tested the correlation between the income and income inequality of urban residents with the panel data of two surveys and found that according to the change of urban per capita income and its Gini coefficient, a single and built-in relation between economic growth and income distribution was not justified.

Some scholars also looked into the impact of some economic variables or new policies on urban income inequality. Zhang Lijun and Zhan Yong (2006) found by constructing VAR model that the expanding size of financial development would soften urban income inequality, but the improving efficiency of financial development would enlarge urban income inequality. Li Yonghui and Xiu Zerui (2005) on the other hand analyzed the impact of such polices as housing accumulation fund system, economically affordable housing, purchase of public housing on favorable terms, and cheap renting system on resident's income distribution. Their research showed that the housing reform did not take into account the special housing interest relation and interest pattern in conventional housing system, and was therefore flawed, for it contributed to the enlargement of urban income inequality.

Some other scholars were interested in the income inequality among urban population groups of differing features. Xiao Shu and Yanjie Bian investigated the wage inequality between male and female workers by household survey data by CASS in 1988 and 1995 and found that in these 2 years, the wage gap was relatively stable because such contributing factors as human capital, politic capital, and professional features between male and female were relatively stable. But from 1988 to 1995, these contributing factors varied in their influence degree, in particular that the contribution of human capita and professional features had increased, a necessary outcome in a transitional economy. On the other hand, the political capital saw a shrinking influence with the speeding marketization process.

1.1.2.2 Present Research on Rural Income Inequality

Griffin was one of the earliest scholars doing empirical study on China's rural income inequality. In his research on the impact of rural reform on income distribution, he concluded that because the system reform provided more income sources for poor households, the end of collectivization reduced, not enlarged income inequality (Griffin 1984). His finding was later supported by Zhu (1991) who, based on three counties in Henan Province, disclosed that the system reform centering on household responsibility countervailed inequality within counties, but at the same time increased inequality across counties.

About the relation of non-farming income to rural income inequality, a popular notion is that non-farming income is the main factor to enlarge rural income inequality, for the distribution of non-farming activities are unevenly distributed (Hare 1999; Rozelle 1994, 1996; Zhang 1992). Athar Hussain et al. (1994) decomposed the rural income inequality by income structure based on survey data of 10,000 urban and rural households in 1986 made by CASS and found that in general, the contribution of non-farming income to total income inequality was more than its share in total income. Income from the employment of town–village ownership enterprise took an average share of 7% in total income, but contributed 17% to total income inequality. In the ten provinces under review, there were six provinces and municipalities where the contribution of non-farming income to total income inequality surpassed its share in total income. Obviously, the rise of non-farming income's share in total income contributes to the widening of rural income inequality. Chen Zongsheng and Zhou Yunbo (2002) once examined the impact of non-farming income on rural income inequality from the perspective of the dual structural transformation in rural areas, using the household survey data of 1994–2000 made by Tianjin Rural Social Economy Survey Team. The research showed that in the time under review, non-farming income, though still on the heels of farming income, was making an increasing contribution to rural income inequality in tandem with the advance of the dual structural transformation. However, for the increased income inequality from 1994 to 2000, the largest contribution came from non-farming income, and farming income came next. Li Shi and Zhao Renwei (1999) made a systemic study on the main factors impacting rural income inequality by using sample survey data. They found that an important factor was the fast but asymmetric growth of non-farming income. Duan Qinglin (1999) in his research concluded that the main factor impacting of rural income inequality was the unequal distribution of wage income. Sha Zhifang and Sun Jingliang (2004), taking Yangzhou in Jiangsu province as an example, argued that family business income and level of management, non-farming employment opportunity, non-farming wage level, and labor's professional technique and quality were the main factors impacting rural income inequality, of which non-farming income was the top one. In the same way, Tang Ping (2006) held the asymmetric distribution of family business income and regional income inequality to be the main body of rural income inequality, and the increasing inequality of rural wage and property income in recent years was a significant contributor to rural income inequality. Opposite to the above views, Nong Zhu and Xubei Luo (2006) surveyed 787 households in Hebei and Liaoning provinces and found that farmers' farming and non-farming activities were not separated from each other; instead, they interacted. Some farmers took up non-farming business partly because they were badly advantaged in farming. To compensate for their loss in farming income, these low-income and poor farmers tended to move to non-farming business. So compared to the rich households, they went to non-farming sectors with more enthusiasm and benefited accordingly. In this sense, non-farming business offset rural income inequality. Taken as a whole, non-farming income exerts certain influence on rural income inequality, but with varied degree in relation to local economic growth level. Generally speaking, the higher the economic development, the higher degree of it's influence.

Another important area of research is the impact of regional inequality on rural income inequality. A study based on surveys on urban and rural residents in 1988 and 1995 by Gustafsson and Li Shi (2001) revealed that of the rural income inequality in 1988, 59–57% was from within county, and 41–43% across counties. Further decomposition of the latter showed that 17% was from within province, 12% from within the east, middle, and west of China, and 12% from regional inequality. In 1995, 20–53% rural inequality was countywide, 50–47% was across counties. Further decomposition of the latter suggested that 18% was from within province, 6% from within the three big regions, and 27% from between the three big regions. Of the added values of income inequality from 1988 to 1995, 36–48% was from within counties, 52–64% from across counties of which 19% came from within province, 36–50% from between the three big regions, and the inequality across provinces in the three regions contributed to reducing rural income inequality.

Since the kick-off of household responsibility, farmers became the subject of production and distribution. By looking into how rural income inequality is related to household features, the factors impacting rural income inequality can be investigated. A study of this kind based on Tianjin household survey data in 1996–1999 by Chen Zongsheng and Zhou Yunbo (2002) showed that the fixed production assets, average number of family labors, size of fishery, and percentage of non-farming labors came to be the main factors impacting rural income inequality, and the fixed production assets was the only factor that enlarge rural income inequality in the years of 1996–1999.

Government polices and some macroeconomic variables, like the change of dual economic structure and level of financial development in rural areas, also have their own impact. Ding Renzhong et al. (2003) analyzed the impact of government polices and system reform on rural income inequality and found that the implementation of tax policy in rural areas produced regressive effect, which consequently widened rural income inequality, whereas such polices as raising the procuring prices of agricultural produce in the early stage of system reform and the great strategy of developing the west of China at the turn of the century helped to soften the inequality. The disintegration of People's Commune and the implementation of household responsibility phased out the institutional base of egalitarianism, but at the same time brought about enlargement of rural income inequality. A study on the impact of the rural dual structural transformation on rural income inequality from 1978 to 2002 indicated that the constant enlargement of dual contrast in rural areas helped to enlarge rural income inequality (Zhou Yunbo 2004). Yang Jun et al. (2006) examined the relation between the magnitude of financial development and rural income inequality with the time series data from 1978 to 2003. They found that the former considerably contributed to the latter's enlargement. The special dual structure of Chinese finance system, they believed, came out of the strategic priority of developing heavy industry to the disadvantage of rural economy. Together with credit binding, farmers, having to pay for financial service, were restricted to the privilege and rural income inequality was accordingly widened.

The system reform, with its built-in defects, has spawned rent-seeking income. Jonathan Moroduch and Terry Sicular (2000) examined the influence of political rent on rural income inequality. Their research showed that village cadres were in some degree politically privileged to either create employment opportunities for their family members in village–town ownership enterprises or manage to seize production factors including land with high added value. In this way, they obtained some political rent, but with slight impact on rural income inequality. A similar research was done by Andrew G. Walder (2002) by using the 1996 household survey data. He concluded that political rent obtained by the Party and government officials in rural areas exerted steady impact on rural income inequality. Some scholars used data from *China Yearbook of Statistics* and representative surveys to measure quantitatively the impact of such rent-seeking income as the tax-dodging of self-employed and private businesses, corruption of the Party and government officials, and smuggling in rural areas on rural income inequality from 1988 to 1999. According to their study, the rent-seeking income as a whole pushed up the rural income inequality by around 23%, and the Gini coefficient in 1995 surpassed the benchmark of polarization for public economy (Chen Zongsheng and Zhou Yunbo 2002).

1.1.2.3 Research on the Urban–Rural Gap

As an important issue in the study of income distribution, the urban–rural inequality has attracted much attention. One of the authors of the book once measured quantitatively its dynamics before and after the system reform in light of the urban-to-rural income ratio, the Gini of urban–rural inequality and urban–rural income structural coefficient, with priority given to analyzing the phasic growth of urban–rural gap and its drivers since the system reform (Chen Zongsheng and Zhou Yunbo 2002).

Many studies showed that the urban–rural gap was proved to be a significant kind of income inequality (Lin Yifu et al. 1998; Zhao Renwei and Li Shi 1999; Chen Zongsheng and Zhou Yunbo 2002; Li Shi and Yue Ximing 2004). Khan and

Riskin (1998) pointed out that ever since 1980s, income inequality of Chinese residents has been considerably enlarged, and the contribution of the urban–rural inequality to income inequality of Chinese total residents has been increasing. A study on the urban–rural inequality in terms of its impact on income inequality of Chinese total residents and its dynamics during the years of 1988–1999 suggested that the urban–rural gap made up more than 50% in income inequality of Chinese total residents, and its contribution to the added value of income inequality of Chinese total residents was above 80% (Chen Zongsheng and Zhou Yunbo 2002). Sporadic measurements were also made by scholars. Li Shi et al. (1999) in their decomposition with Theil Index showed that in 1988 about 40% of income inequality of Chinese total residents came from the urban–rural gap, in 1995 the share, though down a bit, was still one third, and the increment of urban–rural gap that year took about 16.5% of the increment of income inequality of Chinese total residents.

To the causes of the sustainable enlargement of urban–rural gap, scholars reacted differently. Lin et al. (1994, 1999) attributed it to the industry policies targeted at overtaking and biased social policies intended to maintain the overtaking strategy and prevent social crisis, such as household registration system intended for controlling population flow. Li Shi (2001) held that the institutional transformation was responsible for enlargement of urban–rural gap, for the change of dual structure did not change the inverted-U process of the urban–rural gap. Some scholars (Zhang Qi et al. 2003) believed that thanks to government intervention, Chinese financial development rolled on to the disadvantage of the intermediate and small enterprises' financing and rural economic development, thus exerting negative influence on the urban–rural gap. According to them, in the beginning of the reform, the negative influence was slightly felt because the size of financial departments was small and the government intervention was carried out mainly through fiscal means. Anyway, after 1990s it began to be felt quite strong and led to worsening urban–rural gap. They also believed that the urban–rural gap could be reduced with expanded exports and comparative advantages of trade in provinces being played to the full, but it worked only after mid-1980s. Hou Yongzhi pointed out another driver which worsening urban–rural gap, that is, the fiercer competition caused by trade capital liberalization and substitution of capital for labor in the context of a large amount of surplus rural labors. Chen Zongsheng and Li Defu (2007), using the panel data of provinces from 1978 to 2002, analyzed in detail the determinants of urban–rural gap under dual economy and measured their contribution. Their research located the dual contrast coefficient between farming and non-farming, urban-to-rural employment burden coefficient ratio, urban-to-rural distribution coefficient ratio, and the level of rural industrialization as the main determinants. Econometric analysis showed that these four factors could account for 90% of the urban–rural gap from 1978 to 2002. Among them, the dual contrast coefficient reflecting the productivity gap between the two sectors was the fundamental driver, and the level of rural industrialization was a key factor which worked to the contrary. According to their estimation, if the level of rural industrialization in 2002 remained the same with that in 1978, the urban–rural gap in 2002 would be 3.75, 20% more than the actual 3.11.

1.1.2.4 Research on Income Inequality of Chinese Total Residents

Limited by inadequate data and method, research on *income inequality of Chinese total residents* is not so diversified as that on urban and rural income inequality, and urban–rural gap and most of it is focused on *income inequality of Chinese total residents* estimation. Adelmen and Sunding (1987) estimated the *income inequality of Chinese total residents* in the beginning stage of system reform. According to their estimation, if various subsidies in kind for urban residents were not accounted for, the Gini coefficient of income of Chinese total residents in 1978 was 0.317, and in 1983 was 0.284. If subsidies in kind were accounted for, the Gini coefficients of the 2 years were up to 0.438 and 0.412. For the 2 years, the Gini coefficient of income of Chinese total residents in 1983 was slightly down mainly because the urban–rural gap was reduced. The Income Distribution Project Panel of Nankai University (1990) established a standard equation between income inequality and Gini coefficient by using regression method by means of which they worked out the Gini coefficients of income of Chinese total residents in 1980 and 1988 to be 0.25 and 0.30. Chen Zongsheng (1991) measured the Gini coefficients of income of Chinese total residents of the period from 1981 to 1988 by using "hierarchical weighted method." One of the authors of the book, with the same method in combination with "Urban/Rural Weighted Method," also calculated the Gini coefficient of normal income of Chinese total residents from 1988 to 1999 systematically. His measurement showed that in 1988 the Gini coefficients of income of Chinese total residents were somewhere between 0.32 and 0.34, and in 1999 it rose to 0.41 or so (Chen Zongsheng and Zhou Yunbo 2002). If reckoning the abnormal and illegal income from tax-dodging and avoidance, Party and government officials' corruption, transfer of group spending to personal income, and smuggling, the Gini coefficient of income of Chinese total residents would multiply by more than 17% and cross the benchmark of polarization for public economy, that is, 0.4262.

Some organizations also came up with their estimations. The World Bank (1997), after adjusting the rural residents' net income and urban dwellers' living cost, estimated the Gini coefficient of income of Chinese total residents in 1981 to be 0.29 and in 1995 to be 0.39. Other scholars (Zhao Renwei and Griffin 1994; Zhao Renwei et al. 1999) estimated the Gini coefficient of income of Chinese total residents in 1988 to be 0.382 and in 1995 to be 0.452, up 7%, 1% each year. Xiang Shujiang (1998a, b), using Urban/Rural Weighted Method, calculated the Gini coefficients of income of Chinese total residents in the 15 years from 1980 to 1995 in a systemic and complete way. According to calculation of the experts in the World Bank (Martin and Chen 2004), the Gini coefficients of income of Chinese total residents rose from 0.31 in 1981 to 0.447 in 2001. Khan and Riskin found that the Gini coefficient of income of Chinese total residents in 2002 hit 0.46.

1.2 Main Characteristics of the Book and Its Structure

1.2.1 Main Characteristics of the Book

The book is a research of theoretical analysis and empirical study combined. Theoretical analysis provides the basis on which empirical study, in particular quantitative and econometric analysis, is built up. As a whole, the book is an empirical study which features as follows.

Firstly, the book makes a point of introducing methods of studying income distribution and indexes for measuring income inequality. Apart from those indexes given by one of the authors of the book (Chen Zongsheng and Zhou Yunbo 2002), it presents some requisite conditions to be met for an ideal index, and added some other indexes, especially that based on social welfare theory. In Chap. 2, we present various indexes in great detail, including four based on social welfare theory and social welfare function. Focus is given on Lorentz curve and Gini coefficient and some popular distribution functions and estimation equations used to calculate Gini coefficient. Also introduced are several numerical indexes for judging the degree of polarization and two methods to test whether a trend of polarization is in shape or not. Besides, through all the chapters, we punctuate some frequently used decomposition methods in the field of income inequality study, such as decomposing the Gini coefficient by income structure and household features. Meanwhile, we develop some other methods, extending the decomposition methods by income structure and household features from single static application to more dynamic application for instance, or, using the methods to decompose the added values of Gini coefficient. Also, we give a concise and clear reply to questions against the methods, which was put forward by some scholars.

Secondly, a fair amount of urban and rural household survey data is employed for empirical study, including the urban household survey data from 2002 to 2006 and the rural household survey from 2000 to 2003. These data included many indexes, such as household population structure, labor quality, employment structure, amount of production means to one's possession, and all kinds of income sources and spending. All these data lay a solid basis for our research and well justify our tentative conclusion.

The book examines not only microscopic household features with regard to their impact on income inequality, but also a few macroscopic variables such as economic development level, inflation rate, foreign trade dependency, urbanization, and the structural transformation of labor employment in rural areas, with special emphasis on the impact of the double dual structural transformation of Chinese economy on income inequality. For this purpose, econometric method is employed to measure the influence of urbanization on income inequality of Chinese total residents and the impact of the structural transformation of labor employment in rural areas on rural income inequality. Compared to previous studies only aimed at looking into the impact of general variables on urban and rural income inequality, this study is no doubt a great step forward and portrays Chinese economic life with more accuracy.

Finally, the study is an empirical study in combination with theoretical analysis. By means of theoretical analysis, some hypotheses are drawn to be tested against empirical data with quantitative and econometric methods. For instance, when studying the impact of the urbanization on income inequality of Chinese total residents in the process of the dual structural transformation, we first apply mathematical model to theoretical analysis from which to derive two hypotheses. Then we put them into empirical test by means of empirical models. Econometric method, though still in debate in economic studies, is by far the most reliable and scientific. With the maturing of econometrics, the method itself is being improved.

1.2.2 Structure of the Book

The book is made up of eight chapters. Chapter 1 introduces the backdrop of the study, present researches on Chinese residents' income inequality both at home and abroad, main characteristics of the book, and its structure.

Chapter 2 falls into three sections, mainly dealing with some key concepts such as income inequality and polarization. Special importance is attached to introducing main indexes for measuring income inequality and polarization, especially the Gini coefficient and its measurement. We can say with every justification that this chapter covers almost all the indexes and measurement methods in the field of income distribution study.

In Chap. 3, we first discuss the change of urban income distribution system after the system reform and measure the dynamics of urban income inequality by means of Gini coefficient. Next, we decompose the main drivers of urban income inequality and its dynamics by income structure and household features. At the same time, some macroscopic economic variables are examined in terms of their impact on urban income inequality, such as economic development level, inflation, and foreign trade.

Chapter 4 is divided into four sections. It first compares the rural income distribution system before and after the system reform and analyzes the dynamics of rural income inequality. Then it proceeds to examine the main drivers of rural income inequality and its dynamics by income structure, with special attention given to the main variables influencing rural income inequality and its dynamics. In the end, the chapter investigates some macroscopic economic variables, especially the structural transformation of rural labor employment, with respect to their impact on rural income inequality and its dynamics.

Chapter 5 includes three sections. Section 5.1 introduces the method of calculating Gini coefficients of income of Chinese total residents and applies it to measuring the status quo of income inequality of Chinese total residents and its dynamics since the system reform. Section 5.2, after reviewing the dynamics of urban–rural gap since the system reform, measures the contribution of urban–rural gap to income inequality of Chinese total residents and its dynamics. Section 5.3, in the wake of briefly introducing the urbanization process since the system reform, constructs a theoretical model to analyze the impact of population flow on income inequality of Chinese total residents and then goes on to put into empirical test for the hypothesis derived from theoretical analysis based on the level of urbanization and data of DII since the reform.

Chapter 6 mainly looks into the impact of various rent-seeking incomes on income inequality of Chinese urban, rural, and total residents. Firstly, it presents how the nature and forms of rent-seeking income are defined and describes the birth and expansion of such rent-seeking activities as tax-dodging, corruption, and smuggling in China. Secondly, it estimates quantitatively the impact of a few main rent-seeking incomes on income inequality of Chinese urban, rural, and total residents. Finally, the chapter tries to offer economic explanation for the birth and development of rent-seeking income in transitional economy from both subjective and objective perspectives.

Chapter 7 is about prediction in three sections. First, it introduces the main factors that influence income inequality of Chinese urban, rural, and total residents, as well as factors that determine the future direction of the urban–rural income inequality, including both factors enlarging income inequality and factors reducing income inequality. Secondly, it presents the major methods for prediction, viz., exponential smoothing. Finally, the chapter applies this method to predict the income inequality of Chinese urban, rural, and total residents, and urban–rural income gap.

In the concluding chapter, main conclusions derived from the forgoing chapters are given, and policy implications of regulating China's income distribution are offered from such aspects as promoting the income levels of the poor, controlling the too-fast income rise of the rich, developing mid-income group, reducing the urban–rural gap, and rooting out sundry rent-seeking income.

Chapter 2
Concept of Income Distribution and Indexes and Methods for Measuring Income Inequality

In this chapter, some basic concepts useful in studying income distribution are analyzed, such as income distribution, income inequality, and polarization. In addition, a great body of this chapter is also devoted to discussing some indexes and formulas, Gini Coefficient, and several distribution functions in particular, which are mainly employed to measure income inequality and polarization.

2.1 Income Distribution and Major Indexes for Its Measurement

Firstly, we will introduce some key concepts related to income distribution as well as some indexes used to measure income inequality.

2.1.1 Income Distribution and Its Studies

As one of the vital fields in economics, income distribution falls into two categories: functional distribution of incomes and size distribution of incomes. Functional distribution of incomes, also known as factor income distribution, involves relations between various production factors and the revenues they produce, like landlord getting rents, capital investors getting profits, and laborers earning wages, etc. The study of functional distribution of incomes takes as its main task the ratio of income on each kind of production factors to gross national incomes. So it is a macroscopic distribution. Size distribution of incomes, also called individual or household income distribution, is concerned with the ratio of individual or household income to the gross national income. It studies income distribution from the relation between the size of income earners and the size of their income, so it is a microscopic distribution. A concept closely related to size distribution of incomes is

Y. Zhou and Y. Qin, *Empirical Analysis on Income Inequality of Chinese Residents*, Gu Shutang Acad Fund Econ, DOI 10.1007/978-3-642-24952-5_2,

income inequality, which signifies the difference degree of the ratio of the income earned by economic entities to the gross national income. It is at this point where inequality comes.

What concerns the early classic economists is functional distribution of income, namely how the national income is distributed among land owners, labor owners, and capital owners. They believe that functional distribution is closely related to economic growth. Later, economists' interest is gradually diverted to individual or household income, namely, size distribution of incomes. One factor which underpins this change is the large poverty population in developing countries. In the early years after World War II, pervading poverty was considered as a major evidence of a country's low income and the way to tackle this problem was to quicken economic growth and increase national income, or in other words, to make a larger cake. However, since 1960s, people began to question whether pure economic growth could eliminate poverty in developing countries and economists began to seek after ways to alleviate and even eliminate poverty by means of improving distribution of individual or household income. Naturally, size distribution of incomes enters into economists' vision, especially that of development economists.

To study size distribution of incomes is to deal with the following issues: how is gross national income distributed among residents or households? How can we mathematically describe this distribution pattern? How to use a quantitative index to measure income inequality among individual residents or households and assess the change of income inequality for a period of time? What are those economic, social, and cultural factors behind income inequality? What policies can be adopted by a government to regulate the structure of income distribution and help establish one which is conducive to economic growth and social stability at once? This book is confined to deal with such issues like the status quo of Chinese residents' income inequality, factors, and course of change in the setting of China's reform and development.

2.1.2 Major Indexes for Measuring Income Inequality

One of the key issues in the study of income distribution is measuring income inequality. Suppose $Y(y_1, y_2, y_3, \ldots, y_n)$ stands for vector space of a group of incomes, and at the same time $y_1 \leq y_2 \leq y_3 \leq \ldots \leq y_N$, then to measure its income inequality is to effectuate a transformation from N dimensional space to a real number, or, to express the difference among the data of the incomes with a real number.

2.1.2.1 Requirements for Measurement Indexes

In general, measurement indexes should meet the following requirements: (a) Pigou–Dalton transfer sensitivity. When income is transferred from one person or household to another richer person or household, the index for measuring income inequality must be increased. (b) Symmetry. When any two people or households switch their orders in the income sequence, the index for measurement keeps unchanged. In other words, the index value is influenced by the numerical value of the observed item, but not its rank and standing. (c) Mean independence, also called homogeneity. When all incomes vary by the same rate, the index for measurement does not change. Or, if all the observed values are multiplied or divided by the same constant, the index value remains unchanged. (d) Sample size independence of population or household. Any change to the scale of the observed population or household does not exert impact on income inequality. A sample of 20 persons with varying incomes, for instance, is measured for the income inequality among them. If the sample is doubled to 40 persons, the index value should be the same regardless. (e) Decomposibility. The index for measuring income inequality may be decomposed according to different population or household features and income sources. (f) Strong Lorenz consistent. The index should agree Lorenz Curve. Suppose A and B are two Lorenz Curves, when A and B are completely overlapping, they have the same inequality degree; when A is completely in the lower right of B, it suggests a larger degree of inequality than B. A telling index should be able to describe these relations. This requires that when measuring income inequality, all observed values and information of the samples, instead of part of them, should be taken into consideration.

2.1.2.2 Major Indexes for Measurement[1]

Many indexes and formulas have been used to study income inequality. In general they are divided into two categories: one that excludes any welfare and the other that includes welfare. The following are more often adopted.

Range (R_m)

The simplest statistical measure of dispersion is the Range, the difference between the largest and the smallest of the observed values. When we compare the different value of net income levels among various units, individuals, families, or income groups, the reference for comparison may be either relative value or mean value. If more than two units are compared, a method of two by two is needed. However, this method usually entails over-elaborate computation and does not help researchers find patterns. In this case, we can regard the various income levels as a frequency distribution, from which to select the largest and the smallest values and compare their net difference which

[1] One of the authors of this book introduced some indexes in his former book (Chen Zongsheng and Zhou Yunbo 2002), and some new indexes are supplemented in this book.

reflects the income inequality, or the Range. Suppose $Y(y_1, y_2, y_3, \ldots, y_N)$ represents a group of income distribution, the Range is measured by the following formula:

$$R_{\mathrm{m}} = X_{\max} - X_{\min}, \tag{2.1.1}$$

where $X_{\max}$ refers to the top income in a distribution and $X_{\min}$ the lowest. The great part of this measurement is direct and can be computed very easily. However, only two extreme values are considered in this measurement, and the information of values between the extreme values is not reflected, so it cannot reflect the whole status of income inequality.

Mean Deviation (MD)

Given an income distribution (x_1, x_2,. . ., x_n) and its egalitarian distribution (μ, μ,. . .,μ), the mean deviation is constructed by taking the summation of all the difference between the income y_i and the mean income of all population and making the summation be divided by the number of population, so that is,

$$\mathrm{MD} = \frac{\sum_{i=1}^{N} y_i - \mu}{N}. \tag{2.1.2}$$

The bigger the mean deviation is, the more dispersive the income distribution is, and the higher the degree of inequality. Here N stands for the number of incomes compared, or the number of individuals (or households), and μ stands for the average value of the incomes in the group. When we divide population into groups, we need p_i, the proportion of each group in total population, to measure the mean deviation by

$$\mathrm{MD} = \sum_{i=1}^{N} P_i(y_i - \mu). \tag{2.1.3}$$

The economic significance of the mean deviation is that a unit, selected at random from the high- or and low-income population (or households), should transfer (if he is rich) to or receive (if he is poor) from others *MD* amount of income to realize equal distribution.

Standard Deviation (S)

$$S = \sqrt{\frac{\sum (y_i - \mu)^2}{N}}. \tag{2.1.4}$$

The minimum value of S is zero, and there is no upper limit. The bigger the standard deviation, the larger the income inequality. However, this index has two drawbacks. For one, it does not have maximum value, which is the basis for value analysis on income inequality. For the other, it does not take the weight of each group into account, so it is only applicable for equivalent grouping.

Variation Coefficient

$$\mathrm{CV} = \frac{1}{u}\sqrt{\sum_{i=1}^{N} f_i (y_i - \mu)^2}, \tag{2.1.5}$$

f_i is the percentage of population (household) in group i to total population (household). Similar to standard deviation, the minimum value of CV is zero, and there is no upper limit. So it has similar drawbacks except that it is applicable for both equivalent grouping and non-equivalent grouping because the population (household) share of each group is the weight.

Kuznets Measure

It demonstrates the degree of income inequality by computing the income percentage of the richest 20% of population or households in a country's distribution system. Its minimum value is 0.2, and the higher the value, the larger the income inequality. However, this index is partial in measuring the whole society's income inequality because it represents only the percentage of the high-income group, disregarding the overall income distribution of a whole country.

Ahluwalia Index

Opposite to Kuznets measure, Ahluwalia index takes the income percentage of 40% of the poorest population or households in a country's distribution system to show the degree of income inequality. Its maximum value is 0.4, and the smaller the value, the larger the income inequality. Likewise, this index is partial since it represents only the status of the low-income group.

Income Worsening Index

This index points to the ratio of 20% of the highest income to 20% of the lowest income. Its minimum value is 1, and the bigger the value, the larger the income inequality. Combining Kuznets measure and Ahluwalia index, the index is able to show a contrast between the high-income group and the low-income group, but leaving out those in between. When using this index to measure income inequality, we can divide the whole population into five hierarchical rankings: the lowest income, the lower income, the middle income, the higher income, and the highest income. In the case of large population, seven or ten rankings may be adopted. The more rankings, the larger the ratio of the highest income group to the lowest income group.

Theil Index

P represents the total population (households), and it is divided into I groups. P_i stands for the population (households) of each group. Each group is again divided into J subgroups, the population (households) of each subgroups is P_j. $\bar{y}$ represents the general average income, $\bar{y}_i$ the average income of group i, and $\bar{y}_j$ the average income of subgroup j in group i. Theil index is formulated as follows:

$$T = \sum_{i=1}^{I} \frac{P_i}{P} \mathrm{Log} \frac{\bar{y}_i}{\bar{y}} + \sum_{i=1}^{I} \frac{P_i}{P} \sum_{j=1}^{J} \frac{P_j}{P_i} \mathrm{Log} \frac{\bar{y}_j}{\bar{y}}. \tag{2.1.6}$$

The first part of the formula suggests the difference between the average income per capita in each group and the general average income per capita. The second part of the formula indicates the difference within a group. This index is good for analysis based on grouping the samples according to different features, but it fails to make comparison because it has neither lower limit nor upper limit.

Gini Coefficient

The above-mentioned indexes come into use in different ways, but the most frequently employed tools in measuring income inequality are Lorenz Diagram and Gini Coefficient, which will be analyzed in detail in Sect. 2.2.

All these indexes mentioned above are used to measure income inequality exclusive of welfare content. In other words, they do not involve any value judgment. Now, we will introduce another group of indexes which contain social welfare, and whose underlining construction is social welfare function. These indexes share a fundamental supposition that when the total income is equally distributed to each member of the society, the overall social welfare level reaches the highest, and the social welfare function amounts to the maximum. The following is a brief introduction of these groups of indexes.

Dalton Index

Posited by Dalton in 1920, this index is the first one based on social welfare function to measure income inequality. Suppose the total number of social population is N, y_i stands for individual income level, $u(y_i)$ is individual utility function, and $\frac{\mathrm{d}u}{\mathrm{d}y_i} > 0$, $\frac{\mathrm{d}^2 u}{\mathrm{d}y_i^2} < 0$. According to Dalton, if the income of the rich is transferred to the poor, the general welfare level of the whole society will rise, because the transfer will bring about more gains than loss. At the same time, when all members of the society enjoy the same level of income, the general social welfare level hits the summit, which is equal to $Nu(\mu)$. Here, μ stands for the average income. The index can be formulated as follows:

$$D = 1 - \frac{\sum_{i=1}^{N} u(y_i)}{Nu(\mu)}. \tag{2.1.7}$$

The index points out the percentage of social welfare loss caused by the actual income inequality in real life. In effect, it does not measure the utility distribution. So it is flawed by its heavy reliance on the supposed utility function form, and a simple linear transformation will lead to a change.

Atkinson Index

Unlike Dalton Index, Atkinson Index does not depend on utility function form. In order to better describe his theory, Atkinson introduced the concept of equally distributed equivalent level of income per capita, Y_{EDE}. Given a certain social average income level, he supposed, the overall social welfare level based on equal distribution is higher than that based on unequal distribution. Since in reality income inequality of one kind or another always exists, the actual overall social welfare level is always lower than that in ideal condition. Therefore, if the actual overall social welfare level remains stable, the equally distributed equivalent level of income per capita (Y_{EDE}) must be less than/equal to the average income per capita, namely $Y_{\mathrm{EDE}} \leq \mu$. Atkinson Index may by formulated as follows:

$$A = 1 - \frac{Y_{\mathrm{EDE}}}{\mu}. \tag{2.1.8}$$

Herein, A represents Atkinson Index, Y_{EDE} equally distributed equivalent level of income per capita, and μ average income per capita.

Sen Index

The above indexes, however, only concern themselves with the social welfare inequality caused by unequal income distribution of the whole society. As a matter of fact, social welfare is related not only to income distribution of the whole society, but also to the overall income level. Obviously a society with a high-income level and a relatively equal income distribution institution is more popular than one with a low-income level and a large income inequality. But if both the social income level and the income inequality in one society are higher than those in another society, how should we judge which society is more ideal? To answer this question, some scholars have attempted to incorporate the average income and income inequality into one evaluating index. Sen, for one, posited such index in 1970:

$$S = \mu(1 - G). \tag{2.1.9}$$

Herein, S means Sen Index, μ average income, and G Gini Coefficient.

Kakwani Index

Enlightened by Sen Index, Kakwani put forward another index in 1980:

$$K = \frac{\mu}{1 + G}. \tag{2.1.10}$$

In the formula, K represents Kakwani Index, μ average income, and G Gini Coefficient.

Indexes based on social welfare theory to measure income inequality are problematic mainly in two aspects: first, in the process of adding overall social utility function, the heterogeneity of individual utility is ignored; second, how to construct a utility function which can be accepted by the whole society? All the social welfare indexes are limited in that they suppose individual welfare is dependent on economic entity alone, and social welfare is dependent on individual welfare determined by individual income of economic entity. However, in practice, another significant feature of income inequality is that the individual welfare of economic entity relies on not only his own income, but also a comparison with his peers.

2.2 Lorenz Curve and Gini Coefficient and Their Estimation

In the last section, we discussed the concept of income distribution and some major indexes for measuring income inequality. In this section, we will go into Lorenz Curve and Gini Coefficient, two tools frequently used to measure income inequality, and the relations between the two.

2.2.1 General Meaning of Lorenz Curve and Gini Coefficient

Lorenz Curve is the most frequently employed tool to measure income inequality, and most indexes for this purpose are deduced from Lorenz Curve. Suppose $X(x_1, x_2, x_3, \ldots, x_i, \ldots, x_n)$ is the vector space of a group of incomes, x_i is the income of number i person, and $X(x_1 \leq x_2 \leq x_3 \leq \ldots \leq x_i \leq \ldots \leq x_n)$. $f(x_i)$ is an income density function and $f(x_i)\mathrm{d}x$ stands for the number of heads or households with incomes ranging from x to $x\mathrm{d}x$. The ratio of the heads or households with incomes less than x to the total population or households can be represented by $P(x)$:

$$P(x) = \int_0^x f(t)\mathrm{d}t. \tag{2.2.1}$$

Their income is formulated by

$$\mu(x) = \int_0^x tf(t)\mathrm{d}t.$$

The ratio of their income to the total income is $Q(x)$:

$$Q(x) = \mu(x)/\mu_0(x) = (1/\mu_0)\int_0^x tf(t)\mathrm{d}t. \tag{2.2.2}$$

Here, $\mu_0(x)$ stands for average income, and its formula is

$$\mu_0(x) = \int_0^\infty xf(x)\mathrm{d}x.$$

Lorenz Curve indicates the relations between $P(x)$ and $Q(x)$. As seen in the following Fig. 2.2.1, the horizontal axis stands for head or household ratio, while the vertical axis stands for income ratio.

Here line *OA* is the absolute equality line, and each point on the line has the same head percentage and income percentage, that is to say, incomes are equally distributed to each head or household. Line *OEA* is the absolute inequality line, which suggests that all the incomes go to the last person or household on the line. In practice, Lorenz Curve goes between *OA* and *OEA*. The closer it is to *OA* and the farther to *OEA*, the smaller the income inequality, whereas the farther it is to *OA* and the nearer to *OEA*, the larger income inequality. As shown in the figure, the two Lorentz Curves of *OCA* and *ODA* indicate a higher degree of income inequality than that of *OBA* curve. From the general definition, it is easy to conclude four natures of Lorentz Curve[2]:

[2] The four natures are also indexes to assess the eligibility of Lorentz Curve's estimation equation.

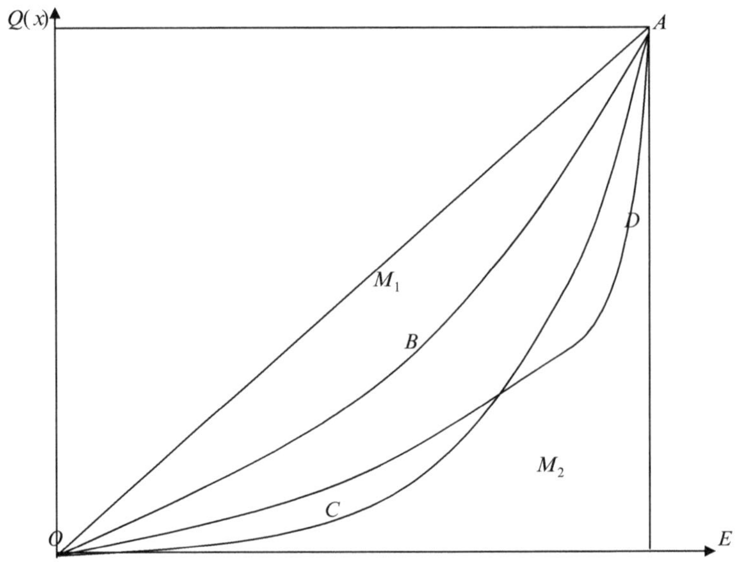

Fig. 2.2.1 Graph of Lorenz Curve

1. If $P = 0$, then $Q = 0$
2. If $P = 1$, then $Q = 1$
3. $\mathrm{d}Q/\mathrm{d}P > 0$
4. $\mathrm{d}^2Q/\mathrm{d}P^2 > 0$.

$\mathrm{d}Q/\mathrm{d}P > 0$ and $\mathrm{d}^2Q/\mathrm{d}P^2 > 0$ means that Lorenz Curve is monotonically increasing and features marginal growth rate increasing. Lorenz Curve has the merit of being simple and direct, but it also has demerit. When two Lorenz Curves intersect, it is not easy to compare the inequalities reflected by them. As seen in 2.2.1, we know for certain that both curve *OCA* and curve *ODA* show a larger income inequality than curve *OBA*, but we cannot know which of the two curves suggests a larger income inequality, *OCA* or *ODA*? Consequently, some scholars find another method to measure income inequality through the ratio of the square enclosed within Lorenz Curve and absolute equality line to the square enclosed within absolute equality line and absolute inequality line. The ratio value is called Gini Coefficient. Suppose the square within *OBA* and absolute equality line *OA* is M_1, the square within *OBA* and absolute inequality line *OEA* is M_2, then Gini Coefficient is formulated as follows:

$$G = \frac{M_1}{M_1 + M_2}.$$

Or in the form of integral:

$$G = \frac{1}{2} - \int_0^1 f(x)\mathrm{d}x. \tag{2.2.3}$$

The value of Gini Coefficient ranges from zero to unit. In general, the smaller value, the smaller income inequality, and the more equal the distribution. Likewise, a larger value of Gini Coefficient suggests a larger income inequality and a less equal distribution system. Due to the definite value range, Gini Coefficient is able to provide a ground for value judgment of income inequality. The internationally accepted standard is that if the Gini Coefficient value is less than 0.2, the income distribution observed is a highly equal one, if the value varies between 0.2 and 0.3, the income distribution is relatively mean, if the value is between 0.3 and 0.4, the income distribution is moderately reasonable, while if the value is more than 0.4, the income inequality tends to be large (You Hongbing 1998). Some scholar has pointed out that Gini Coefficient is the best single index for measuring income inequality because of several advantages: first, it is very comprehensive, and one value may embody the overall picture of income inequality; second, its geometric meaning is simple and direct; third, it has definite range of value, namely definite maximum and minimum, which enables comparison. At the same time there are some pitfalls: first, some calculations of Gini Coefficient attach less importance to the weight of the low income, and are not sensitive to their ratio change; second, the change of Gini Coefficient cannot mirror the change of each income group; third, it is difficult to do calculation if fed with empirical data; fourth, similar to other indexes, it falls short of direct economic meaning; last, it is not allowed to divide the subject into groups according to certain feature and find the overall Gini Coefficient by means of footing the dividing Gini Coefficients. This is the biggest limitation.

2.2.2 *Estimation of Lorenz Curve and Gini Coefficient*

It is not far from enough to give a theoretic meaning of Lorenz Curve and Gini Coefficient, for in empirical study, we have to estimate the Curve by empirical data. The key to estimation is to locate the probability density function of income, $f(x)$. Only with that can we have the accumulative distribution functions $P(x)$ (for describing the population or household) and $Q(x)$ (for describing income), and produce Lorenz equation. Since the probability density function is unknown, in practical estimation, scholars tend to use some existing probability distribution functions for reference, Burr distribution function, Pareto function, exponent normal function, and GAMMA function, for instance. Some conventional probability functions are to be introduced first.

2.2.2.1 Conventional Probability Functions

Burr distribution function. Its mathematical expression is as follows:

$$F(x) = 1 - \left(\frac{1}{(1 + \alpha x^{\beta})}\right)^{\gamma}. \tag{2.2.4}$$

α, β, and γ are parameters to be estimated. The formula to compute Gini Coefficient is as follows:

$$G = 1 - \frac{\Gamma\left(2\gamma - \frac{1}{\beta}\right)\Gamma(\gamma)}{\Gamma\left(1 - \frac{1}{\beta}\right)\Gamma(2\gamma)}. \tag{2.2.5}$$

Γ refers to GAMMA distribution function and its value can be looked up in tables.

GAMMA function. It is a member of Pearson distribution function family, and its probability density function is formulated as follows:

$$f(x, \alpha, \lambda) = \frac{\lambda^{\alpha}}{\Gamma(\alpha) x^{\alpha-1} \mathrm{e}^{-\lambda x}}. \tag{2.2.6}$$

α and λ are parameters greater than 0, $\Gamma(\alpha)$ refers to GAMMA function, and its formula is as follows:

$$\Gamma(\alpha) = \int_0^{\infty} \mathrm{e}^{-\alpha} u^{\alpha-1} \mathrm{d}u.$$

Based on the formula of GAMMA density function given above, we can develop the accumulative distribution function of population (household) $P(x)$ and that of income $Q(x)$:

$$P(x) = \frac{1}{\Gamma(\alpha)} \int_0^x \lambda^{\alpha} t^{\alpha-1} \mathrm{e}^{-\lambda t} \mathrm{d}t, \tag{2.2.7}$$

$$Q(x) = \frac{1}{\mu_0 \Gamma(\alpha)} \int_0^x \lambda^{\alpha} t^{\alpha-1} \mathrm{e}^{-\lambda t} \mathrm{d}t. \tag{2.2.8}$$

The computational formula of Gini Coefficient is as follows:

$$G = 2\alpha \frac{\mathrm{B}_{0.5}(\alpha, \alpha + 1)}{\lambda}. \tag{2.2.9}$$

$\mathrm{B}_{0.5}(\alpha, \alpha + 1)$ is incomplete Beta function.

When these probability distribution functions are used to fit Lorenz Curve, three requirements should be generally observed: it is well fit, parameter estimation is simple, and the parameters to be estimated have certain economic value. However, the three conditions are somewhat contradictory, so it is difficult to meet them at once. Given that in real economic life, the real data on $P(x)$ and $Q(x)$ are more available, some scholars come up with equations directly expressing the relation between $P(x)$ and $Q(x)$, and proceed to make parameter estimation with the real data on $P(x)$ and $Q(x)$. We will introduce some popular estimation equations below.

2.2.2.2 Some Popular Equations

$R-J-A-N$ estimation equation. Proposed by R.H. Rasche, J. Gaffney, A.Y.C. Koo and N. Obst in 1980, the equation is expressed mathematically as follows:

$$Q = [1-(1-P)^{\alpha}]^{\frac{1}{\beta}} \quad Q, P \in [0,1]. \tag{2.2.10}$$

Q and P refer to the accumulative income percentage and population (household) percentage, respectively, and α and β are parameters to be estimated. From the equation, it is easy to see that when $P=0$, $Q=0$, and $P=1$, $Q=1$. Obviously, nature (i) and nature (ii) of Lorenz Curve are satisfied. When $\alpha=\beta=1$, then $P=Q$, and it is absolute equality line. The first derivative and second derivative of Q with respect to P are as follows respectively:

$$Q' = \frac{\alpha}{\beta}[1-(1-P)^{\alpha}]^{\frac{1}{\beta}-1}(1-P)^{-(1-\alpha)},$$

$$Q'' = \left\{\frac{\alpha}{\beta}[1-(1-P)^{\alpha}]^{\frac{1}{\beta}-1}(1-P)^{-(1-\alpha)}\right\}\left\{\frac{1-\alpha}{1-P}+\frac{\alpha(1-\beta)}{\beta}\left[\frac{(1-P)^{\alpha}}{1-(1-P)^{\alpha}}\right]\right\}.$$

If we put the estimated value of α and β into the formula, and if $Q'>0$ and $Q''>0$, nature (iii) and nature (iv) of Lorenz Curve are satisfied, so the Lorenz Curve equation derived is valid. Accordingly the computational formula of Gini Coefficient is as follows:

$$G = 1-\frac{2B\left(\frac{1}{\alpha},\frac{1}{\beta+1}\right)}{\alpha}, \tag{2.2.11}$$

B refers to Beta distribution.

Put forward as a group of distribution functions by N.C. Kakwani and N. Podder in 1973, the equation was originally formulated as follows:

$$Q = P\mathrm{e}^{-\beta(1-P)}, \quad Q, P \in [0,1], \tag{2.2.12}$$

β is parameter to be estimated, and the first derivative and second derivative are as follows:

$$Q' = \mathrm{e}^{-\beta(1-P)}(1+P\beta),$$

$$Q'' = \beta e^{-\beta(1-P)}(2 + P\beta).$$

Similarly, when $P = 0, Q = 0$; and when $P = 1, Q = 1$. Evidently nature (i) and nature (ii) of Lorenz Curve are satisfied. Also if we put the estimated value of β into the formula, and if $Q' > 0$ and $Q'' > 0$, nature iii and nature iv are satisfied, so the *K − P estimation equation I.* Lorenz Curve equation derived is valid. Generally, if $\beta > 0$, then $Q' > 0$ and $Q'' > 0$, proving the estimation equation is valid, and with it the computational formula of Gini Coefficient is as follows:

$$G = 1 - \frac{2(\beta - 1) + 2e^{-\beta}}{\beta^2}. \tag{2.2.13}$$

To generalize formula (2.2.12) as

$$Q = P^{\alpha} e^{-\beta(1-P)}. \tag{2.2.14}$$

α and β are parameters to be estimated, and their first derivative and second derivative are as follows respectively:

$$Q' = e^{-\beta(1-P)}\left(\alpha P^{\alpha-1} + \beta P\right),$$

$$Q'' = \beta e^{-\beta(1-P)}\left(\alpha\beta P^{\alpha-1} + \beta^2 P + \alpha(\alpha - 1)P + \beta\right).$$

If we put the estimated value of α and β into the above formula, and if $Q' > 0$ and $Q'' > 0$, then nature iii and nature iv are satisfied, so the Lorenz Curve equation derived is valid and with it the computational formula of Gini Coefficient is as follows:

$$G = 1 - \frac{2e^{-\beta}}{1 - \alpha} F(1 + \alpha, 2 + \alpha, \beta). \tag{2.2.15}$$

Herein $F(1 + \alpha, 2 + \alpha, \beta)$ is confluent hypergeometric function.

K − P estimation equation II. It is another type of Lorenz equation proposed by N.C. Kakwani and N. Podder in 1973. Suppose $P(x)$ and $Q(x)$ still refer to accumulative population (household) percentage and accumulative income percentage in a distribution respectively, then

$$P(x) = \int_0^x f(x)dx, \tag{2.2.16}$$

$$Q(x) = \frac{1}{\mu_0} \int_0^x xf(x)dx, \tag{2.2.17}$$

and

$$\pi = \frac{1}{\sqrt{2}}(P+Q), \quad \eta = \frac{1}{\sqrt{2}}(P-Q).$$

Since $Q, P \in [0,1]$ and $Q > P$, so $\eta > 0$, $\pi \in [1, \sqrt{2}]$. The geometric meaning of η and π is shown in Fig. 2.2.2, where A is a random point on Lorenz Curve OAD, η refers to the distance from point A to OD, and π refers to the distance from point O to point B. The mathematical expression of Lorenz Curve equation about η and π is as follows:

$$\eta = g(\pi). \tag{2.2.18}$$

If $f(x)$ is continuous, and Q and P are differentiable with respect to x, then $\mathrm{d}Q/\mathrm{d}x = (x/\mu_0)f(x)$, $\mathrm{d}P/\mathrm{d}x = f(x)$. From it we can make out η's derivative with respect to π:

$$\frac{\mathrm{d}\eta}{\mathrm{d}\pi} = \frac{\mu_0 - x}{\mu_0 + x}, \quad \frac{\mathrm{d}^2\eta}{\mathrm{d}\pi^2} = \frac{-2^{\frac{3}{2}}\mu_0^2}{f(x)(\mu_0 + x)^3}.$$

It can be inferred that when $x = \mu_0$, η gets the maximum. If Lorenz Curve is symmetrical with respect to diagonal QP, then η gets equal values in the case of π and $2^{\frac{1}{2}} - \pi$:

$$g(\pi) = g\left(2^{\frac{1}{2}} - \pi\right).$$

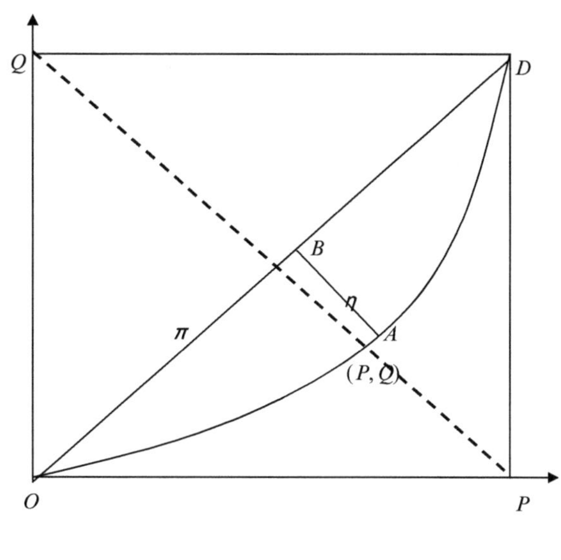

Fig. 2.2.2 Geometric graph of η and π

In the case of $\pi < 1/\sqrt{2}$, if $g(\pi) > f(2^{\frac{1}{2}} - \pi)$, then Lorenz Curve deflects to point (1,1); in the case of $\pi < 1/\sqrt{2}$, if $f(\pi) < g(2^{\frac{1}{2}} - \pi)$, then the Curve deflects to point (0,0).

Suppose the curve equation is:

$$\eta = \alpha\pi^{\alpha}(2 - \pi)^{\beta}, \tag{2.2.19}$$

and α and β are parameters to be estimated. If $\alpha > 0$ and $\beta > 0$, and when $\pi = 0$ or $\pi = \sqrt{2}$, $\eta = 0$. Nature i and nature ii of Lorenz Curve are satisfied. If $\alpha > 0$, then $\eta \geq 0$, and Lorenz Curve is below absolute equality line; if $\alpha = \beta$, then Lorenz Curve is symmetrical with respect to diagonal QP; if $\alpha < \beta$, the Curve deflects to point (0,0); if $\alpha > \beta$, it deflects to point (1,1). For (2.2.19), we have the first and second derivatives of η with respect to π:

$$g'(\pi) = 1 - \frac{\sqrt{2}Q + (1-\alpha)\eta}{\pi} + \frac{\beta\eta}{\sqrt{2} - \pi},$$

$$g''(\pi) = -\eta\left(\frac{\alpha(1-\alpha)}{\pi^2} + \frac{\beta(1-\beta)}{\sqrt{2} - \pi} + \frac{2\alpha\beta}{\pi(2^{\frac{1}{2}} - \pi)}\right).$$

And with it Gini Coefficient is formulated as follows:

$$G = 2\alpha\left(\sqrt{2}\right)^{1+\alpha+\beta} B(1+\alpha, 1+\beta). \tag{2.2.20}$$

General Quadratic Equation. Also called GQ estimation equation, it is proposed by Villasenor and Arnold in 1984 and improved in 1989. Suppose a general Lorenz equation is formulated as follows:

$$Q = Q(P, \pi). \tag{2.2.21}$$

Herein, Q stands for accumulative income percentage and P accumulative population (household) percentage, and π is the vector space for the estimated parameter. According to GQ estimation equation, Q is related to P in the following way:

$$Q(1-Q) = a\left(P^2 - Q\right) + bQ(P-1) + c(P-Q). \tag{2.2.22}$$

a, b, and c are parameters to be estimated. This equation is good for its simple computation with general regression. Besides, by estimating the relations between coefficients, an assessment may be made on the validity of estimated result. For detailed conditions, see Table 2.2.1.

Table 2.2.1 Conditions for assessing validity of GQ estimation equation

Theoretical conditions	GQ-model estimation equation
(1) $Q(0,\pi)=0$	$e<0$
(2) $Q(1,\pi)=1$	$a+c\geq 1$
(3) $Q'(P,\pi)\geq 0$	$c\geq 1$
(4) $Q''(P,\pi)\geq 0$	(i) $m<0$, or (ii) $0<m<\frac{n^2}{4e^2}, n\geq 0$, n ≥ 0 or (iii) $0<m<-\frac{n}{2}, m<\frac{n^2}{4e^2}$
$e=-(a+b+c+1)$, $m=b^2-4a$, $n=2be-4c$	

Source: Gauray Datt (1998), "Computational tools for poverty measurement and analysis", Discussion paper of food consumption and nutrition division of International Food Policy Research Institute, October, p. 12

The first and second derivatives of Q with respect to P are as follows:

$$Q'(P)=-\frac{b}{2}-\frac{(2mP+n)(mP^2+nP+e^2)^{-\frac{1}{2}}}{4}.$$

$$Q''(P)=\frac{r^2(mP^2+nP+e^2)^{-\frac{3}{2}}}{8}.$$

And with it if the computational formula of Gini Coefficient is $m<0$, then

$$G=\frac{e}{2}-\frac{n(b+2)}{4m}+\frac{r^2}{8m\sqrt{-m}}\left[\sin^{-1}\left(\frac{2m+n}{r}\right)-\sin^{-1}\frac{n}{r}\right]. \tag{2.2.23}$$

If $m>0$, then

$$G=\frac{e}{2}-\frac{n(b+2)}{4m}-\frac{r^2}{8m\sqrt{m}}\ln\left\{abs\left[\frac{2m+n+2\sqrt{m}(a+c-1)}{n-2e\sqrt{m}}\right]\right\}. \tag{2.2.24}$$

The concrete calculation for e, m, and n is shown in Table 2.2.1, $r=(n^2-4me^2)^{\frac{1}{2}}$. As for GQ equation, only in the condition of $a+c\geq 1$ are the computational formulas (2.2.23) and (2.2.24) valid.

Beta estimation equation. It is proposed by Kakwani in 1980. Suppose the form of Lorenz Curve equation is identical with (2.2.21), then according to Beta estimation equation, the relation between Q and P is as follows:

$$Q=P-\theta P^{\gamma}(1-P)^{\delta}. \tag{2.2.25}$$

θ, γ, and δ are parameters to be estimated. Table 2.2.2 gives the conditions which make Beta estimation equation valid.

The first and second derivatives of Q with respect to P are as follows:

Table 2.2.2 Conditions for assessing the validity of Beta estimation equation

Theoretical conditions	GQ-model estimation equation
(1) $Q(0, \pi) = 0$	Equation (2.2.25) itself meets the requirement
(2) $Q(1, \pi) = 1$	Equation (2.2.25) itself meets the requirement
(3) $Q'(P, \pi) \geq 0$	$Q'(0.001, \theta, \gamma, \delta) \geq 0$
(4) $Q''(P, \pi) \geq 0$	$Q''(P, \theta, \gamma, \delta) \geq 0, P \in \{0.01, 0.02, \ldots, 0.99\}$

Source: The same with Table 2.2.1

$$Q'(P) = 1 - \theta P^{\gamma}(1-P)^{\delta}\left(\frac{\gamma}{P} - \frac{\delta}{1-P}\right),$$

$$Q''(P) = \theta P^{\gamma}(1-P)^{\delta}\left[\frac{\gamma(1-\gamma)}{P} + \frac{2\gamma\delta}{(1-P)P} + \frac{\delta(1-\delta)}{(1-P)^2}\right].$$

The computational formula of Gini Coefficient is as follows:

$$G = 2\theta B(1+\gamma, 1+\delta). \tag{2.2.26}$$

Herein, $B(1+\gamma, 1+\delta)$ is Beta function, which can be formulated as follows:

$$B(1+\gamma, 1+\delta) = \int_0^1 P^{\gamma}(1-P)^{\delta}\mathrm{d}P.$$

The weakness of Beta estimation equation is that it needs to solve a recessive nonlinear equation, making the computation difficult.

In fact, apart from the above calculations, there are still others. For instance, Professor Chen Zongsheng (1991) suggested two types of calculation methods, "unequal grouping" and "equal grouping", based on whether the observed population or household data are equally divided. In this book his methods are not introduced in detail.

2.3 Meaning of Polarization and Its Measurement

In previous section we dealt with such concepts of income distribution and income inequality as well as some major indexes for its measurement. Among them, Lorenz Curve and Gini Coefficient and their estimation and computation are given prominence. In the following part, we will go into polarization, another issue inseparable from income distribution. And some indexes and methods for its measurement will be presented.

2.3.1 Meaning of Polarization[3]

In the field of income distribution study, in addition to income inequality, another focus is on polarization. Before arguing whether there is a phenomenon of polarization in income distribution, we need to clarify its meaning. What is polarization? How to judge polarization?

Some scholars hold that generally speaking, polarization is not equal to enlargement of income inequality. First, in terms of the content of the two concepts, polarization attaches much importance to comparison between income of the poor and that of the rich. Or put in another way, polarization focuses on the two extremes in income distribution system, whereas enlargement of income inequality points out a whole picture of income distribution, with all groups included. In the latter case, the factors leading to enlarged income inequality are complex, they may be either the rise of the high-income, or the reduction of the low-income, or both, or change of the middle-income. Second, an enlarged income inequality does not necessarily result in polarization, and vice versa. Take an example. It could be that the high-income group sees a rise in their income with the middle- and low-income groups' incomes remaining stable. It could also be that the low-income group sees a cut in their incomes with the high- and middle-income groups' incomes remaining stable. The two cases will lead to an enlarged income inequality, but not necessarily polarization. Again, suppose there is a rise in high-income group's incomes and a decline in low-income group's incomes, and at the same time a change to the middle-income group's incomes, then it could be that the income inequality will remain stable and even decrease a bit. In this sense, we cannot simply regard polarization as a special example of enlarged income inequality. They cross each other, but remain different. We cannot call any enlarged income inequality polarization.

Some scholars divide polarization into absolute one and relative one. Absolute polarization means an absolute increase in the high-income group's incomes along with a concurrent absolute reduction in low-income group's incomes, or what is so called "the rich being richer, the poor being poorer." Relative polarization refers to a parallel increase in both high- and low-income groups' incomes, but with the former more rapid in its rise and thus leading to a relatively enlarged inequality; or in another case, a parallel decrease in both high- and low-income groups' incomes, but with the latter diving more quickly and thus leading to a relatively enlarged inequality.

Some scholars suggest that polarization should be investigated from dynamic and static perspectives. That is, we have to judge an income distribution by separately analyzing the trend of polarization and the state of polarization. Failure in this account will cause mistake in policymaking. Static perspective demands we put the investigation in the absolute and relative inequality between the

[3] This part of analysis is partly borrowed from Hong Xingjiang and Li Jinchang (2007).

high-income and low-income in the context of a specific period, 1 year, for instance. To fulfill this, we need to construct an assessment indicator and delimit it. Any state beyond the mark is deemed polarization. Dynamic perspective refers to the change course of the absolute and relative inequality between the high-income and the low-income in a certain period of time. Again, we need to specify a certain assessment tool and the time span for comparison.

Of course, some scholars (Joan-Maria Esteban and Debraj Ray 1994) think differently. They assume that only two extremes or two opposite sides can be defined as polar, and so-called division means that homogeneous entity changes into heterogeneous one. In this respect, polarization may be understood as the transformation of homogeneous entity into its extremes or its opposite. Based on this understanding, polarization in income distribution means an originally balanced income distribution changes into one with sharp rise in both high-income and low-income groups and increasing reduction in middle-income group. When it comes to the pattern of income distribution, polarization should indicate a dumb-bell-like distribution pattern, with a large number of people crowding in the two ends of high-income and low-income and less people in between. From this assumption, it can be reasoned that a complete polarization should suggest the complete disappearance of the middle-income, the whole income goes equally to one half of the population and the other half's income is zero. Obviously this theory on polarization is unscientific; it describes the wealth gap at best. Wealth gap analysis is conducted by comparing the rich to the poor, whereas polarization aims at all members of the society, classing them and judging the degree of polarization according to the difference between the last two groups as well as the aggregation in each group.

Of course, they also distinguish income inequality from polarization. Income inequality, they say, refers to the dispersion degree of income distribution for a group of people. It emphasizes the mean deviation of individual from the ensemble average and takes no account of local clustering degree of individuals. As mentioned before, we know that the fundamental principle in measuring income inequality is Pigou–Dalton Axiom, that is, if other conditions remain unchanged, any income transfer from the rich to the poor—not altering the original income order—will effectuate a reduction in inequality. Polarization focuses more on local clustering of income. It is contradictory with Pigou–Dalton Axiom. Suppose the incomes of four people are in arithmetic progression, shown as a, b, c, and d in Fig. 2.3.1. Now if given a redistribution between a and b, c and d, then the two groups are equally distributed, shown as e and f in Fig. 2.3.2. It is obvious that after redistribution, the overall income gap is shortened, but the whole society sees an intensified aggregation in two ends and the disappearance of the middle-income,

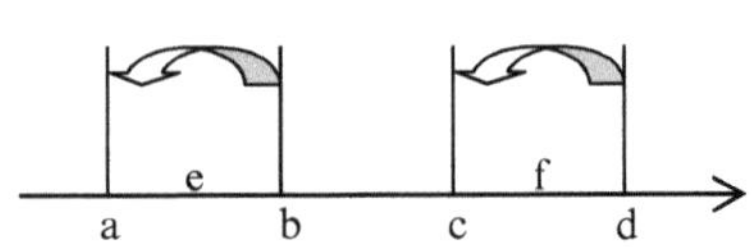

Fig. 2.3.1 Original income distribution

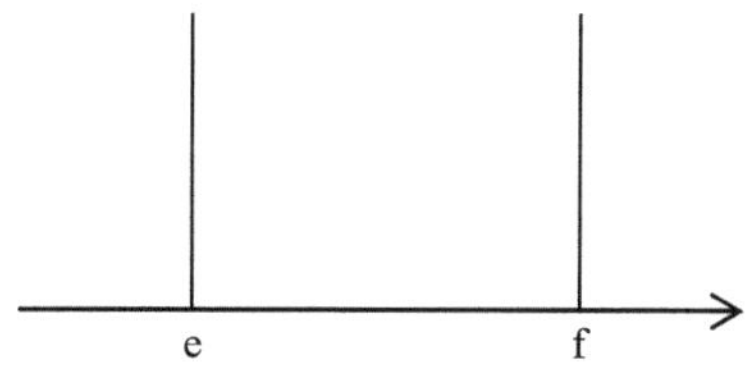

Fig. 2.3.2 Income redistribution

thus a more serious polarization. The two figures demonstrate a direct difference between polarization and income inequality. It is probable that a severe polarization does not necessarily result in a large index of income inequality, and vice versa.

They propose that polarization should be judged on quantitative analysis, including drawing probability density distribution graph and calculating some indexes. They pay much attention to the quantitative attribute, while putting aside factors behind. To answer this question, many qualitative explanations come to be useful, such as social system, development mode, ethnic issue, and religious issue. Some countries in Latin America and Africa witness a flaring polarization, and some countries like Canada and North European countries do not see much of polarization. In some transition countries, due to the function of market and possible policy defects, polarization also occurs. Unfair distribution leads to polarization, so do unequal initial resources and difference in working skills. Certainly they should be handled differently. The former, unfair distribution should be eliminated, while the latter could be improved by means of indirect mediation. So, polarization has something to do with social system, but it has more to do with economic development strategies and ways and levels of social security.

2.3.2 Indexes for Measuring Degree of Polarization

Gini Coefficient. Gini Coefficient is a popular method to measure degree of polarization. It is well accepted that if Gini Coefficient is larger than 0.5, then the income distribution is polarized. Some scholars argue that this standard, based on private economy, is not applicable to public economy like China. According to them, the factors influencing income distribution in public economy and private economy are different, and the primary difference is that in private economy capital receipts directly determine individual or family income. Obviously, income inequality of the two economies cannot be compared immediately. Only after taking away the factor of capital receipts in private economy, can the rest factors reflecting the inequality of income from labor be compared with those in public economy. If data are available, we may also compare the inequality of income from labor in private economy with that in public economy. By rigorous comparison, they find that with the same level of income, the degree of capital's influence on income inequality is about 0.1477 (Chen Zongsheng 1991). Deducting 0.1477 from 0.5, the remaining 0.3523 could be set as standard value of Gini Coefficient to judge polarization in public economy. However, with the rapid development of self-employed and private businesses, current Chinese economy is no longer public out and out, but a mixed economy with public ownership being the center. Capital receipt has been playing a vital role in Chinese residents' income inequality. Some scholars suggest that a deduction of 50% of 0.1477 may be more appropriate with Chinese mixed economy. After the deduction, the standard value of Gini Coefficient for judging polarization in Chinese residents' income inequality is 0.4262 (0.5–0.07385), and is used to test polarization in income distribution among urban and rural residents since the late 1980s.[4] A question arises when judging polarization with Gini Coefficient: how much should we set its standard value? In effect, it is difficult to find one fit for all countries. Different countries with different population, geography, economic system, and social custom have varying perceptions of income inequality. Basically, countries with larger territory and population are more tolerant with income inequality, and have a higher standard value for judging polarization, while countries with smaller territory and population are less tolerant and have a lower standard value. In the same way, countries and regions with a long tradition of predominant private economy may hold a higher standard for polarization, whereas income inequality is less tolerated in countries like China who has a long tradition of egalitarianism and is undergoing transformation from a single public economy to a mixed one. In these countries, a relatively low standard for judging polarization works better. Of course, perceptions of income inequality change with social development, and so will the standard for judging polarization.

It is because of such problems with Gini Coefficient standard that some scholars believe that since polarization is different from income inequality and wealth gap, all indexes including Gini Coefficient for measuring inequality do not work well with polarization. A new method, they suggest, must be introduced. Current indexes measuring income polarization fall into two basic categories. One is W-mode indexes, first put forward by Wolfson (1994) and developed later by Wang and Tusi (2000), Chakravarty and Majumder (2001), and Rodriguez and Salas (2003). This type of index divides all members into two groups besides the median, high-income and low-income, measures how much the income of members of each group is deviated from the median, and sums up all the deviations. Another type of index is called ER index, first proposed by Esteban and Ray (1994) and later improved by Esteban et al. (1999) and Duclos et al. (2003). This type of index groups all members according to certain standard for the first time, then proceeds to measure the difference between groups and similarity among members of each group, and finally figures out the index with specific form construction. It is safe to say *W*-mode index is used specifically for measuring polarization, and ER index can also be used for measuring multipolarization. Next we will go into these two types of index in detail.

[4] In fact, the Income Worsening Index mentioned before may also serve as an index to judge polarization.

W Index. Inspired by the important function of Lorentz Curve in measuring income inequality, Foster and Wolfson (1992) advanced concept of polarization curve and expounded the relation between polarization curve and Lorentz Curve. Wolfson (1994) gave a formula for measuring polarization:

$$W = \frac{2(2T - G)}{\left(\frac{m}{\mu}\right)}. \tag{2.3.1}$$

Here, m and μ stand for the median and arithmetical mean of all members' incomes, G is Gini Coefficient, T refers to the difference between population share of 50% low-income members and their income share, namely, $T = 0.5 - L(0.5)$, and $L(0.5)$ refers to income share of 50% lowest income members. Of course formula (2.3.1) can be further simplified. Mookherjee and Shorrocks (1982) gave the decomposition formula of Gini Coefficient as follows: $G = \sum_k {v_k}^2 \lambda_k G_k + \frac{1}{2} \sum_k \sum_h v_k v_h |\lambda_k - \lambda_h| + R$. v_k here refers to population share of group k, λ_k means percentage of the average income in group k to the overall average income, and G_k means Gini Coefficient of group k. The first item on the right of the formula refers to weighted average of Gini Coefficient inside group, indicating the contribution of inequality inside group to the overall inequality, marked as G_W. The second item is Gini Coefficient based on the average income of groups, indicating the contribution of inequality between groups to the overall inequality, marked as G_B. The third item R points to the interaction between groups due to their overlapping. If the median is set as demarcating point, we have two groups on both sides. In this case, $R = 0$, $V_1 = V_2 = 0.5$, $\lambda_1 = L(0.5)/0.5$, and $\lambda_2 = 1 - L(0.5)/0.5$. Then, $G_B = 0.5 - L(0.5)$ and $G_B = G - 0.5 - L(0.5)$, which are put into formula (2.3.1):

$$W = \frac{2\mu(G_B - G_W)}{m}. \tag{2.3.2}$$

From (2.3.2), it not difficult to detect the difference between polarization measurement and income inequality measurement based on W-mode index. They approach inequality inside group differently. With the former approach, inequality inside group is detracted from that between groups, while with the latter, inequality inside group is added to that between groups. Suppose the inequality between two groups remains unchanged, and if the inequality inside group declines, then income distribution of members within each group tends to be fair. If the inequality between groups remains unchanged and that within group is reduced, then it suggests that income distribution on the part of each member tends to be fair, but inequality between groups is liable to enlargement, and sharper the contrast, the larger the polarization. Anyhow, the overall income inequality is reduced. Therefore, in light of W-mode index, measuring polarization does have something to do with income inequality, but they are different in nature.

W index is operated on two conditions: the median as the grouping criterion and Gini Coefficient as the measurement index for income inequality. In recent years some scholars have developed these two conditions. Rodríguez (2005) analyzed the measurement formula with other grouping criterion. If it is an average μ, the formula for measuring polarization is $W_\mu = 2[2(p(\mu) - L(p(\mu))) - G] = 2\left(G_B^\mu - G_W^\mu\right)$, in which G_B^μ and G_W^μ refer to respectively the Gini between groups and the Gini within a group with μ as the cutoff point, and $P(\mu)$ and $L(p(\mu))$ represent population share and income share lower than average μ. Since $P(\mu) - L(p(\mu))$ has the largest value relative to other division points, so for the same income distribution, *W* index has the largest value with average μ as division point. If the division point is set on random income z, the measurement formula for polarization is $W_z = \frac{2\mu}{z}(G_B^z - G_W^z) + (1 - 2p(z))(\mu - z)$. Some other scholars also borrowed other indexes instead of Gini Coefficient to measure W index. Rodríguez and Salas (2003), by replacing Gini Coefficient with single parameter Gini index, offered a formula of measuring extended bipolarization: $W^v = G_B^v - G_W^v$, in which G_B^v and G_W^v stand for inequality between groups and inequality within a group based on single parameter Gini index measurement, namely, $G_B^v = v(v-1)\int_0^1 (1-p)^{v-2} [p - L_B(p)]\mathrm{d}p$ and $G_W^v = v(v-1)\int_0^1 (1-p)^{v-2}[L_B(p) - L(p)]\mathrm{d}p$, respectively. Here $L_B(p)$ refers to irregular Lorenz curve linking the average incomes of groups. Other scholars like Chakravarty and Majumder (2001), by comparing income inequality, polarization, and welfare, pointed out that any income inequality index determined by the homothetic function of social welfare corresponds to polarization index, and their formula of measuring extended bipolarization is as follows:

$$\mathrm{CM} = \frac{\Xi(x_+) + 2\mu(x_+)}{2m} + \frac{\Xi(x_-) + B(m)\cdot\mu(x_-)}{2m} + H(m). \tag{2.3.3}$$

Herein, x_- and x_+ refer to income vector below the median and income vector above the median, respectively, while $\mu(x_-)$ and $\mu(x_+)$ refer to their average incomes, respectively. $B(m)$ and $H(m)$ are functions about the median, some axioms that satisfy polarization by selecting appropriate forms proportionate to differing social welfare functions. Ξ means social welfare function of equal distribution of the same income, $\Xi(x_-)$ means all population (households) below the median enjoy an equal distribution of the same income, and the consequent social welfare function value is equal to that of the real income distribution x_-. Aiming at the general form of polarization index, Chakravarty and Majumder (2001) gave polarization indexes under Atkinson index and Theil index. In theory, extended polarization index has enriched our understanding of polarization, but due to its intricate structure and not being illustrative, it is seldom given priority in practical measurement.

Duclos and Échevin (2005) proposed the dominant method of the polarization curve, which is very illustrative but will fall short when polarization curves in different income distribution patterns cross. A surprising parallel with Lorenz Curve. When it comes to real measurement index, Wang and Tusi (2000) offered a visual one, based on two given axioms[5]:

$$\mathrm{WT} = \frac{\theta}{n}\sum_{i=1}^{n}\left|\frac{x_{(i)} - m}{m}\right|^{r}. \tag{2.3.4}$$

Herein, n is the number of samples, m is the median income, $x(i)$ stands for individual income of number i in an ascending sequence of income levels, θ and γ are two positive invariables, and $\gamma \in (0, 1)$. When sorting polarizations in varying income distributions, the same θ does not affect the sorting result. So, given the generality, we may suppose $\theta = 1$. But different values of γ will affect the sorting, because a larger γ will give more weight to income above $2m$, and at the same time less weight to income below $2m$.[6] As a result, if income of some very rich people is enormously farther from the median, WT index will become sensitive to parameter γ; that is, different values of γ will effectuate different polarization sorting.

ER Index. Esteban and Ray (1994) put forward another measurement after defining identification and alienation. Identification is the increasing function of population (household) number within group. The more people in the same group, the stronger identification they have. Alienation is a contrast born from income inequality between groups. The larger the inequality, the stronger alienation they have. Suppose $x(i)$ is the average income per capita in group i, and p_i is the population share of group i, then its identification function in Esteban and Ray's term is p_i^{α} and its alienation function is $|x_i - x_j|$. Multiply the two and add all groups, we have ER index as follows:

$$\mathrm{ER} = K\sum_{i=1}^{n}\sum_{j=1}^{n} {p_i}^{1+\alpha} p_j |x_i - x_j|. \tag{2.3.5}$$

Herein, $K > 0$ is a constant for the function of standardization, α is a parameter indicating the degree of polarization sensitivity, and at the same time $\alpha \in [1, 1.6]$. We can see that ER index has a similar formula with that of Gini Coefficient. If $\alpha = 0$, then ER index has the same measurement effect with that of Gini Coefficient. In effect, Gini Coefficient is a specific example of ER index. A larger α will

[5] The two axioms are increased spread and increased bipolarization. For any n dimensional income vectors x and y, given the same median, suppose x_- and y_- indicate income vectors below the median, and x_+ and y_+ indicate income vectors above the median. If $y_- \le x_-$ and $x_+ \le y_+$, we will have a more increased spread of y relative to x; this is called increased spread axiom. If y_- and y_+ depend on progressive income transfer of x_- and x_+, respectively, we will have a more polarized y than x; this is called increased bi-polarization axiom.

[6] For index function $y = a^{\gamma}$, since $\mathrm{d}y/\mathrm{d}\gamma = a^{\gamma}\ln a$, so when $a > 1$, $\mathrm{d}y/\mathrm{d}\gamma > 0$; when $a < 1$, $\mathrm{d}y/\mathrm{d}\gamma < 0$. In the case of the book, when $a > 1$, $x(i) > 2m$, and when $a < 1$, $x(i) < 2m$.

result in a larger deviation of ER-based sorting from Gini Coefficient-based sorting. If there is only one object in each group, it does not make difference to the measurement either by ER index or by Gini Coefficient.

However, ER index is based on the assumption that members of a group are completely identified with one another, an assumption that is not satisfied in most cases, for the degree of identification within a group depends on the group's scale and its formation method. For improvement, Esteban et al. (1999) revised ER index in the following way:

$$\mathrm{EGR} = K\sum_{i=1}^{n}\sum_{j=1}^{n} p_i p_j p_i^{\alpha}\left|x_i - x_j\right| - \beta(G - G(x)). \tag{2.3.6}$$

Herein $\beta > 0$, and it is a sensitive parameter to measure the concentration degree within a group, G refers to the Gini coefficient of practical income distribution, and $G(x)$ refers to the Gini which is calculated in the condition that each member's income in a group is equal to the average income of the group, x. The first part in the right side of EGR is ER index, and the second part tells inequality within a group. The larger the second part, the smaller degree of concentration of members of the group, and the smaller the polarization. So a subtraction sign is put before the second part. It is safe for us to conclude that W index and EGR index approach inequality within a group from virtually the same way, only except that the former is suitable for two divisions with a median as the division point, while the latter suits all grouping. As proved by Esteban, Gradín and Ray, W index is just a specific example of EGR index. However, there exists some fallacy with EGR index, though its authors realized that inequality within a group plays a significant role in forming the identification among members of a group. Only when incomes of members of each group do not overlap, can $G - G(x)$, the second part of formula (2.3.6), reflects inequality within a group. Considering the above fallacy of EGR index, Lasso and Urrutia (2006) offered an alternative formula:

$$\mathrm{LU} = K\sum_{i=1}^{n}\sum_{j=1}^{n} p_i p_j p_i^{\alpha}(1 - G_i)^{\beta}\left|x_i - x_j\right|. \tag{2.3.7}$$

Herein G_i means the Gini coefficient of the income of members in group i. It is obvious that with LU index, the impact of inequality within a group is directly reflected in the identification function of ER index, a way to make up for the drawback of EGR index to some degree.

Whether ER index works well or not is dependent on right grouping, which demands that we make a careful and minute analysis on the observed and select the most related grouping mark to better display the difference between groups and the similarity within group. Under some circumstances when grouping is exogenous, ER index works well in measuring polarization from, say, different religions, ethnics, and regions. Duclos et al. (2004) provided another ER index and EGR index of successive income distribution to help people measure polarization by dint of sample theory. W index, though devised specifically for measuring polarization, is also flawed in that its two-division method with median as the cutoff point does not always work well. Suppose, for instance, the income distribution of six people is like (4, 4, 4, 5, 10, 10), it is more scientific to divide them into two groups with the first four items in one group, and the last two in other group than two equal divisions.

Just like measuring income inequality, to measure polarization is to realize a transformation from a N dimensional vector space to a real number, that is, to express the polarization feature of a group of income data with a real number. In this process, loss of information is inevitable. Since each measurement index is flawed in one way or another, so to select a couple of indexes with differing natures is necessary for empirical analysis, which will guarantee more information and reasonable judgment. Polarization measurement study (including multi-polarization) has come into being for about a decade, and there is much room for improvement despite new measurements coming out from time to time. What underpins the problem is an incomplete theoretical foundation and axiom system. No unified framework is available in which current measurement indexes can be judged. This is where it contrasts sharply with the study of income inequality measurement. The priority in the field of measuring polarization should be given to constructing axiom system, and advance a better measurement index according to practical problems.

2.3.3 Measurement for Judging Trend of Polarization

All the indexes introduced in previous parts, Gini Coefficient, W index, and ER index, approach polarization from static perspective. In other words, they measure the degree of polarization. Previous studies (Chen Zongsheng and Zhou Yunbo 2002) suggested that besides measuring the degree of polarization, we should also judge its trend, that is, to approach polarization from dynamic perspective, an approach which may be named as "trend comparing method." The method may be divided into "absolute" and "relative". Absolute approach means the change of average incomes of the highest and the lowest groups at present time relative to those in previous time. If the rise of average income of the highest group is in tandem with the decline of average income of the lowest group, we believe that polarization of absolute income level takes place, which may be expressed in the following mathematical formulas:

$$\frac{\mathrm{d}y_r}{\mathrm{d}t} > 0 \quad \text{and} \quad \frac{\mathrm{d}y_p}{\mathrm{d}t} < 0.$$

Herein, y_r means average income of the highest income group, y_p means average income of the lowest income group, and $\mathrm{d}y_r/\mathrm{d}t$ and $\mathrm{d}y_p/\mathrm{d}t$ represent temporal change rate of respective group. Relative approach claims that if the ratio of average income of the highest income group to that of the middle income group is increased and at the same time the ratio of average income of the lowest income group to that of the middle income group is reduced, we may say a relative polarization happens, which may be expressed in the following mathematical formulas:

$$\frac{y_r(t)}{y_m(t)} > \frac{y_r(t-1)}{y_m(t-1)} \quad \text{and} \quad \frac{y_p(t)}{y_m(t)} < \frac{y_p(t-1)}{y_m(t-1)}.$$

Both are satisfied. $y_m(t)$ refers to per capita average income of the middle-income group in t time, also called total average income or median income.

When putting the two approaches into practical test for polarization, some technical issues should not be neglected.[7] First, how to demarcate two poles? How much percentage should highest income group and lowest income group take in total population? Do we select the highest income group and lowest income group from five equal divisions, or ten equal divisions, or even twenty equal divisions? Different grouping may result in opposite conclusion. Presently, there is no such absolute grouping standard for judging polarization. Conventionally, 5% or 10% of the poorest and the richest population are taken as two poles in income distribution. By comparing the variation trend of income inequality between the two groups, we may judge whether polarization exists or not.

The second question is how to set the median from relative approach to polarization? To fix it on total average income, or on per capita income of the middle group, or on per capita income in mode group.

Taking seven divisions as an example (see Table 2.3.1). We are supposed to judge the trend of polarization in 2010, with 2004 being the base year. We take 10% of the lowest income group and another 10% of the highest income group as the two poles in income distribution, and we set the per capita income of 20% middle group as the median in relative approach. In 2004, the ratio of the per capita income in 10% lowest income group to the median was 0.36, the ratio of the per capita income in 10% highest income group to the median was 2.86; in 2010, the ratios changed to 0.30 and 3.0, respectively. The ratio of the per capita income in the highest income group to the median rose, but at the same time the ratio of the per capita income in the lowest income group to the median decreased, a phenomenon that meets relative polarization standard. So we may conclude that there exists a trend of relative polarization. If we set the total average income as the median, then in 2004, the ratio of per capita income of 10% lowest income group to the median was 0.35, and the ratio of the per capita income of 10% highest income group to the median was 2.81; in 2010 the ratios changed to 0.28 and 2.77, respectively. Though the ratio of per capita income in the lowest income group to the median was reduced, the ratio of

[7] For these technical issues, one of the authors discussed these issues in his former book (Chen Zongsheng and Zhou Yunbo 2002). In this book, we will discuss them in more detail.

Table 2.3.1 Examples of judging trend of polarization

Grouping	2004	2007	2010
1(10%)	100	80	90
2(10%)	–	–	–
3(20%)	–	–	–
4(20%)	280	295	300
5(20%)	–	–	–
6(10%)	–	–	–
7(10%)	800	900	900
Total average	285	300	325

Source: By author's own design

per capita income in the highest income group to the median also declined, which does not meet requirements for relative polarization. So we cannot conclude that a relative polarization occurs in this case.

In addition, when doing comparative study from the two approaches, contradiction will arise. Again take the above table as an example. In 2004 the average incomes per capita of 10% of the poorest and the richest were 100 yuan and 800 yuan, and in 2010 they were 90 yuan and 900 yuan, a good example for absolute polarization. So we can say 2010 saw a trend of absolute polarization. However, if measured by relative polarization, that is to say, if we set the total average income as the median, no polarization took place. It has been generally accepted that absolute polarization has a looser standard than relative polarization, and the former, if ever in existence, will inevitably result in the latter. But this contradicts against the conclusion we just reached. We have to be cautious with the above approaches.

Furthermore, the two approaches belong to comparing method of time trend, so different base periods will bring about different results. In Table 2.3.1, if we set 2004 as the base year, then year 2010 saw a trend of absolute polarization. If we set 2007 as the base year, then there was no absolute polarization in 2010, a conclusion totally to the contrary.

All in all, when we measure trend of polarization from the above mentioned approaches, we have to be very careful about the comparability of conclusion, for differing grouping and selection of the median and base period tend to effectuate different and even contradictory conclusions.

2.3.4 Combined Perspectives to Judge Polarization

In conclusion, either the static indexes for measuring degree of polarization or the dynamic methods for testing trend of polarization is somewhat flawed. Only with a combined approach can we elicit an inclusive and objective judgment on income distribution and polarization. Any wrong judgment will lead to distorted policy. Suppose current income distribution pattern is quite fair and its Gini Coefficient is

0.16, then it implies an egalitarian distribution by international standard. However, seen from dynamic perspective, the pattern suggests a trend of absolute or relative polarization. What should be the policy priority? In view if trend, the policy priority should be given to retaining the enlarged income inequality, but chances are it would get bogged down in egalitarianism and put economic efficiency at stake. Instead, the priority should be put on guiding the income inequality to widen and shaking off egalitarian distribution in order to increase economic efficiency on the one hand, and to keep a close eye on substantial causes for potential polarization, in particular the income change to the low-income group so as to prevent absolute income reduction of the low-income group. Again, suppose current income inequality is quite large and its Gini Coefficient is bigger than 0.5, then its means a state of polarization. Nevertheless, seen from dynamic perspective, no trend of either absolute or relative polarization occurs. If government ignores, social upheaval caused by too widened income inequality will probably break out. The right way for policymakers is to control the sharp income rise of the high-income group and increase earnings of the low-income, but not at the expense of efficiency. As a corollary, to judge whether a society is polarized we should take both dynamic and static perspectives into account. Only in this way can distorted policy priority be avoided.

Chapter 3
Income Inequality of China's Urban Residents and the Factors Which Impact It

This chapter is made up of four sections. Section 3.1 reviews the change of income distribution system in China's urban area (including cities and towns) since its reform and opening up to the world. The analysis focuses on the dynamics of income inequality of urban residents. Sections 3.2 and 3.3 are devoted to analyzing main determinants of income inequality and its dynamics in light of income structure and household features, respectively. Section 3.4 looks into some macroscopic economic variables in terms of their influence on the change of urban residents' income inequality.

3.1 Economic System and Structure in China's Urban Area and Change of Income Inequality of Urban Residents Since Reform

Since the reform and opening-up policy, cities and towns in China have seen great change in economic system and structure. It has brought about change in income distribution pattern, and an increasingly widened income inequality in particular. This chapter will go into them in detail.

3.1.1 Change of Urban Income Distribution System

In view of economic system, one change that is mostly related to income distribution in cities and towns is the internal wage system reform in state-owned and collective enterprises and institutions. Up to now, there have been three major wage system reforms in state-owned enterprises, institutions, and government administrations. The first reform started in 1985, when the wage system in state-owned enterprises was gradually separated from that in administrations and institutions,

Y. Zhou and Y. Qin, *Empirical Analysis on Income Inequality of Chinese Residents*, Gu Shutang Acad Fund Econ, DOI 10.1007/978-3-642-24952-5_3,

and a new one was formulated to meet the demand of the emerging market economy. A worker's wage income became to be linked with his enterprise's economic efficiency and personal contribution. Piece rates and hour wage came out successively, which to some degree contributed to the enlarged income inequality within and between state-owned enterprises. On the other hand, administrations and institutions maintained the original structural wage system featuring pay according to one's post.

The second wave of wage reform began in 1993 in administrations and institutions. The administrative departments instituted placement wage system based on ranking of the post. By adding part of welfare subsidies into the income, placement wage system regulated the structure of wage income and built up a new subsidy system and a normal mechanism of wage raise. Institutions adopted another wage system characteristic of their own sectors. That is to say, fives types of wage system took effect in different institutions, namely, grading wage system for academic and technical titles, rank and post wage system, structural wage system for arts, allowance and bonus wage system for sports, and worker's wage system. In this way clerks and workers in administrations and institutions began to have somewhat hierarchical yet as a whole equal wages. In state-owned enterprises, leasing, contracted responsibility, and annual pay were put into force; some even began to give out partial stock rights and options to the leaders and high-level management. A group of high income cropped up. In parallel, since the end of 1996 a new policy of reshuffling for higher efficiency in state-owned enterprises has spewed out hordes of laid-off and unemployed, who constitute another group of low income. Income inequality between entrepreneurial leaders and high-level management on the one hand and common employees on the other was enlarged.

The third reform came in 2002 and was targeted at administrations and institutions. In provinces of Guangdong, Zhejiang, Liaoning, and municipalities of Beijing and Tianjin, a system called "sunlight wage" has been in action in Party and government departments since 2002 by standardizing allowances and subsidies. This wage system reform for civil servants has the following characters: first, their salary is raised by a large margin through such measures like simplifying the salary structure, increasing rankings, and improving salary regulation. The incentive function of wage is highlighted. Second, salary gap between different ranks and posts is widened. Third, some favor is given to grassroot organizations. Some low posts are given a higher rank to permit civil servants in low post to have adequate potential for promotion. Fourth, favor is also given to remote areas and hardship-post allowances are introduced therein. With more people included, standard of allowance raised, and the variety of allowances increased, a dynamic wage regulating mechanism was put in motion. In parallel, the institutions adjusted their wage system in five aspects. First, a worker's salary was linked with his post responsibility, performance, and achievement. Second, a new system of classified salary management was formulated for institutions which provide the public service. Third, a normal wage regulating mechanism in line with the workplace was set up, which ran in a somewhat different way from that of administrations. Fourth, incentive mechanism of income distribution for highly talented people was further developed and incentive restraining mechanism for income distribution among leaders in institutions was laid down. At the same time, the income distribution of some institutions will be guided. Finally, a control mechanism for income distribution was improved. Classified management, regulation at different levels, bettered regulating policy, and salary payment management were coordinated for the purpose of establishing a working macroscopic regulating mechanism.

3.1.2 *Change of Urban Economic Structure*

Urban economic structure has been through significant swings since the system reform due to the accelerated degree of market orientation and opening the door. One of them is the multiple forms of ownership structure, including foreign-owned enterprises, joint ventures, joint cooperatives, private enterprises, and self-employed, which have gained sustainable development and taken growing share in national economy and offered multitudinous opportunities for a large number of labors (see Table 3.1.1).

The table shows that in 1978 the number of the employed in state-owned and collective economic units (SCEU) was 94.97 m, occupying as high as 99.82% of total urban labors, whereas the number of the employed in non-state-owned

Table 3.1.1 Ownership structure of the employment of urban labors (1978–2010)

Year	Total number of urban labor (10,000)	State-owned and collective economic units		Non-state-owned economic units	
		Number of employed (10,000)	Share to total urban labors (%)	Number of employed (10,000)	Share to total urban labors (%)
1978	9,514	9,497	99.82	17	0.18
1980	10,525	10,444	99.23	81	0.77
1985	12,808	12,314	96.14	494	3.86
1990	17,041	13,610	81.54	3,146	18.46
1995	19,040	14,408	75.67	4,632	24.33
1998	21,616	11,021	50.99	10,595	49.01
1999	22,412	10,284	45.89	12,128	54.11
2000	23,151	9,601	41.47	13,550	58.53
2001	23,940	8,931	37.31	15,009	62.69
2002	24,780	8,285	33.43	16,495	66.57
2003	25,639	7,876	30.72	17,763	69.28
2004	26,476	7,607	28.73	18,869	71.27
2005	27,331	7,298	26.70	20,033	73.30
2006	28,310	7,194	25.41	21,116	74.59
2007	29,350	7,142	24.33	22,208	75.67
2008	30,210	7,109	23.53	23,101	76.47
2009	31,120	7,038	22.62	24,082	77.38

Source: *China Yearbook of Statistics 2010*

Table 3.1.2 Employment in computer, real estate, and financing sector (2003–2009)

	Information transmission, computer service and software		Property		Financing	
	Figure (10,000)	Share to total urban employment (%)	Figure (10,000)	Share to total urban employment (%)	Figure (10,000)	Share to total urban employment (%)
2003	116.8	0.46	120.2	0.47	253.3	0.99
2004	123.7	0.47	133.4	0.50	356.0	1.34
2005	130.1	0.48	146.5	0.54	359.3	1.31
2006	138.2	0.49	153.9	0.54	367.4	1.30
2007	150.2	0.51	166.5	0.57	389.7	1.33
2008	159.5	0.53	172.7	0.57	417.6	1.38
2009	173.8	0.56	190.9	0.61	449.0	1.44

Source: *China Yearbook of Statistics 2010*

economic units (NSEU) was only 170,000, a small share of 0.18% in total urban labors. In 1985, the number of the employed in SCEU grew to 123.14 m and its ratio to total urban labors decreased to 96.14%, while the number of the employed in NSEU rose to 4.94 m, occupying 3.86% of total urban labors. The year 1995 was a tipping point where the number of the employed in SCEU reached its record level of 144.08 m, but its share in total urban labors was down to 75.67%, whereas the number of the employed in NSEU rose to 46.32 m, taking 24.33% of total urban labors. Since then, the absolute number of SCEU employment is a descending line until 1999, when the number of SCEU employment declined to 102.84 m, and its share in total urban labors was below 50%, while the number of NSEU employment rose to 121.28 m, taking more than 54% of total urban labors. It is recorded that up to 2009, the number of SCEU employment as 70.38 m, taking only 22.62% of total urban labors, and the number of NSEU employment as 240.82 m, taking up to 77.38% of total urban labors.

The second change was that many new sectors were emerging with technology progress, economic development, and improvement of market system, including computer, real estate, and financing, etc., which are drawing a growing number of labors. Statistics show that in 2003 these three sectors attracted, respectively, 1.168 m, 1.202 m, and 2.533 m labors, and in 2009 the numbers rose, respectively, to 1.738 m, 1.909 m, and 4.49 m, seeing a growth of 48.8%, 58.82%, and 77.26% correspondingly. The percentages of the employed in the three sectors to total urban labors ascended from 0.46%, 0.47%, and 0.99% in that order in 2009 to 0.56%, 0.61%, and 1.44% in 2009 correspondingly (see Table 3.1.2).

3.1.3 Change of Income Inequality of Urban Resident

The system reform and the change of economic structure have exerted great impact on Chinese urban resident's income distribution, and the dominant impact manifests in the gradually enlarged income inequality. Before the system reform, a highly egalitarian pattern of income distribution was prevalent, and it is estimated by SBS that the Gini coefficient of urban residents' income in 1978 was 0.16, and according to Adelman and Sunding (1987) the figure was 0.165. In 1980, the figure was still 0.16 according to the World Bank. After the system reform, affected by the dual changes in economic system and structure, income distribution pattern has seen a great change too, mainly in a constantly enlarged income inequality. Statistics show that in 2008 the Gini coefficient of urban income inequality was 0.38 (see Fig. 3.1.1).

From the figure, we can see that urban income inequality has been through three stages of swing. 1978–1981 was the first stage, when income inequality was spectacularly enlarged, and the Gini coefficient rose by 29% from 0.1621 in 1978 to 0.2092 in 1981. The second stage of 1981–1989 did not see much change in income inequality, and the Gini coefficient in 1989 was 0.2259, a growth of 8% relative to 1981. The third stage, since 1989 till now, again saw a large increase in income inequality and its Gini coefficient in 2008 was 0.3801, a rise of more than 68% relative to 1989.

Taken as a whole, the enlarged income inequality is attributed to two major factors: change of economic system for one and change of economic structure for the other. The first factor includes reform of income distribution pattern in SCEU, for instance, piece rating, hour wage, annual pay, stock rights and options in state-owned enterprises, and introduction of "sunlight wage" for civil servants. The development of market economy system including stock market, technology market, and leasing market contributes to diversified income sources. The second factor is related to change of economic structure, the diversification of ownership structure in particular. As a result, non-state-owned economy with various forms has developed rapidly. Wage system therein is a typically market-oriented distribution in which employees negotiate with the managers about their salaries and other benefits. All these are done in the full principle of market economy and conventions and signing labor agreement on the basis of equality and voluntariness. Within the

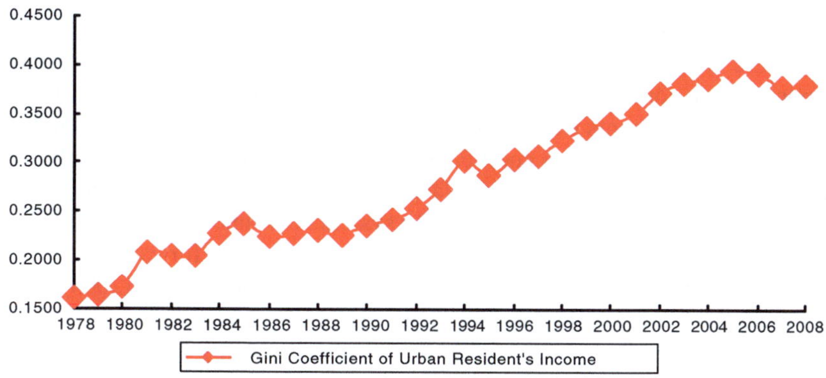

Fig. 3.1.1 Gini coefficients of urban residents' income (1978–2008). Source: Author's calculation according to *China Yearbook of Statistics* 1978–2009

enterprise, between managers and workers, base manager and high-level managers, there exists a large salary gap. Also, foreign-owned enterprises tend to offer a higher salary to their employees than their state-owned counterparts do. Besides, newly emerged sectors like computer and software industry, property, and financing enterprises outside banks have a generally higher salary than traditional sectors. All these changes all step up the continuous enlargement of income inequality among urban residents.

3.2 Main Factors Impacting Income Inequality of Urban Resident and Its Change: Analysis from Income Components

In the previous section, we introduced how reforms in economic system and structure have contributed to enlarging income inequality in urban residents. In the following parts, we will go on to find out some major drivers of income inequality from various perspectives. After the reform, the income components of China's urban residents are more and more diversified. First, we are going to do it by income structure. The same perspective was adopted by the author to study the state of income inequality and its contributing factors from 1988 to 1998 in Tianjin residents (Chen Zongsheng and Zhou Yunbo 2001a, b, c, 2002). Based on that research and for the purpose of further improvement, this section will discuss the exact drivers of urban income inequality since the new millennium. Meanwhile, we will take credit income into consideration as was never done in previous studies. The method used below will be improved and a brief and tentative reply will be given to questions against it.

3.2.1 Method and Its Development

In the field of income distribution, decomposing income inequality by income components is a conventional method. The idea of decomposing income inequality from income components was originally put forward by Rao (1969), and the factual method of decomposing Gini coefficient was brought forward successively by Fei et al. (1978). Later, Pyatt et al. (1980) elaborated and developed this method in detail, and Lerman and Yitzhaki (1985) provided a systematic framework systematic for the empirical analysis. Some decomposition principles were put forward by Shorrocks (1982, 1983), and they were complemented further by Satya Paul (2004). In fact, many indexes measuring income inequality may come into use, for instance, standard deviation, variation coefficient, and generalized entropy index, etc. However, Gini Coefficient is the most useful index in many empirical studies (see Podder 1993; Cheng 1996; Tusi Kai-yuen 1998a, b; Khan and Azizur 1999; Chen Zongsheng and Zhou Yunbo 2001a, b, c, 2002). But some scholars (Podder and Tran-Nam 1991;

Podder 1993, Podder and Mukhopadhaya 2001; Satya Paul 2004) pointed out that there was some fallacy to decompose Gini coefficient by income structure and inappropriate explanation and application would lead to misleading policy suggestion. We are going to see in detail the concrete method, if taking Gini Coefficient as the decomposing object.

Suppose Y represents the total income of a resident or household, and $Y_1, Y_2 \ldots Y_k \ldots Y_K$ represent incomes from various sources, then we have:

$$Y = \sum_{k=1}^{K} Y_k. \tag{3.2.1}$$

Suppose G refers to Gini coefficient of Y, and $G_1, G_2 \ldots G_k \ldots G_K$ stand for pseudo Gini coefficient[1] of $Y_1, Y_2 \ldots Y_k \ldots Y_K$,respectively, μ stands for total average income, and $\mu_1, \mu_2 \ldots \mu_k \ldots \mu_K$ stand for average income of each source, then we have:

$$G = \sum_{k=1}^{K} \left(\frac{\mu_k}{\mu}\right) \times G_k. \tag{3.2.2}$$

Suppose there are N households or individuals, then we have:

$$\mu = \frac{Y}{N} = \frac{\sum_{k=1}^{K} Y_k}{N} = \sum_{k=1}^{K} \frac{Y_k}{N} = \sum_{k=1}^{K} \mu_k. \tag{3.2.3}$$

And:

$$\sum_{k=1}^{K} \frac{\mu_k}{\mu} = 1. \tag{3.2.4}$$

[1] It is necessary to add that G_k is calculated by the descending order of resident's total income. Unlike the Gini coefficient calculated by the order of the income of item k itself, G_k reflects the gap between the income of item k and total income, so it is called Pseudo Gini coefficient, or concentration rate of the income of item k by some scholars. It indicates, however, the exact relation of kth income to total income, that is, what it suggests in the formula. In general, Pseudo Gini coefficient of kth income is related to the Gini coefficient of total income inequality in three ways: first, Pseudo Gini coefficient of kth income is positive and larger than the Gini coefficient of total income. In this case, the inequality of kth income is larger than total income inequality, so kth income enlarges the inequality of the total income; second, Pseudo Gini coefficient of kth income is positive but lower than the Gini coefficient of total income. In this case, the kth income inequality is lower than the inequality of total income, and decreases the inequality of total income relatively; third, Pseudo Gini coefficient of kth income is negative, indicating that it is concentrated in low-income group and contributes to decrease inequality of total income absolutely. When kth income is in the same order as in total income, G_k then is the real Gini coefficient of kth income.

Formula (3.2.2) may be transformed as follows:

$$\Phi_k = \left[\frac{(\mu_k/\mu) \times G_k}{G}\right] \times 100, \tag{3.2.5}$$

$$\sum_{k=1}^{K} \Phi_k = 100. \tag{3.2.6}$$

Φ_k stands for contribution rate of income sources $Y_1, Y_2 \ldots Y_k \ldots Y_K$ to total income inequality (Y). The above formulas show the complete calculation process of this method. In any case, some scholars (Podder and Tran-Nam 1991; Podder 1993; Podder and Mukhopadhaya 2001; Satya Paul 2004) pointed out that a wrong understanding of the decomposed result would lead to misleading policy. For example, suppose government supplies an equal subsidy S for each household or individual, we know from the meaning of Gini Coefficient that regardless of the sorting, the subsidy's Gini Coefficient and Pseudo Gini Coefficient are all zero, namely, $G_s = 0$. From (3.2.5), we may infer that the contribution of the subsidy to total income inequality is zero, namely, $\Phi_s = 0$. In theory, government's subsidy does not help reduce income inequality, but in practice, it does. Where is the problem? Take the same example for further illustration. Suppose a household or individual has incomes from as many as K sources, namely, $Y_1, Y_2 \ldots Y_k \ldots Y_K$, then total income inequality is as shown in (3.2.2). If government adds an equal subsidy $S$to the original incomes for each household or individual, then his total income becomes Y^*, made up of incomes from $K + 1$sources, namely, $Y_1, Y_2 \ldots Y_k \ldots Y_K, S$. According to (3.2.2), the Gini Coefficient of individual total income Y^* is as follows:

$$G^* = \sum_{k=1}^{K} (\frac{\mu_k}{\mu + S}) \times G_k + \frac{S}{\mu + S} \times G_s. \tag{3.2.7}$$

Herein G^* refers to the Gini Coefficient of total income Y^* inclusive of subsidy. Since S is equally given, so $G^* = 0$, and (3.2.7) may be simplified as follows:

$$G^* = \sum_{k=1}^{K} \left(\frac{\mu_k}{\mu + S}\right) \times G_k. \tag{3.2.8}$$

Since $S{>}0$, so $\frac{\mu_k}{\mu+S} < \frac{\mu_k}{\mu}$, and we have:

$$\frac{\mu_k}{\mu + \pi} \times G_k {<} \frac{\mu_k}{\mu} \times G_k.$$

Further we have

$$\sum_{k=1}^{K} \left(\frac{\mu_k}{\mu + S}\right) \times G_k {<} \sum_{k=1}^{K} \frac{\mu_k}{\mu} \times G_k. \tag{3.2.9}$$

That is, $G^* < G$. From the above derivation, we may see that added by government subsidy, the Gini coefficient (G^*) of total income Y^* is smaller than the Gini coefficient (G) of total income before subsidy (Y). We may conclude that government subsidy works indirectly in softening income inequality. Its working mechanism is like this: after government subsidy, total income is increased, and those incomes with their Gini coefficient larger than zero see a reduced percentage in total income, which results in reduced total income inequality.

Next we will work out variation percentage of Gini coefficient caused by the variation percentage of an income source with other sources remaining unchanged, or, in other words, the elasticity of Gini coefficient with respect to income source variation. Using (3.2.2), we may find G's total derivative with respect to μ_k:

$$\frac{\mathrm{d}G}{\mathrm{d}\mu_k} = \frac{\partial G}{\partial \mu_k} + \frac{\partial G}{\partial \mu} \times \frac{\mathrm{d}\mu}{\mathrm{d}\mu_k}. \tag{3.2.10}$$

From (3.2.2), we may have $\frac{\partial G}{\partial \mu_k} = \frac{G_k}{\mu}$ and $\frac{\partial G}{\partial \mu} = -\sum_{k=1}^{K} \frac{\mu_k}{\mu^2} G_k = -\frac{G}{\mu}$, and from (3.2.3), we may have $\frac{\mathrm{d}\mu}{\mathrm{d}\mu_k} = 1$. So we have

$$\frac{\mathrm{d}G}{\mathrm{d}\mu_k} = \frac{G_k - G}{\mu}.$$

Since $\eta_k = \frac{\frac{\mathrm{d}G}{G}}{\frac{\mathrm{d}\mu_k}{\mu_k}} = \frac{\mu_k}{G} \times \frac{\mathrm{d}G}{\mathrm{d}\mu_k}$, then

$$\eta_k = \frac{1}{G}\left[\frac{\mu_k}{\mu}(G_k - G)\right]. \tag{3.2.11}$$

Further we may have

$$\eta_k = \frac{1}{G}\sum_{k=1}^{K}\left[\frac{\mu_k}{\mu}(G_k - G)\right] = \frac{1}{G}\left(\sum_{k=1}^{K}\frac{\mu_k}{\mu}G_k - \sum_{k=1}^{K}\frac{\mu_k}{\mu}G\right).$$

From (3.2.2) and (3.2.4), we have

$$\sum_{k=1}^{K}\eta_k = \frac{G - G}{G} = 0. \tag{3.2.12}$$

Formula (3.2.12) means that if all incomes vary at the same rate, the Gini coefficient of total income is invariable, or, income inequality keeps the same. Formula (3.2.11) is of great importance to income redistribution policy and provides a good reference for government to adjust residents' income structure and improve income distribution, since it displays the relative contribution of each income source to inequality variation of total income. In addition, because

$$\frac{\partial G}{\partial \mu} = -\frac{G}{\mu}, \tag{3.2.13}$$

so,

$$\frac{\Delta G}{G} = -\frac{\Delta \mu}{\mu}. \tag{3.2.14}$$

Since (3.2.14) indicates the correspondence between average income change rate and Gini coefficient change rate, it serves as a very handy tool for us to investigate total income inequality change caused by one income source change. What we just discussed is mainly for static study. Next, we will expand it for a comparatively static analysis, that is, to study impact of each income source variation on total income inequality variation by income structure. First, we will make some adjustment to (3.2.2). In fact, in (3.2.2), $\frac{\mu_k}{\mu}$ also means the percentage of each income source $(Y_1, Y_2 \ldots Y_k \ldots Y_K)$ to total income (Y). Therefore, it can be expressed as follows:

$$G = \sum_{k=1}^{K} P_k G_k. \tag{3.2.15}$$

Herein, P_k refers to the percentage of each income source $(Y_1, Y_2 \ldots Y_k \ldots Y_K)$ to total income (Y), and $\sum_{k=1}^{K} P_k = 1$. Suppose sometime later, the distribution pattern of each income source and its share to total income vary, and their change values are ΔG_k and ΔP_k, respectively, then the Gini coefficient (G^n) of new total income (Y^n) is as follows:

$$G^n = \sum_{k=1}^{K} (P_k + \Delta P_k)(G_k + \Delta G_k). \tag{3.2.16}$$

Formula (3.2.16) is expanded into

$$G^n = \sum_{k=1}^{K} (P_k G_k + \Delta P_k G_k + \Delta G_k P_k + \Delta P_k \Delta G_k).$$

Variation value of the Gini coefficient of total income, ΔG, is

$$\Delta G = G^n - G = \sum_{k=1}^{K} (P_k G_k + \Delta P_k G_k + \Delta G_k P_k + \Delta P_k \Delta G_k) - \sum_{k=1}^{K} P_k G_k,$$

$$\Delta G = \sum_{k=1}^{K} P_k G_k + \sum_{k=1}^{K} \Delta P_k G_k + \sum_{k=1}^{K} \Delta G_k P_k + \sum_{k=1}^{K} \Delta P_k \Delta G_k - \sum_{k=1}^{K} P_k G_k.$$

After further simplification, we have

$$\Delta G = \sum_{k=1}^{K} \Delta P_k G_k + \sum_{k=1}^{K} \Delta G_k P_k + \sum_{k=1}^{K} \Delta P_k \Delta G_k. \quad (3.2.17)$$

Herein, $\sum_{k=1}^{K} \Delta P_k G_k$ represents the variation value of total income inequality caused by the percentage variation of each income source to total income, or named structural effect. $\sum_{k=1}^{K} \Delta G_k P_k$ represents the variation of total income inequality caused by variation of each income source's distribution pattern, and we name it distribution effect. $\sum_{k=1}^{K} \Delta P_k \Delta G_k$ refers to the inequality variation of total income due to both factors, also called interaction effect. In this way, total income inequality variation (ΔG) is decomposed into structural effect, distribution effect, and interaction effect.

3.2.2 Main Factors that Impact Income Inequality of Urban Resident: Analysis by Income Components[2]

In the following part, using survey data of urban household, we will examine major factors behind urban income inequality since the new century by income structure. The data are from a survey on 3,000 urban households in Shandong Province from 2002 to 2006. These households are regularly investigated and the data in question are obtained through stratified sampling. The samples of investigated localities whose samples are less than 100 households are renewed every 3 years, and for more than 100 households, one third of their samples are renewed. According to the above formulas, we can work out how much resident's income sources contribute to total household income inequality from 2002 to 2006.

At first, we will take a look into the share of each income source to total household income, as shown in Table 3.2.1.

Seen annually, (1) wage income plays a dominant role in urban households, whose largest 1-year share is 62.95% and smallest 1-year share is 51.88%, averaging about 55.53%. This indicates that labor income is the main source of livelihood, quite in character with socialist China. However, given the variation trend, we can see that labor income share is falling as a result of the reform of market economy. (2) Credit income, with average percentage of 29.19%, stands next to wage income,

[2] One of the authors (Chen Zongsheng and Zhou Yunbo 2002) did a similar research on Tianjin residents, taking individual resident as analyzing unit, a little different from the study here which takes households as analyzing unit.

Table 3.2.1 Contribution of income sources to total family income of urban residents (%)

Year	2002	2003	2004	2005	2006	平均	2002–2006
1. Wage income	62.95	57.04	52.80	52.99	51.88	55.53	−11.07
1.1. Salary and subsidy	62.17	56.32	51.77	51.89	50.95	54.62	−11.22
1.2 Other labor income	0.78	0.72	1.03	1.10	0.93	0.91	0.15
2. Net business income	1.39	1.44	1.69	2.57	2.72	1.96	1.33
3. Income from assets	0.69	1.03	0.75	0.88	1.01	0.87	0.32
3.1. Interests and dividend	0.52	0.52	0.49	0.54	0.61	0.54	0.09
3.2. Rental income	0.17	0.52	0.26	0.34	0.40	0.34	0.23
4. Transfers income	12.91	11.10	9.97	12.65	11.33	11.59	−1.58
4.1. Old age pension	10.74	8.91	8.04	11.04	9.91	9.73	−0.83
4.2. Social security income	0.24	0.17	0.12	0.17	0.12	0.16	−0.12
4.3. Other transfers income	1.92	2.03	1.82	1.44	1.30	1.70	−0.62
5. Income from property sales	0.31	0.76	0.15	0.12	0.30	0.33	−0.01
6. Credit income	21.04	28.05	34.25	30.23	32.37	29.19	11.33
6.1. Retrieving lending	16.94	25.38	32.10	28.66	29.98	26.61	13.04
6.2. Income from loan	3.13	1.87	1.94	1.38	2.32	2.13	−0.81
6.3. Other credit income	0.97	0.80	0.21	0.18	0.07	0.45	−0.90
7. Other incomes	0.71	0.57	0.39	0.56	0.38	0.52	−0.33
Total income	100	100	100	100	100	100	–
Number of samples	2,617	2,623	2,584	2,741	2,954	–	–

Source: Household surveying data in Shandong Province (2002–2006)

and has great potential for growth. It is up 11% from 21.04% in 2002 to 32.37% in 2006. (3) The third is transfers income, which occupies 11.59% of total income and is falling a bit. (4) The fourth is net income from business, which takes an average percentage of 1.96% and is rising rapidly, nearly doubled from 2002 to 2006. (5) Income from assets, though a share of as small as less than 1%, has a large space for growth. (6) Other incomes including that from property sales have a very small share.

Next, we will investigate the pseudo Gini coefficient of income sources for the purpose of discussing the relation between their distribution pattern and total income, as shown in Table 3.2.2.

From the table, we can see that (1) as a whole, the Gini coefficient of total income, though fluctuating, tends to rise. That is, income inequality among urban residents is seeing a continuous widening ever since the last century; (2) as for the relation between distribution pattern of income sources and total income, pseudo Gini coefficient of wage income, business income, and transfers are smaller than the Gini coefficient of total income. This implies that these three income sources are relatively equally distributed as opposed to total income, so they function as flattening inequality of total income. Pseudo Gini coefficient of social security income of transfers income, in particular, is negative in these years, indicating that this kind of income is mostly distributed to low-income and the poor population, and facilitates reduction in income inequality; (3) income from assets, income from property sales, and credit income each have a larger pseudo Gini coefficient than Gini coefficient of total income, indicating a more unequal distribution of these

Table 3.2.2 Pseudo Gini coefficient of urban income sources

	2002	2003	2004	2005	2006	Relation to total income inequality
1. Wage income	0.25903	0.27708	0.26412	0.27085	0.26536	–
1.1. Salary and subsidy	0.26066	0.27979	0.26722	0.27402	0.26866	–
1.2. Other labor income	0.12917	0.06645	0.10755	0.12157	0.08473	–
2. Net business income	0.00425	−0.01648	0.02598	0.12491	0.16240	–
3. Income from assets	0.42907	0.66948	0.47678	0.48897	0.47537	+
3.1. Interests and dividend	0.49956	0.55690	0.52799	0.55100	0.52621	+
3.2. Rental income	0.21858	0.78211	0.38148	0.39078	0.39832	+
4. Transfers income	0.30975	0.32402	0.31464	0.34118	0.32822	–
4.1. Old age pension	0.29114	0.28491	0.26941	0.34304	0.32208	–
4.2. Social securities	−0.02978	−0.31267	−0.31414	−0.25366	−0.25477	–
4.3. Other transfers income	0.45593	0.54998	0.55521	0.39591	0.42675	+
5. Income from property sales	0.67250	0.93377	0.73125	0.75794	0.86512	+
6. Credit income	0.64450	0.55456	0.51368	0.51317	0.55955	+
6.1. Retrieving lending	0.62358	0.54199	0.49640	0.50208	0.53692	+
6.2. Income from loan	0.80036	0.74654	0.82547	0.74227	0.86617	+
6.3. Other credit income	0.50615	0.50502	0.26657	0.51865	0.13162	+
7. Other incomes	0.30268	0.39336	0.16558	0.25694	0.09728	–
Total income	0.34590	0.36556	0.35252	0.35168	0.36821	–
Number of samples	2,617	2,623	2,584	2,741	2,954	–

Source: Household surveying data in Shandong Province (2002–2006)
Note: (1) The Gini coefficient of each income source should be added directly; (2) the last line in the table is the Gini coefficient of total income for convenience of comparison; (3) in "relation to the inequality of total income", "+"suggests a larger Pseudo Gini coefficient than the Gini coefficient of total income, "–"suggests a smaller Pseudo Gini coefficient than the Gini coefficient of total income, and even a negative value

three income sources relative to total income. Among them, income from property sales and credit income have an even more unbalanced distribution pattern.

Finally, let us take a look into the contribution rate of income sources to the inequality of total income and their marginal effect, as shown in Tables 3.2.3 and 3.2.4.

(1) Credit income contributes the most to the inequality of total income thanks to its high degree of inequality, a share of 44.99% on average, in which retrieving lending makes the largest contribution, as large as 39.60% on average. They have the tendency to increase by 9.99% and 13.18% correspondingly. (2) Wage income comes next, its contribution rate being 41.63% on average, of which salary and subsidy are the main contributors, as large as 41.36% on average. The two have the tendency to decline by 9.75 points and 9.68 points, respectively. (3) Transfers income comes third, with contribution rate averaging 10.53%, showing slight decline. Among them, old age pension is responsible for 8.31% of contribution rate, while social security income has a negative contribution rate, indicating that

Table 3.2.3 Contribution of income sources to family total income of urban residents (%)

	2002	2003	2004	2005	2006	平均	2002–2006
1. Wage income	47.14	43.24	39.56	40.81	37.39	41.63	−9.75
1.1. Salary and subsidy	46.85	43.11	39.24	40.43	37.17	41.36	−9.68
1.2. Other labor income	0.29	0.13	0.31	0.38	0.21	0.26	−0.08
2. Net business income	0.02	−0.07	0.12	0.91	1.20	0.44	1.18
3. Income from assets	0.86	1.89	1.02	1.22	1.30	1.26	0.44
3.1. Interests and dividend	0.75	0.79	0.73	0.85	0.87	0.80	0.12
3.2. Rental income	0.11	1.11	0.28	0.38	0.43	0.46	0.32
4. Transfers income	11.56	9.84	8.90	12.27	10.10	10.53	−1.46
4.1. Old age pension	9.04	6.95	6.14	10.77	8.67	8.31	−0.37
4.2. Social security income	−0.02	−0.14	−0.10	−0.12	−0.08	−0.09	−0.06
4.3. Other transfers income	2.53	3.05	2.87	1.62	1.51	2.32	−1.02
5. Income from property sales	0.60	1.94	0.31	0.26	0.71	0.76	0.11
6. Credit income	39.20	42.55	49.91	44.11	49.19	44.99	9.99
6.1. Retrieving lending	30.54	37.63	45.20	40.92	43.72	39.60	13.18
6.2. Income from loan	7.24	3.82	4.55	2.92	5.45	4.80	−1.79
6.3. Other credit income	1.42	1.11	0.16	0.27	0.03	0.60	−1.39
7. Other incomes	0.62	0.61	0.18	0.41	0.10	0.38	−0.52
Total income	100	100	100	100	100	100	–
Number of samples	2,617	2,623	2,584	2,741	2,954	–	–

Source: Household surveying data in Shandong Province (2002–2006)

Table 3.2.4 Marginal effect of income sources to total income inequality of urban residents (%)

	2002	2003	2004	2005	2006	平均
1. Wage income	−15.81	−13.81	−13.24	−12.18	−14.49	−13.91
1.1. Salary and subsidy	−15.32	−13.21	−12.53	−11.46	−13.77	−13.26
1.2. Other labor income	−0.49	−0.59	−0.71	−0.72	−0.72	−0.65
2. Net business income	−1.37	−1.50	−1.57	−1.66	−1.52	−1.52
3. Income from assets	0.17	0.86	0.26	0.34	0.29	0.38
3.1. Interests and dividend	0.23	0.27	0.24	0.31	0.26	0.26
3.2. Rental income	−0.06	0.59	0.02	0.04	0.03	0.12
4. Transfers income	−1.35	−1.26	−1.07	−0.38	−1.23	−1.06
4.1. Old age pension	−1.70	−1.97	−1.90	−0.27	−1.24	−1.41
4.2. Social security income	−0.27	−0.32	−0.22	−0.29	−0.20	−0.26
4.3. Other transfers income	0.61	1.02	1.05	0.18	0.21	0.61
5. Income from property sales	0.29	1.18	0.16	0.14	0.41	0.44
6. Credit income	18.16	14.50	15.66	13.88	16.82	15.81
6.1. Retrieving lending	13.60	12.25	13.10	12.26	13.74	12.99
6.2. Income from loan	4.11	1.95	2.61	1.54	3.13	2.67
6.3. Other credit income	0.45	0.31	−0.05	0.09	−0.05	0.15
7. Other incomes	−0.09	0.04	−0.21	−0.15	−0.28	−0.14

Source: Household surveying data in Shandong Province (2002–2006)

this income source helps reduce inequality of total income, but too little effect. (4) Business income and assets income have a small contribution rate, but they are increasing by a large margin. As a whole, to income inequality of Chinese urban residents, labor income is the dominant driver, while credit income is increasingly affecting income inequality, and showing a momentum of surpassing wage income.

First, the marginal effect of wage income remains negative during the observed years, averaging −13.91%, indicating that every increase of 1% of the share wage income in total income will result in nearly 14% of reduction in the inequality of total income. Among wage income, salary and subsidy have a marginal effect of −13.26% on average, and every increase of 1% share in total income will lead to 13% of reduction in the inequality of total income. However, the marginal effect of these two income sources tends to erode. Second, credit income has a positive marginal effect of 15.81% on average thanks to its highly unequal distribution pattern. That means every increase of 1% share in total income will bring about 15.81% enlargement of the inequality of total income. Third, transfers income has a negative marginal effect of −1.06%, indicating that every increase of 1% share in total income will lead to more than 1% reduction in the inequality of total income. However, this income source is slipping. Therein, the marginal effects of old age pension and social security income are 1.41% and −0.26%. Other transfers income has a marginal effect of 0.61%. Fourth, the marginal effect of net business income averages 0.38%, indicating that every increase of 1% share in total income will lead to 1.52% reduction in inequality of total income, and its contribution rate is going through a spiral growth. Finally, assets income has a marginal effect of 0.38% on average, indicating that every increase of 1% share in total income will result in a growth of 0.38% in inequality of total income and that the effect is increasing.

3.2.3 The Main Factors that Impact the Change of Income Inequality of Urban Resident: Analysis by Income Components

Just now we discussed income sources in light of their share to total income, their distribution pattern, their contribution to inequality of total income, and their marginal effect. There arises a new problem, namely, during the observed period, income inequality of Shandong's urban residents is further enlarged. Seen from income structure, what role do income sources play in the enlarged income inequality? Is it more determined by the variation of income sources' share in total income or by the variation of their own distribution pattern, or both? We will test it by means of cross multiplication. First we multiply the percentages of income sources in total income in 2006 with their pseudo Gini coefficient in 2002 one by one and find the sum, and then we multiply the percentages of income sources in total income in 2002 with income sources in 2006 one by one and find the sum. Compare the results:

$$G_1 = \sum_{i=1}^{N} G_i(2002) \times Y_i(2006) = 0.38578,$$

$$G_2 = \sum_{i=1}^{N} G_i(2006) \times Y_i(2002) = 0.33606.$$

In the first formula, $G_1 = 0.38578$, a rise of 0.01757 from the Gini coefficient of total income in 2006 and a rise of 0.03988 from the Gini coefficient of total income in 2002. In the second formula, $G_2 = 0.33606$, a rise of 0.03215 from Gini coefficient of total income in 2006 and a rise of 0.00984 from the Gini coefficient of total income in 2002. It is apparent that G_1 is closer to the Gini coefficient of total income in 2006 and G_2 is closer to the Gini coefficient of total income in 2002. If we compare G_1 and G_2 with the real Gini coefficient of total income in 2002, that is, 0.34590, we find that relative to the real Gini coefficient, G_1 is larger and G_2 smaller. We may infer that as a whole, it is the variation of distribution pattern of income sources that causes a reduced total income inequality, and it is the variation of their share in total income that causes an enlarged total income inequality, a conclusion different from my previous research (Chen Zongsheng and Zhou Yunbo 2001a, b, c, 2002). We decompose the increment of total income inequality using (3.2.17) with the following result (Table 3.2.5).

The outcome of decomposing agrees with our previous analysis. (1) The contribution of structural effect to the increment of income inequality is positive, as much as 159.22%, which widens income inequality, whereas the contribution of distribution effect and interaction effect is negative, to be −39.17% and −20.05%, respectively, which help reduce income inequality. (2) Distribution effect of wage income makes a contribution of 15.86% to the increment of income inequality to the effect of the latter's enlargement, while structural effect and interaction effect of wage income contribute, respectively, −114.55% and −2.79% to the increment of income inequality to the effect of reducing income inequality. As a whole, the contribution rate of wage income is −101.48%, that is, variation of this part of income has mitigating effects on total income inequality. (3) Credit income makes a positive contribution, as large as 181.96%, especially its structural effect contributes the most, as large as 291.67%, while its distribution effect and interaction effect make negative contribution of −71.30% and −38.41%, respectively. (4) Net business income makes a positive contribution of 17.43% as a whole, of which 8.78%, 0.24%, and 8.40% go to the three effects in that order. (5) The three effects of assets income, with contribution rates of 1.24%, 5.48%, and 0.58% in that order, are a driving force for enlarged inequality. As a whole, the overall contribution rate of assets income is 7.30%. (6) Transfers income has a negative contribution rate to total income inequality increment, −11.00%, which countervails to some degree the increase of inequality. Among them, distribution effect, with its contribution rate of 9.68%, helps widen the inequality. It is obvious that transfers income is in the high-income's favor during the observed years. By contrast, structural effect and interaction effect offset the inequality, their contribution rates being −19.50% and −1.18%, respectively. (7) Income from property sales and other incomes show a slight impact, not in our discussion here.

Table 3.2.5 Decomposition of increment of income inequality of urban household

	Distribution effect		Structure effect		Interaction effect		Total	
	Value	Share (%)	Value	Share (%)	Value	Share (%)	Value	Share (%)
1. Wage income	0.00397	15.86%	−0.02868	−114.55%	−0.00070	−2.79	−0.02541	−101.48
1.1. Salary and subsidy	0.00402	16.06%	−0.02907	−116.11%	−0.00071	−2.83	−0.02576	−102.88
1.2. Other labor income	−0.00005	−0.20%	0.00039	1.56%	0.00001	0.04	0.00035	1.39
2. Net business income	0.00220	8.78%	0.00006	0.24%	0.00210	8.40	0.00436	17.43
3. Income from assets	0.00031	1.24%	0.00137	5.48%	0.00014	0.58	0.00183	7.30
3.1. Interests and dividend	−0.00041	−1.64%	0.00038	1.52%	−0.00019	−0.76	−0.00022	−0.88
3.2. Rental income	0.00072	2.88%	0.00099	3.97%	0.00033	1.34	0.00205	8.18
4. Transfers income	0.00242	9.68%	−0.00488	−19.50%	−0.00030	−1.18	−0.00275	−11.00
4.1. Old age pension	0.00510	20.38%	−0.00256	−10.22%	−0.00062	−2.49	0.00192	7.67
4.2. Social security income	−0.00026	−1.05%	−0.00042	−1.66%	0.00003	0.13	−0.00065	−2.58
4.3. Other transfers income	−0.00242	−9.65%	−0.00191	−7.63%	0.00030	1.18	−0.00403	−16.10
5. Income from property sales	0.00060	2.40%	−0.00004	−0.16%	−0.00001	−0.05	0.00055	2.18
6. Credit income	−0.01786	−71.30%	0.07303	291.67%	−0.00962	−38.41	0.04556	181.96
6.1. Retrieving lending	−0.00100	−4.01%	0.08405	335.68%	−0.00054	−2.16	0.08251	329.51
6.2. Income from loan	−0.01201	−47.95%	−0.00524	−20.94%	−0.00647	−25.83	−0.02372	−94.72
6.3. Other credit income	−0.00485	−19.35%	−0.00578	−23.06%	−0.00261	−10.42	−0.01323	−52.83
7. Other incomes	−0.00146	−5.83%	−0.00099	−3.95%	0.00336	13.40	0.00091	3.62
Total	−0.00981	−39.17%	0.03987	159.22%	−0.00502	−20.05	0.02504	100.00

Source: Household surveying data in Shandong Province (2002–2006)

3.3 Main Factors Impacting Income Inequality of Urban Resident and Its Change: Analysis by Household Characteristics

In the previous section, we examined main drivers of urban income inequality by income structure. We are going to examine other drivers by household feature. One of the authors (Chen Zongsheng and Zhou Yunbo 2002) did a similar research based on surveys on Tianjin households from 1988 to 1998, only that he took population as analysis unit, a little different from the study here which takes households as analysis unit.

3.3.1 *Basic Method for Analysis*

Fei et al. (1979) offered a decomposing method as follows:

$$G_1 = \phi_1 R_1 G_1 + \ldots + \phi_i R_i G_i + \ldots \Delta, \quad i = 1, 2, 3 \ldots \tag{3.3.1}$$

Herein, R_i refers to the feature-income correlation coefficient of ith household feature, pointing to how much ith household feature is related to its income. G_i refers to the Gini coefficient of ith household feature, reflecting distribution pattern of ith household feature. ϕ_i is the income weight of ith household feature, indicating income rate of ith household feature. Δ is the rank-weighted error term. The computation process of ϕ_i as follows is comparatively complicated:

$$\phi_i = a_i \frac{\bar{I}_i}{\bar{Y}}. \tag{3.3.2}$$

Herein a_i stands for income of ith household feature, $\bar{I}_i$ stands for the mean of ith household feature, and $\bar{Y}$ stands for the mean of total income. First we measure the income of ith household feature, which means the contribution of each household feature to its per capita income, or the increase or reduction of household per capita income when alteration happens to a feature with other features remaining the same. First we have to measure feature income by multiple linear regression shown as the following:

$$Y = \alpha_0 + \alpha_1 X_1 + \ldots \alpha_i X_i + \ldots + \alpha_n X_n + \Delta. \tag{3.3.3}$$

Y stands for per capita income, X_i explanatory variable, namely, household feature, n the number of explanatory variables, namely, the number of household features, Δ stochastic error, and α_i regression coefficient, representing household feature income.

3.3.2 Impact of Some Main Household Characteristics on Income Inequality of Urban Resident

Since it is unpractical to put all household features as explanatory variables into regression equation, we just select some of them in the principle of (1) strong comprehensive power, (2) strong explaining power, (3) simple and direct implication, and (4) non-relatedness as much as possible between variables, with a view to avoiding multicollinearity. The chosen features include regional level of economic development, share of persons with income in household, share of workers of state enterprise in household, and some other information like householder's nationality, householder's gender, householder's age, character of householder's employment, industry of householder's employment, householder's duty, householder's seniority, householder's education, and householder's time of moving into the city. We put data of these features into (3.3.3) for OLS estimation of multiple regression in order to find income rate of these features. For detailed outcome, see Table 3.3.1.

The data show a moderately good effect of regression model in general and a moderately high level of significance of each feature's regression coefficient. With household feature income measured, the income weight of household feature, ϕ_i,

Table.3.3.1 Household feature income of urban residents

	2002		2006	
	Regression coefficient	t-Statistics	Regression coefficient	t-Statistics
Constant	−17,837.11	−7.72	−36,625.20	−9.07
Regional economic development level	262.97	12.08	224.07	10.77
Householder's time of moving into city	−25.86	−2.11	−21.64	−0.99
Householder's nationality	−1,027.09	−0.81	−1,113.00	−0.46
Householder's gender	1,339.34	4.02	1,774.78	2.76
Householder's age	100.64	2.73	266.92	5.65
Character of householder's employment	103.52	0.93	81.98	0.44
Industry of householder's employment	237.02	5.47	237.02	3.78
Householder's duty	938.17	1.96	2,065.50	2.15
Householder's seniority	29.65	0.90	−56.70	−1.46
Householder's education	474.22	6.70	1,204.35	9.29
Share of persons with income in household	13,399.72	14.18	23,682.92	14.03
Share of workers of state enterprise in household	1,535.79	2.81	3,286.79	3.39
Overall evaluation of equation	$R^2 = 0.1969$ $F = 53.22$		$R^2 = 0.1850$ $F = 55.63$	

Source: Household surveying data in Shandong Province (2002 and 2006)

can be calculated according to (3.3.2), while feature-income correlation coefficient R_i and Gini coefficient of ith household feature G_i are easy for calculation. Therefore according to (3.3.1) we can work out how much household features both as a whole and as individual item can explain income inequality of urban resident, as shown in Table 3.3.2:

The table tells some facts. First, in 2002 the Gini coefficient of urban income inequality in Shandong Province that could be explained by above 12 features was 0.0846, a share of 24.46% of the Gini coefficient that year, that is, 0.34590. In 2006, the explained Gini coefficient by above 12 features was 0.07961, a share of 21.62% of the Gini coefficient that year, 0.36821. We can say urban household features as a whole can explain total income inequality by 1/5 to 1/4, and of the 2 years, 2006 saw a slight drop in its explanatory power.

Second, in 2002 the household features contributing the most to income inequality were, by descending order, share of persons with income in household, regional economic development level, and householder's education, industry of householder's employment, householder's age, and share of workers of state enterprise in household, whose contribution rates to total income inequality were 8.74%, 6.02%, 2.96%, 2.71%, 1.07%, and 1% correspondingly. Other features, such as householder's age, householder's duty, householder's gender, householder's seniority, character of householder's employment, householder's nationality, and householder's time of moving into city, had less influence. In 2006, the greatest contributing features were, by descending order, share of persons with income in household, householder's education, regional economic development level, industry of householder's employment, share of workers of state enterprise in household, and householder's age, with contribution rates being 7%, 4.96%, 4.04%, 1.76%, 1.51%, and 1.44% correspondingly. Other features were of minor influence.

Third, for the explained income inequality, the contribution rates of household features saw some change during the observed years. Among them, the contribution rate of householder's education sees a sharp rise, from 2.96% in 2002 to 4.96% in 2006 and that of share of workers of state enterprise in households, householder's age, and householder's duty climbed up a little from 1%, 1.07%, and 0.82% in 2002 to 1.51%, 1.44%, and 0.90% in 2006. On the contrary, that of regional economic development level witnessed a sharp fall, from 6.02% in 2002 to 4.04% in 2006. Other features like share of persons with income in household, industry of householder's employment, householder's gender, and character of householder's employment underwent some slip also, from 8.74%, 2.71%, 0.57%, and 0.30% in 2002 to 7%, 1.76%, 0.25%, and 0.18% in 2006, respectively. One feature worth special mentioning is householder's seniority, whose contribution rate dived from 0.37 in 2002 to −0.36 in 2006.

Taken as a whole, share of persons with income is the greatest determinant for income inequality, implying that to increase urban employment, especially for low-income households, proves the most efficient measure to reduce inequality. Regional economic development level also plays an important role, indicating that regional inequality is responsible for China's urban income inequality to a

Table 3.3.2 Influence of household feature on income inequality of urban resident

Variable	Code	2002		2006	
		Value	Percentage (%)	Value	Percentage (%)
Income weight of household feature					
Regional economic development level	ϕ_1	0.34474		0.31004	
Householder's time of moving into city	ϕ_2	−0.07508		−0.03354	
Householder's nationality	ϕ_3	−0.09219		−0.05565	
Householder's gender	ϕ_4	0.04907		0.03550	
Householder's age	ϕ_5	0.40447		0.58188	
Character of householder's employment	ϕ_6	0.11074		0.04345	
Industry of householder's employment	ϕ_7	0.15196		0.10429	
Householder's duty	ϕ_8	0.15381		0.16524	
Householder's seniority	ϕ_9	0.06365		−0.06463	
Householder's education	ϕ_{10}	0.54855		0.73465	
Share of persons with income in household	ϕ_{11}	0.87135		0.71049	
Share of workers of state enterprise in household	ϕ_{12}	0.09706		0.09860	
Feature-income correlation coefficient					
Regional economic development level	R_1	0.21233		0.18230	
Householder's time of moving into city	R_2	0.01709		0.02187	
Householder's nationality	R_3	0.00318		0.01165	
Householder's gender	R_4	0.06697		0.04049	
Householder's age	R_5	0.07164		0.06934	
Character of householder's employment	R_6	0.11005		0.14106	
Industry of householder's employment	R_7	0.16481		0.15264	
Householder's duty	R_8	0.12737		0.13741	
Householder's seniority	R_9	0.07927		0.07522	
Householder's education	R_{10}	0.15935		0.21539	
Share of persons with income in household	R_{11}	0.27887		0.27269	
Share of workers of state enterprise in household	R_{12}	0.12061		0.13640	
Gini coefficient of household feature					
Regional economic development level	G_1	0.28439		0.26313	
Householder's time of moving into city	G_2	0.27967		0.28372	
Householder's nationality	G_3	0.01567		0.01523	
Householder's gender	G_4	0.5961		0.63879	

(continued)

Table 3.3.2 (continued)

Variable	Code	2002		2006	
		Value	Percentage (%)	Value	Percentage (%)
Householder's age	G_5	0.12791		0.13186	
Character of householder's employment	G_6	0.08484		0.10664	
Industry of householder's employment	G_7	0.37506		0.40711	
Householder's duty	G_8	0.14428		0.14541	
Householder's seniority	G_9	0.25485		0.27207	
Householder's education	G_{10}	0.11713		0.1155	
Share of persons with income in household	G_{11}	0.12444		0.13302	
Share of workers of state enterprise in household	G_{12}	0.29577		0.41287	
Contribution of household feature to income inequality of urban resident	$\sum \phi_i R_i G_i$	0.08460	100	0.07961	100
Regional economic development level	$\phi_1 R_1 G_1$	0.02082	6.02	0.01487	4.04
Householder's time of moving into city	$\phi_2 R_2 G_2$	−0.00036	−0.10	−0.00021	−0.06
Householder's nationality	$\phi_3 R_3 G_3$	0.00000	0	−0.00001	−0.00
Householder's gender	$\phi_4 R_4 G_4$	0.00196	0.57	0.00092	0.25
Householder's age	$\phi_5 R_5 G_5$	0.00371	1.07	0.00532	1.44
Character of householder's employment	$\phi_6 R_6 G_6$	0.00103	0.30	0.00065	0.18
Industry of householder's employment	$\phi_7 R_7 G_7$	0.00939	2.71	0.00648	1.76
Householder's duty	$\phi_8 R_8 G_8$	0.00283	0.82	0.00330	0.90
Householder's seniority	$\phi_9 R_9 G_9$	0.00129	0.37	−0.00132	−0.36
Householder's education	$\phi_{10} R_{10} G_{10}$	0.01024	2.96	0.01828	4.96
Share of persons with income in household	$\phi_{11} R_{11} G_{11}$	0.03024	8.74	0.02577	7.0
Share of workers of state enterprise in household	$\phi_{12} R_{12} G_{12}$	0.00346	1.00	0.00555	1.51
Household/income Gini	G	0.34590	100	0.36821	100
Gini coefficient explained	G_j	0.08460	24.46	0.07961	21.62
Gini coefficient unexplained	Δ	0.26130	75.54	0.28860	78.38

Source: Household surveying data in Shandong Province (2002 and 2006)

large degree. Householder's education is seeing more and more influence on urban income inequality, indicating that urban labor market is gradually maturing. Industry of householder's employment also affects income inequality in a remarkable way, which shows that industry income inequality remains an important driver of urban income inequality.

3.3.3 Main Factors that Impact the Change of Income Inequality of Urban Resident: Analysis by Household Characteristics

We just analyzed the contribution of household features to urban income inequality. The next thing we are going to do is to examine the contribution of household features to the variation of income inequality, namely, for the added values of income inequality from 2002 to 2006, how much can be explained by household features? The decomposing formula is as follows:

$$\frac{\partial G}{\partial t}=\sum_{i=1}^{n}\left[\frac{\partial\phi_i}{\partial t}R_iG_i+\frac{\partial R_i}{\partial t}\phi_iG_i+\frac{\partial G_i}{\partial t}\phi_iR_i\right]. \quad (3.3.4)$$

Each code in the formula has the same denotation with that mentioned above, only that n refers to number of household features. For detailed measurement, see Table 3.3.3.

From the table, we find that, from 2002 to 2006, in the added value of the Gini coefficient of urban resident's income, 0.02231, householder's education contributed the most, as large as 31.06%; share of workers of state enterprise in household came next, as large as 8.43%; householder's age came third, 7.26%; with 2.02% householder's duty rounded out the top four. By contrast, features like regional economic development level, share of persons with income in household, industry of householder's employment, householder's seniority, and householder's gender helped to reduce inequality, their contribution rate being −29.58%, −18.69%, −12.73%, −11.52%, and −5.29%, respectively.

In conclusion, the biggest factor behind the widening urban income inequality is householder's education, whereas regional economic development level plays a predominant role in reducing income inequality.

3.4 Main Factors Impacting Income Inequality of Urban Resident: Analysis by Population Characteristics[3]

In the previous two sections, we made a careful investigation into main drivers of urban income inequality by urban income structure and household features. This section provides another approach to drivers of income inequality, namely, from the perspective of population features and with population as the basic unit. In fact, one of the authors of this book analyzed the impact of population feature on income

[3] The main content of this section was published on *Nankai Economic Studies*, 2005 (6), coauthored with Xue Shougang.

Table 3.3.3 Contribution of household features to income inequality variation

Variable	Code	Numeric value in 2002	Numeric value in 2006
Income weight of household feature			
Regional economic development level	ϕ_1	0.34474	0.31004
Householder's time of moving into city	ϕ_2	−0.07508	−0.03354
Householder's nationality	ϕ_3	−0.09219	−0.05565
Householder's gender	ϕ_4	0.04907	0.03550
Householder's age	ϕ_5	0.40447	0.58188
Character of householder's employment	ϕ_6	0.11074	0.04345
Industry of householder's employment	ϕ_7	0.15196	0.10429
Householder's duty	ϕ_8	0.15381	0.16524
Householder's seniority	ϕ_9	0.06365	−0.06463
Householder's education	ϕ_{10}	0.54855	0.73465
Share of persons with income in household	ϕ_{11}	0.87135	0.71049
Share of workers of state enterprise in household	ϕ_{12}	0.09706	0.0986
Feature-income correlation coefficient			
Regional economic development level	R_1	0.21233	0.18230
Householder's time of moving into city	R_2	0.01709	0.02187
Householder's nationality	R_3	0.00318	0.01165
Householder's gender	R_4	0.06697	0.04049
Householder's age	R_5	0.07164	0.06934
Character of householder's employment	R_6	0.11005	0.14106
Industry of householder's employment	R_7	0.16481	0.15264
Householder's duty	R_8	0.12737	0.13741
Householder's seniority	R_9	0.07927	0.07522
Householder's education	R_{10}	0.15935	0.21539
Share of persons with income in household	R_{11}	0.27887	0.27269
Share of workers of state enterprise in household	R_{12}	0.12061	0.13640

Gini coefficient of household features				
Regional economic development level	G_1	0.28439	0.26313	
Householder's time of moving into city	G_2	0.27967	0.28372	
Householder's nationality	G_3	0.01567	0.01523	
Householder's gender	G_4	0.5961	0.63879	
Householder's age	G_5	0.12791	0.13186	
Character of householder's employment	G_6	0.08484	0.10664	
Industry of householder's employment	G_7	0.37506	0.40711	
Householder's duty	G_8	0.14428	0.14541	
Householder's seniority	G_9	0.25485	0.27207	
Householder's education	G_{10}	0.11713	0.1155	
Share of persons with income in household	G_{11}	0.12444	0.13302	
Share of workers of state enterprise in household	G_{12}	0.29577	0.41287	
Increment of 2006 to 2002			Added value	Percentage
Added value of Gini			0.02231	
Regional economic development level	$\partial\phi_1/\partial tR_1G_1+\partial R_1/\partial t\phi_1G_1+\partial G_1/\partial t\phi_1R_1$		−0.00660	−29.58
Householder's time of moving into city	$\partial\phi_2/\partial tR_2G_2+\partial R_2/\partial t\phi_2G_2+\partial G_2/\partial t\phi_2R_2$		0.00009	0.40
Householder's nationality	$\partial\phi_3/\partial tR_3G_3+\partial R_3/\partial t\phi_3G_3+\partial G_3/\partial t\phi_3R_3$		−0.00001	−0.04
Householder's gender	$\partial\phi_4/\partial tR_4G_4+\partial R_4/\partial t\phi_4G_4+\partial G_4/\partial t\phi_4R_4$		−0.00118	−5.29
Householder's age	$\partial\phi_5/\partial tR_5G_5+\partial R_5/\partial t\phi_5G_5+\partial G_5/\partial t\phi_5R_5$		0.00162	7.26
Character of householder's employment	$\partial\phi_6/\partial tR_6G_6+\partial R_6/\partial t\phi_6G_6+\partial G_6/\partial t\phi_6R_6$		−0.00007	−0.31
Industry of householder's employment	$\partial\phi_7/\partial tR_7G_7+\partial R_7/\partial t\phi_7G_7+\partial G_7/\partial t\phi_7R_7$		−0.00284	−12.73
Householder's duty	$\partial\phi_8/\partial tR_8G_8+\partial R_8/\partial t\phi_8G_8+\partial G_8/\partial t\phi_8R_8$		0.00045	2.02
Householder's seniority	$\partial\phi_9/\partial tR_9G_9+\partial R_9/\partial t\phi_9G_9+\partial G_9/\partial t\phi_9R_9$		−0.00257	−11.52
Householder's education	$\partial\phi_{10}/\partial tR_{10}G_{10}+\partial R_{10}/\partial t\phi_{10}G_{10}+\partial G_{10}/\partial t\phi_{10}R_{10}$		0.00693	31.06
Share of persons with income in household	$\partial\phi_{11}/\partial tR_{11}G_{11}+\partial R_{11}/\partial t\phi_{11}G_{11}+\partial G_{11}/\partial t\phi_{11}R_{11}$		−0.00417	−18.69
Share of workers of state enterprise in household	$\partial\phi_{12}/\partial tR_{12}G_{12}+\partial R_{12}/\partial t\phi_{12}G_{12}+\partial G_{12}/\partial t\phi_{12}R_{12}$		0.00188	8.43

Source: Household surveying data in Shandong Province (2002 and 2006)

inequality of urban resident using Tianjin's household survey data from 1988 to 1998. In this book, we will continue the similar research.

3.4.1 Grouping by Population Characteristic

First we group urban residents by population features, and, using Theil Index, measure in-group income inequality and that between groups. The formula of Theil Index is as follows:

$$T = \sum_{i=1}^{I} \frac{P_i}{P} \mathrm{Log} \frac{\bar{y}_i}{\bar{y}} + \sum_{i=1}^{I} \frac{P_i}{P} \sum_{j=1}^{P_i} \frac{1}{P_i} \mathrm{Log} \frac{\bar{y}_{ij}}{\bar{y}_i}. \tag{3.4.1}$$

Herein P refers to the number of total population, $\bar{y}$ total average income, I number of groups, P_i number of ith group population, $\bar{y}_i$ average income of ith group, and y_{ij} income of jth person in ith group. The first part in (3.4.1) expresses income inequality between groups, and the second part the in-group income inequality. Next, we decompose it by some major population features, including sexuality, age, education, character of employment, industry of employment, and duty. Our data are from the large sample survey in 2004. The survey was done within 18 districts and counties of Tianjin by means of multistage stratified sampling. The ultimate valid samples total 3,108 households and 6,567 population.

1. *Decomposing by gender*. Putting the survey data into (3.4.1), we have the outcomes in Table 3.4.1

The data show that in general income inequality of male in-group and female in-group is most responsible for total income inequality, nearly 89.06%, of which 45.96% goes to male in-group inequality, and 43.10% to female in-group inequality; the former's contribution is more 2.86% than that of the latter. Inequality between groups contributes 10.94% to total inequality. Further decomposition finds that concerning absolute income inequality, that of male in-group is smaller than that of female in-group. It is the former's large share of population that

Table 3.4.1 Theil Index and its constitution by gender grouping

Gender	Theil Index constitution			Contribution (%)
	T_i	$P_i(100)$	$\frac{T_i \times P_i}{100}$	
Male in-group inequality	0.5391	51.83	0.2794	45.96
Female in-group inequality	0.5439	48.17	0.2620	43.10
Total in-group inequality			0.5414	89.06
Inequality between groups			0.0665	10.94
Total			0.6079	100

Source: Household surveying data in Tianjin (2004)

Note: T_i means in-group Theil Index unweighted, $P_i$means population percentage of each group

Table 3.4.2 Theil Index and its constitution by urban resident's age grouping

Age grouping	Theil Index constitution			Contribution (%)
	T_i	$P_i(100)$	$\frac{T_i \times P_i}{100}$	
Below 20	0.7138	0.80	0.0057	0.96
21–30	0.4952	12.27	0.0608	10.29
31–40	0.6311	15.56	0.0982	16.63
41–50	0.5976	26.28	0.1571	26.58
51–60	0.5052	20.83	0.1052	17.81
Above 60	0.4661	24.26	0.1131	19.15
Aggregate in-group inequality			0.5400	91.42
Inequality between groups			0.0507	8.58
Total			0.5907	100

Source: Household surveying data in Tianjin (2004)
Note: T_i means in-group Theil Index unweighted, P_i means population percentage of each group

answers for its relative larger contribution than the latter. The fact implies that considering income inequality, urban females suffer a more unequal income distribution than males.

2. *Decomposing by age*. As shown in Table 3.4.2, total in-group inequality is the dominant contributor to total income inequality, more than 90%, while inequality between groups contributes less than 10%. Further decomposition finds that inequality between 30 and 60 age bracket is mainly responsible for total income inequality, as large as more than 60%, because people of this age bracket constitute the majority of social labor force and are the main family income source. On account of their differing education, industry, and duty, there must be sizable income inequality among them as well as sizable contribution to total income inequality. Those above 60 are low-income group, for they are usually aged people either on old age pension or on unfixed payments. Their population percentage reaches 25%, not a small share, but they do not differ much from one another in income. A slight contribution to total income inequality is a natural outcome for them. For those below 20, though showing a quite large income difference, their contribution to total income inequality is almost unnoticeable, less than 1%, mainly because of their slight population share, as little as 0.8%.

3. *Decomposing by education*. As shown in Table 3.4.3, in-group inequality and between-group inequality contribute to total income inequality by 80.10% and 19.90%, respectively, and the latter sees a sharp increase relative to 1988 and 1998.[4] The survey implies that the past several years have seen a rapid enlargement of income inequality among people of different educations, another evidence of what we have concluded just before.

[4] We have done similar research on Tianjin Urban households with survey data of 1988 and 1998. The outcome shows that the inequality among urban residents of differing educations contributes to total income inequality by 6.28% in 1988 and 8.01% in 1998. For detailed information, see Chen Zongsheng and Zhou Yunbo (Chen and Zhou 2001a, b, c).

Table 3.4.3 Theil Index constitution by urban resident's education grouping

Degree of education	Theil Index constitution			Contribution (%)
	T_i	$P_i(100)$	$\frac{T_i \times P_i}{100}$	
Ph.D	0.2941	0.09	0.0003	0.05
Master	0.3163	0.47	0.0015	0.26
Bachelor	0.4153	9.01	0.0374	6.56
Associate	0.4455	13.75	0.0613	10.75
Technical	0.4290	13.64	0.0585	10.26
Senior h.s	0.5342	21.23	0.1134	19.89
Junior h.s	0.4509	28.32	0.1277	22.39
Primary school	0.3176	8.55	0.0272	4.77
Illiterate	0.5988	4.92	0.0295	5.17
Total in-group inequality			0.4567	80.10
Between-group inequality			0.1135	19.90
Total			0.5702	100

Source: Household surveying data in Tianjin (2004)
Note: T_i means in-group Theil Index unweighted, $P_i$means population percentage of each group

Further decomposing the in-group inequality finds that the top five contributors to total income inequality are the in-group inequalities of junior high school, senior high school, associate degree, technical secondary school, and bachelor group, with respective contribution rates of 22.39%, 19.89%, 10.75%, 10.26%, and 6.56%, amounting to almost 70% to total income inequality. This can be answered for by the 9-year compulsory education system in China, which guarantees that the majority of the population can finish their junior high schooling or above. In parallel, some of them receive college or associate college education through entrance examination and self-taught examination. Consequently they form the majority of urban population. Furthermore, thanks to a stratified employment makeup, this group of people features large income inequality, which leads to sizable contribution to total income inequality. Ph.D, Master, primary schooling, and illiterate group make up minor part of the population, and contribute slightly to total income inequality.

4. *Decomposing by Character of employment.* The measurement in Table 3.4.4 shows that in-group inequality and between-group inequality contribute to total income inequality by 82.19% and 17.81%, respectively. Compared with 1998, the contribution of between-group inequality is reduced to some degree.[5] By adding depth to reform in administrations and state-owned enterprises and institutions, these sectors have seen a more accelerated income inequality within themselves

[5] In 1998, measured by Theil Index, inequality among different employments contributed to total income inequality by 18.61%. (For detailed analysis, see Chen Zongsheng and Zhou Yunbo, *More Remarks on Income Distribution During China's Reform and Development*. Economics and Science Publisher, 2002: p. 168.)

Table 3.4.4 Theil Index constitution by character of urban resident's employment grouping

Character of employment	Theil Index			Contribution (%)
	T_i	$P_i(100)$	$\frac{T_i \times P_i}{100}$	
Unemployed	0.4909	45.14	0.2216	37.21
Administrations	0.3873	1.86	0.0072	1.21
Institutions	0.3424	7.71	0.0264	4.43
State-owned enterprises	0.4624	18.07	0.0836	14.04
Collective enterprises	0.3943	1.81	0.0071	1.19
Shareholding enterprises	0.5462	3.56	0.0194	3.26
Private enterprises	0.5631	7.30	0.0411	6.90
Three-funding enterprises	0.5148	4.18	0.0215	3.61
Self-employed proprietor	0.6179	8.26	0.0511	8.58
Others	0.4969	2.12	0.0105	1.76
Total in-group inequality			0.4895	82.19
Between-group inequality			0.1061	17.81
Total			0.5956	100

Source: Household surveying data in Tianjin (2004)
Note: T_i means in-group Theil Index unweighted, $P_i$means population percentage of each group

than that between these sectors and other non-state sectors, Sino-foreign joint venture enterprises in particular.

After further decomposition of in-group inequality, we find that people in administrations, institutions, and state-owned enterprises and collective enterprises have a remarkably smaller income inequality than their counterparts in shareholding enterprises, three-funding enterprises, and self-employed and private economies. It is well known that state-ownership sectors are still imbued with traditional egalitarian distribution system. At the same time reforms in administrations and institutions lag far behind state-owned enterprises. Among state-ownership sectors, people in administrations and institutions have less income inequality than their peers in state-owned enterprises. Next, contribution of unemployed population to total income inequality is on rapid rise, up to 37.21%, a growth of almost 20% relative to 1998. One reason for this rise is that Tianjin has long been China's industrial base, with public economy holding dominant share in the city's aggregate economy. Since 1998 when strategic economic consolidation and upgraded corporate reform spewed out a larger number of layoffs and early retirement, their share in urban population rockets and their contribution to total income inequality rockets too. Third, population group employed in state-owned enterprise contributes the most to total income inequality, as much as 14.04%, thanks to the large number of state-owned enterprises and employees. Finally, next to population group employed in state-owned enterprise, self-employed and private enterprises altogether contribute to total income inequality by 15.48%, 10% higher than 4.7% in 1998. The growth is attributed to the rapid development of the two sectors and sharp increase of employment therein since the new century.

5. *Decomposing by Industry of Employment*. With economic development and the optimization of industrial structure, some traditional sectors are gradually edging

Table 3.4.5 Theil Index constitution by industry of urban resident's employment grouping

Industry of employment	Theil Index constitution			Percentage (%)
	T_i	$P_i(100)$	$\frac{T_i \times P_i}{100}$	
Unemployed	0.4909	45.14	0.2216	37.60
Agriculture, forestry, animal husbandry, fishery	0.4617	0.20	0.0009	0.15
Mining	0.5794	0.80	0.0047	0.78
Manufacturing	0.4497	17.07	0.0768	13.03
Fuel and power, water production and supply	0.3652	1.06	0.0039	0.66
Construction industry	0.6012	2.01	0.0121	2.05
Transport, storage, postal service	0.4747	4.85	0.0230	3.90
Information transmission, computer service, software	0.4891	1.04	0.0051	0.87
Wholesale, retail, accommodation, catering	0.5613	9.68	0.0544	9.21
Banking, securities, insurance	0.4284	1.06	0.0045	0.76
Real estate	0.5769	0.95	0.0055	0.93
Leasing and commercial service	0.4826	0.97	0.0047	0.80
Scientific research, technological service	0.3671	0.69	0.0025	0.43
Water conservancy, environmental and public facility stewardship	0.3876	1.02	0.0040	0.69
Social service	0.5333	5.14	0.0274	4.65
Health care, sporting, social welfare	0.3806	2.01	0.0076	1.31
Education, cultural arts, broadcasting, film and TV	0.3616	4.36	0.0158	2.68
Public management and Social organization	0.4851	1.95	0.0095	1.61
Total in-group inequality			0.4838	82.11
Between-group inequality			0.1054	17.89
Total			0.5892	100

Source: Household surveying data in Tianjin (2004)
Note: T_i means in-group Theil Index unweighted, $P_i$means population percentage of each group

out, and some emerging industries are taking their stead, so incomes of different industry must vary, which play a key role in influencing urban resident's income. Table 3.4.5 shows that in-group inequality and between-group inequality contribute to total income inequality by 82.11% and 17.89%. Compared with 1998, the contribution of between-group is reduced by 4.5%. It implies that between-group inequality increases more slowly than in-group inequality. It may be explained from two aspects. For one, with further reform of market economy and opening of all economic fields, industry inequality due to administrative monopoly is reduced to some degree; for the other, internal institutional reform of each sector has eliminated the income distribution characteristic of egalitarianism, and brought about substantial rise of internal income inequality.

For in-group inequality, it can be observed that (1) unemployed group contributes the most to total income inequality for the same reason as above mentioned, as large as 37.60%; (2) manufacturing group comes next, contributing 13.03%, because Tianjin as an old industrial base has built up a solid manufacturing foundation and offers much employment; (3) wholesale, retail, accommodation, catering group, and social service group come third and fourth, contributing, respectively, 9.21% and 4.65%. This indicates that in tertiary industry, traditional

Table 3.4.6 Theil Index constitution by urban resident's duty grouping

Duty	Theil Index			Contribution (%)
	T_i	$P_i(100)$	$\frac{T_i \times P_i}{100}$	
Unemployed	0.4909	0.4514	0.2216	37.83
Department principle	0.6205	0.0237	0.0147	2.51
Senior technicians	0.4140	0.0230	0.0095	1.62
Primary and junior technicians	0.3690	0.0547	0.0202	3.45
General management and clerks	0.4171	0.1395	0.0582	9.94
Workers	0.4430	0.2717	0.1204	20.55
Other	0.6456	0.0359	0.0232	3.96
Total in-group inequality			0.4678	79.86
Between-group inequality			0.1180	20.14
Total			0.5858	100

Source: Household surveying data in Tianjin (2004)
Note: T_i means in-group Theil Index unweighted, $P_i$means population percentage of each group

services remain dominant and draw a number of employment; (4) modern service sectors represented by banking, insurance, securities, information transmission, computer, software, scientific research, and technological service contribute a little, an evidence of lagging behind on part of these sectors.

6. *Decomposing by Duty*. Contribution of duty and post of urban resident to his income is apparent and it is even more so with the upgrading of urban wage system reform which directly enlarges income gap between different duties. As shown in Table 3.4.6, in-group inequality and between-group inequality contribute to total income inequality by 79.86% and 20.14%. Between-group inequality is more than doubled relative to that in 1998. Different from previous study by one of the authors (Chen Zongsheng and Zhou Yunbo 2002), the table indicates that post-driven income inequality is surpassing that driven by different industry.

After further decomposition, (1) the groups of workers and general management and clerks, being the major body among all kinds of persons with employment, are the first two contributors: 20.55% and 9.94%, respectively. Added together, their contribution is more than 30%; (2) the contribution of the group of primary and junior technician is 3.45%, the groups of department principles and senior technicians make less contribution on account of their limited number.

3.4.2 Decomposition Analysis by Population Characteristics

Based on population features grouping, using Theil Index, we just examined the in-group inequality and between-group inequality and their contribution to total income inequality, and investigated into the impact of China's reform and development on urban income inequality. The following will measure each population feature's contribution to urban income inequality by using Fei–Ranis decomposition.

Concrete computation formulas have been given in Sect. 3.3, namely, (3.3.1), (3.3.2), and (3.3.3). We select five main variables to explain urban income inequality, namely, gender, age, education, industry, and duty. First we work out the income rate of these five features, as shown in Table 3.4.7.

The measurement shows that (1)duty has the largest income rate, indicating one step higher to high-income duty will put additional 240 yuan to urban average income per capita per month; (2) next to it comes gender, namely, male earns 175 yuan more than female does per month; (3) third comes education. One more year in education leads to 40 more yuan per month; (4) industry comes fourth, and one rank higher than high-income industry will secure about 28 yuan for monthly income; (5) age has the least income rate, and 1 year older will lead to only 11 yuan growth of monthly income.

Given feature income rate, we can figure out the income weight of population feature proceeds, while feature-income correlation coefficient and feature Gini coefficient can be worked out directly. Therefore, according to (3.3.1), we can measure how much the urban population features each and in total can explain income inequality. The outcome is shown in Table 3.4.8.

Table 3.4.7 OLS estimation of income rate of population features of urban residents

Variable	Regressive coefficient	T statistic
Constant	−903.72	−19.64
Gender	175.37	9.42
Age	11.00	7.34
Education	39.43	16.22
Industry	27.53	8.02
Duty	240.12	26.28
Overall evaluation of equation	$R^2 = 0.35, F = 694$	

Source: Household surveying data in Tianjin (2004)

Table 3.4.8 Contribution of urban population characteristic to income inequality

Population feature	ϕ_i	R_i	G_i	$\phi_i \times R_i \times G_i$	Explanation degree of population feature to income inequality (%)
Gender	0.2963	0.1934	0.1673	0.0096	2.33
Age	0.5894	0.0174	0.2067	0.0021	0.51
Education	0.4677	0.3879	0.2173	0.0394	9.55
Industry	0.1162	0.4267	0.5513	0.0273	6.62
Duty	0.5555	0.5136	0.3544	0.1011	24.52
Explained Gini coefficient				0.1795	
Explained rate (%)					43.53
Unexplained Gini coefficient				0.2329	
Unexplained rate					56.47
Total				0.4124	100

Source: Household surveying data in Tianjin (2004)

The outcome shows some conclusions. (1) Of the overall Tianjin urban income inequality, 43.53% may be explained by sexuality, age, education, industry, and duty, quite a high explained rate. On the top is duty which contributes as high as 24.52%. Substituting industry, duty has grown to be the primal driver of urban income inequality on account of the internal income distribution reform within state sectors. (2) Education comes next, signaling its growing importance in urban income and income inequality. An increased contribution of education to income inequality suggests a growing knowledge proceed rate and growing social priority to knowledge. It is also a sign for a rational and mature labor market. (3) Coming third is industry, contributing 6.62% or so. The cause that the industry impacts income inequality is the change and grade of industry structure with economic development. With economic development, technology progress, and the change of consumption structure, some new and high technology sectors gradually emerge, and some traditional and backward technology sector degenerate. The change of industrial structure will inevitably have an impact on employees' income and income inequality, and further have an impact on industry income inequality. (4) Sexuality and age make the least contribution, not more than 3% added together.

As a whole, duty, education, and industry are the top three determinants of urban income inequality.

3.5 Impact of Some Macroeconomic Variables on Income Inequality of Urban Resident

The previous section reviewed some main drivers of urban income inequality by income structure, household features, and population features, using survey data on Shandong and Tianjin urban households. This section takes a further look into some macroeconomic drivers of urban income inequality, economic development, opening up, and inflation, to name a few.

3.5.1 Economic Growth Since the System Reform

Since reform and opening up in the late 1970s, China has become a country with the fastest economic growth all over the world. From 1978 to 2010, China saw an annual economic growth rate of about 10%. By 2010, China's GDP reached 3,979.83 billion yuan, 20.4 times that in 1978 at comparable prices, and its per capita GDP reached 29,678 yuan, 14.6 times that in 1978 at comparable prices. The following figure represents the absolute figures of China's per capita GDP and its growth rate in 1978–2010 according to the data given by *China's Yearbook of Statistics 2010* (Fig. 3.5.1).

The figure shows that despite a low growth rate in a couple of years, China's economy as a whole saw a fast growth. The amount of China's national economy

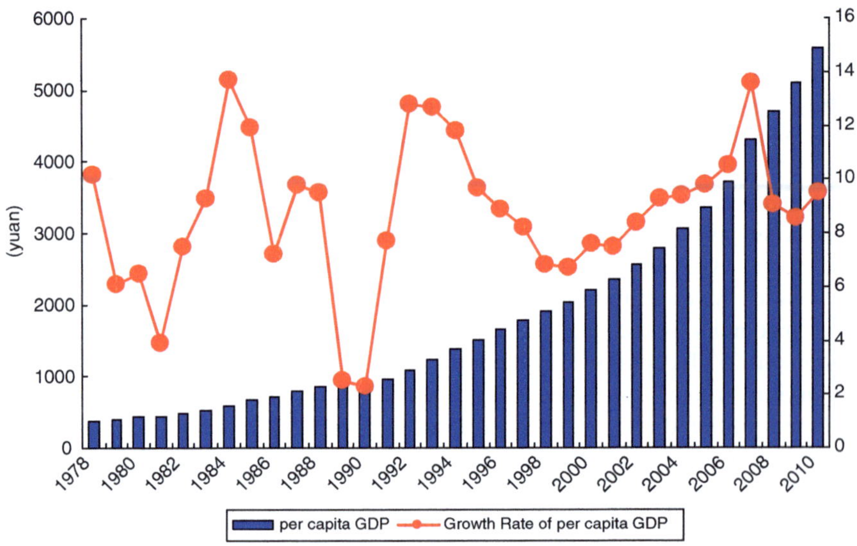

Fig. 3.5.1 China's economic growth trend since reform and opening up. Source: *China's Yearbook of Statistics* 2010

was improved greatly. In 2010 China's total economic output surpassed that of Italy, France,Britain, Japan, and Germany, only next to USA. Since 1978 China's economic growth can be divided into three stages.

From 1978 to 1991 is the first stage when economic growth witnessed up and down, and the growth rate of per capita GDP was 7.72% with the highest 1-year speed of 13.7%, and the lowest 1-year speed of 2.3%; the difference between the highest and the lowest is 11%. This stage proved to be a transition from deficit economy to surplus economy, in character of seller's market in essence. This cycle started from investment expansion, and terminated with total consumption expansion. Its oscillation mode may be simplified as investment expansion, supply expansion, and consumption expansion, and effective supply expansion serves a key mediator.

1992–2000 is the second stage when growth rate of per capita GDP was 9.47%, the highest to be 12.8% and the lowest 6.7%; the difference between the highest and the lowest is 6%. This stage underwent a course from fast development to low development, having ended the transition from deficit economy to surplus economy. Macroeconomy ran at a high level with more stability and sustainability than in the first stage. The oscillation mode in this stage was consumption expansion, supply expansion, investment expansion, and supply expansion, starting from consumption expansion and ending with supply expansion. Since the final demand expansion was missing here, shortage of total demand was to emerge later.

From 2001 till now is the third stage which saw an average growth rate of per capita GDP of 9.56%, the highest 13.6% and the lowest 7.5%; the difference between the highest and the lowest is 6%. The stability of macroeconomic operation was substantially boosted and economic growth underwent a continuous rise. The whole economy belonged to buyer's market with increasing competition among enterprises which impose the enterprise to accelerate the technology progress and foster the kernel competition capability.

3.5.2 *Foreign Trade Since the System Reform*

Since the system reform, China has seen a rapid development of foreign trade. Its total imports and exports increased by 20% per year, from \$20.64 billion in 1978 to \$2972.8 billion in 2010, far higher than present annual growth rate of per capita GDP. It is worth noting that China's foreign trade has seen an accelerated development since the end of 2001 when China joined WTO, with an average growth rate of 25.91%. Consequently, China's foreign trade climbed from the world's No. 32 in 1978 up to No. 2 in 2010, becoming the world's trade power in real terms. China's foreign trade dependency rose in a large scale, from 9.8% in 1978 to 50.24% in 2010. In general, China's foreign trade development falls into three stages; see Fig. 3.5.2.

1978–1993 is the first stage when foreign trade began to see a rapid growth thanks to power decentralization and transfer of profits, implementation of contracted responsibility system in the field of foreign trade, and transformation of foreign trade corporate operation mechanism. The total imports and exports increased from \$20.64 billion in 1978 to \$195.7 billion in 1993, almost up 20% per year, and foreign trade dependency rose from 9.74% to 31.9%. But the years with trade deficit exceeded the years with trade surplus, so all these years were in foreign trade deficit.

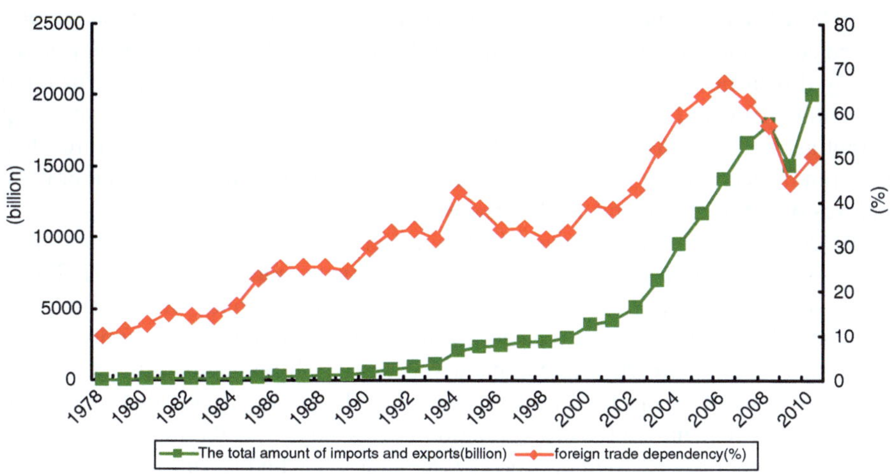

Fig. 3.5.2 Development of foreign trade since China's system reform. Source: *China's Yearbook of Statistics 2011*

1994–1999 is the second stage. In this stage, China's foreign trade developed steadily. A new round of foreign trade institutional reform centering around exchange rate merger took off in 1994 when such economic means as pricing, exchange rate, interest rate, tax rebate, and export credit were used to regulate foreign trade, which as a result increased rapidly. Its total imports and exports grew from $23.662 billion in 1994 to $360.63 billion in 1999 and annual growth rate reached 8.77%. The exchange rate merger and consequent RMB devaluation in 1994, in particular, stimulated the growth of foreign trade, especially that of exports from $121.01 billion in 1994 to $194.93 billion in 1999 with annual growth of more than 10%. During this stage the export amounts exceed import amounts, and trade surplus amounted to $118.4 billion.

2000 till now is the third stage when foreign trade has gained more momentum. Apace with world's economic recovery and especially thanks to its official entry into WTO, China's economy also recovered from deflation. Foreign trade dependency skyrocketed from 33.34% in 1999 to 57.29% in 2008. In 2009, because of global financial crisis China's foreign trade was stroke, the amount of export and import decreased to $2207.5 billion, and the foreign trade dependency decreased to 44.24%. In 2010, China's foreign trade underwent the recovery growth, and the amount of export and import and the foreign trade dependency increased to $2972.8 billion and 50.24%.

3.5.3 *Inflation Since the System Reform*

Since the system reform and opening up, with the accelerated marketization, inflation has become an important part of economic life and the course of inflation may fall into three stages; see Fig. 3.5.3.

1978–1991 is the first stage which is named as "a stage of single-total-supply-driven economic growth" (Liu Jinquan and Zhang Ailian 2003), that is to say, total-supply-driven factor featuring a seller's market was the leading impetus for rapid economic growth. The stage also witnessed efficient use of resources, expanding output and services, as well as noted economic fluctuations. Inflation rate reached its summit successively in 1980, 1985, and 1988 accompanied with consumer price indexes of 7.5%, 9.3%, and 18.8%, respectively.

1992–1996 is the second stage which is named as "a stage of total-demand-and-total-supply-driven economic growth" (Liu Jinquan and Zhang Ailian 2003). Expansion of demand and expansion of supply took place at once, and consumption expansion led to investment expansion, which in turn brought about supply expansion, and economic growth was comparatively fast. No little fluctuation like the first stage was evident except for a marked peak. The data only suggest that because of the impact of demand and supply, inflation in this stage was the most drastic ever since the system reform, and consumer price index reached record level, 24.1%.

From 1997 till now is the third stage which is also dubbed as "a stage of single-total-demand-driven economic growth" (Liu Jinquan and Zhang Ailian 2003), that

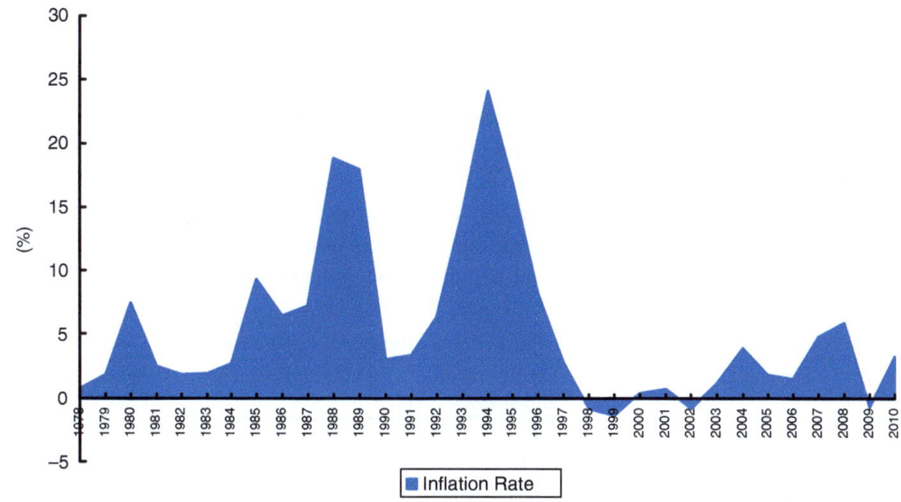

Fig. 3.5.3 China's inflation from 1978 to 2010. Source: *China's Yearbook of Statistics 2011*

is, total demand featuring a buyer's market was the dominant impetus for rapid economic growth. Due to a shortage of demand, the whole economy displayed supply surplus and inadequate total demand. And a couple of years even saw deflation. The highest consumer price index was just 5.9% in 2008 and that in 1998, 1999, 2002, and 2009 was even −0.8%, −1.4%, −0.8%, and −0.7%.

3.5.4 Empirical Analysis of Impact of Macroeconomic Variables on Income Inequality of Urban Resident

Now, using time-series model, we will measure the impact of the above-mentioned macroeconomic variables on income inequality of urban resident from 1978 to 2008 in terms of both the magnitude and the orientation.

1. *Empirical model and selection and test of data*. The empirical model used here is as follows:

$$G_u = C + \alpha_1 \text{RJGDP} + \alpha_2 \text{RJGDP}^2 + \alpha_3 \text{INE} + \alpha_4 \text{INF} + \mu. \qquad (3.5.1)$$

Herein RJGDP refers to the per capita GDP at comparable prices. From 1978 to 2010, China's per capita increased from \$220 to \$4,413 at contemporary exchange rate. According to the experiences of developed and the developing countries, this period proves to be one when economic growth could wield the greatest influence on income inequality. We first introduce per capita GDP to examine the impact of economic development on urban income inequality. In addition, we introduce the square of per capita GDP to test the long-time impact of economic development on income inequality, and the inverted U hypothesis for income inequality under public ownership. INE refers to foreign trade dependency, namely, percentage of total imports and exports in GDP. Foreign trade contributes to forming inequality between foreign trade department and non-foreign trade departments, which in turn affects resident's income inequality. After system reform and opening up, China's foreign trade grew fast, and to downplay the factor of scale, we substitute degree of opening up with foreign trade dependency. INF is consumer price index which is used for investigating the impact of inflation rate on urban income inequality. All

Table 3.5.1 Macroeconomic variables and Gini coefficient of urban resident's income

Year	Per capita GDP (yuan)	Foreign trade dependency (%)	Inflation rate (%)	Gini coefficient of urban income
1978	381.00	9.74	0.7	0.1621
1979	404.24	11.19	1.9	0.1643
1980	430.53	12.54	7.5	0.1733
1981	447.68	15.03	2.5	0.2092
1982	480.82	14.49	1.9	0.2045
1983	525.4	14.42	2.0	0.2050
1984	597.41	16.66	2.7	0.2275
1985	668.66	22.92	9.3	0.2376
1986	717.04	25.11	6.5	0.2240
1987	787.15	25.58	7.3	0.2278
1988	862.2	25.41	18.8	0.2307
1989	883.54	24.46	18.0	0.2259
1990	904.11	29.78	3.1	0.2354
1991	973.84	33.17	3.4	0.2425
1992	1,098.8	33.87	6.4	0.2536
1993	1,237.87	31.90	14.7	0.2724
1994	1,384.17	42.29	24.1	0.3018
1995	1,518.67	38.66	17.1	0.2880
1996	1,653.16	33.91	8.3	0.3034
1997	1,788.41	34.15	2.8	0.3079
1998	1,910.33	31.81	−0.8	0.3230
1999	2,037.97	33.34	−1.4	0.3361
2000	2,192.66	39.58	0.4	0.3417
2001	2,357.25	38.47	0.7	0.3512
2002	2,554.22	42.70	−0.8	0.3726
2003	2,793.11	51.89	1.2	0.3820
2004	3,056.38	59.76	3.9	0.3875
2005	3,348.61	63.86	1.8	0.3956
2006	3,706.75	66.85	1.5	0.3918
2007	4,210.87	62.73	4.8	0.3793
2008	4,594.06	57.29	5.9	0.3801

Source: *China's Yearbook of Statistics* 1980–2009, China Statistics Publisher. The Gini coefficient of urban resident's income from 1978 to 1999 is from *Income Distribution during System Reform and Economic Development* by Chen Zongsheng and Zhou Yunbo. That after 2000 is the author's calculation by data from *China's Yearbook of Statistics*

Table 3.5.2 Statistical properties of economic variables in empirical model

Variable	Mean	Standard deviation	Maximum	Minimum
Gini of urban income	0.28187	0.07457	0.39563	0.16214
Per capita GDP	1,629.26	1,192.45	4,594.06	381.00
Foreign trade dependency	33.66	16.33	66.85	9.74
Inflation rate	5.68	6.46.	24.10	−1.40

Source: The same with Table 3.5.1

Table 3.5.3 Unit root test of economic variables in empirical model

Variable	Type of test (C, T, K)	T statistic	Critical value at 5% significant level	Result
Gini coefficient of urban income	(0, 0, 3)	2.96217	1.95247	Unstable
	(C, 0, 3)	−0.95071	−2.96397	Unstable
	(C, T, 3)	−1.96518	−3.56838	Unstable
Per capita GDP	(0, 0, 3)	3.17113	−1.95291	Unstable
	(C, 0, 3)	3.02407	−2.96777	Unstable
	(C, T, 3)	6.19839	−3.56838	Unstable
Foreign trade dependency	(0, 0, 3)	1.61930	−1.95247	Unstable
	(C, 0, 3)	−0.68373	−2.96397	Unstable
	(C, T, 3)	−2.70641	−3.57424	Unstable
Inflation rate	(0, 0, 3)	−1.65793	−1.95247	Unstable
	(C, 0, 3)	−3.27568	−2.96777	Stable
	(C, T, 3)	−3.36472	−3.57424	Unstable

Source: By author's calculation by data from Table 3.5.1
Note: C in test type (C, T, K) means whether the model includes constant, T means whether the model includes tendency variable, and K stands for lag length

the data on the variables are from *China's Yearbook of Statistics* through the years. The Gini coefficient of urban resident's income, per capita GDP, foreign trade dependency, and inflation rate are given in Table 3.5.1. For statistic characteristics of these variables, see Table 3.5.2.

Because all the data are time series, we first test stability for all variables in model (3.5.1); for detailed test result, see Table 3.5.3.

From the table, we know that the Gini coefficient of urban income, per capita GDP, foreign trade dependency, and inflation rate are unstable at 5% significance level. It is possible that regression of these variables is spurious, and therefore, the outcome may be discreditable. However, some combination of these unstable time variables is stable. It is necessary for us to do cointegration test on these variables with a view to analyzing whether there is a long-standing equilibrium between them. Results of cointegration test are shown in Tables 3.5.4 and 3.5.5.

From Tables 3.5.4 and 3.5.5, we can see that at 5% significance level, there exist at least one cointegration relations between the Gini coefficient of urban income on the one hand and per capita GDP, foreign trade dependency, and inflation rate on the other. It shows that there is a long-standing equilibrium relationship between the Gini coefficient of urban income and the three macroscopic variables, enabling us to make OLS estimation on model (3.5.1), as shown in Table 3.5.6.

Table 3.5.4 Unrestricted cointegration rank test (Trace)

Hypothesized no. of CE(s)	Eigenvalue	Trace statistic	0.05 Critical value	Prob.
None*	0.698429	56.87614	47.85613	0.0057
At most 1	0.435653	22.11243	29.79707	0.2923
At most 2	0.171295	5.521949	15.49471	0.7512
At most 3	0.002518	0.073124	3.841466	0.7868

* rejecting the hypothesis in 5%(1%) significant level
Source: Author's calculation by data from Table 3.5.1
Note: Trace test indicates 1 cointegrating eqn(s) at the 0.05 level

Table 3.5.5 Unrestricted cointegration rank test (Maximum Eigenvalue)

Hypothesized no. of CE(s)	Eigenvalue	Max-Eigen Statistic	0.05 Critical value	Prob.
None*	0.698429	34.76372	27.58434	0.0050
At most 1	0.435653	16.59048	21.13162	0.1922
At most 2	0.171295	5.448825	14.26460	0.6844
At most 3	0.002518	0.073124	3.841466	0.7868

* rejecting the hypothesis in 5%(1%) significant level
Source: Author's calculation by data from Table 3.5.1
Note: Max-eigenvalue test indicates 1 cointegrating eqn(s) at the 0.05 level

2. *Outcome of empirical test.* As far as model I is concerned, regardless of a high goodness of fit and F statistic, the residual is stable at 5% significance level, and the DW statistics is small, suggesting that there is a strong au-correlation in regression model. For this, we introduce foreign trade dependency and the first- and second-order lag term of inflation rate and the first-order lag term of explained variable of Gini coefficient of urban income to the effect demonstrated in model IV. By contrast, model IV has a high goodness of fit and F statistic, and its DW statistic stays close to 2. No au-correlation is observed and the residual at 1% significance level is stable, demonstrating a long-standing cointegration and a creditable regressive outcome. Since cointegration represents a long-term relation between explaining variable and explained variable, the lag length of all lag terms may be considered as zero. The final outcome is shown in model V.

From model V we observe that, first, the regressive coefficient of per capita GDP is positive, suggesting that economic development is to some degree responsible for the increase of income inequality of urban resident, and its square is significantly negative, suggesting that there is a marked inverted U relation between urban income inequality and economic development. In other words, the inverted U hypothesis has been supported by the change of income inequality of urban resident. Second, the impact of foreign trade on the increase of income inequality of urban resident is significant. Foreign trade enlarged the income inequality between foreign trade departments and non-foreign trade departments, and thus enlarged urban income inequality. Finally, inflation rate serves to countervail income inequality of urban resident, but it does not pass the significance test. Two factors may attribute to this. For one, by giving rise to distribution effect to financial assets and physical assets of the high-income group, inflation rate tends to rise to the

Table 3.5.6 OLS estimation of the impact of macroeconomic variables on urban income inequality

Variable and equation test	Model I	Model II	Model III	Model IV	Mode V
Constant	0.12873*** (19.84)	0.07870*** (3.18)	0.08446*** (3.76)	0.09497*** (3.63)	0.14650
Per capita GDP	0.12541*** (10.60)	0.07603*** (3.22)	0.08683*** (3.99)	0.08206*** (3.12)	0.12659
Square of per capita GDP	−0.01710*** (−9.97)	−0.01066*** (−3.46)	−0.01092*** (−3.92)	−0.01118*** (−3.76)	−0.01725
Foreign trade dependency	0.00057 (1.28)	0.00020 (0.48)	0.00102* (2.03)	0.00118** (2.49)	0.00182
First-order lag term of foreign trade dependency	–	–	−0.00144** (−2.40)	−0.00186** (−2.73)	–
Second-order lag term of foreign trade dependency	–	–	–	0.00088 (1.21)	–
Inflation rate	−0.00027 (−0.73)	−0.00024 (−0.71)	9.61E-05 (0.25)	−0.00032 (−0.72)	−0.00049
First-order lag term of inflation rate	–	–	−5.24E-05 (−0.13)	0.00018 (0.38)	–
Second-order lag term of inflation rate	–	–	–	−0.00055 (−1.16)	–
First-order lag term of Gini coefficient of urban resident income	–	0.42700** (2.28)	0.40814** (2.40)	0.35174* (1.89)	–
General assessment of equation	$R^2 = 0.98$ $F = 315.32$ DW = 0.97	$R^2 = 0.98$ $F = 289.36$ DW = 1.86	$R^2 = 0.99$ $F = 254.15$ DW = 1.79	$R^2 = 0.99$ $F = 214.30$ DW = 2.02	–
ADF test of the residue	$T = -3.35$	$T = -5.27$	$T = -5.53$	$T = -5.88$	–

Source: Author's calculation by data from Table 3.5.1

*Suggests 10% significance level, **suggests 5% significance level, and ***suggests 1% significance level

The residues of model I are stable at 5% significance level, and the residues of model II, model III, and model IV are stable at 1% significance level

detriment of their properties and offset urban income inequality. For the other, inflation rate is a significant indicator to economic stability. Facing a high inflation rate, governments always take such policies as raising salary and inflation-proof bank savings so as to maintain economic stability. These measures benefit the low-income group and consequently soften income inequality of urban resident. However, since its regression coefficient does not pass the significance test, inflation rate, as a determinant of urban income inequality, needs more study in light of the direction and magnitude of its influence on income inequality of urban resident.

Chapter 4
Income Inequality of Chinese Rural Resident and the Factors Which Impact It

This chapter is divided into four sections. Section 4.1 presents the change of income distribution system in Chinese rural area before and after the system reform. A detailed description of income inequality of rural resident and its change is given. Sections 4.2 and 4.3 make a careful investigation into main drivers of total income inequality of rural residents and its dynamics and drivers of rural non-agricultural income inequality and its dynamics. Section 4.4 examines the transfer of rural labors to non-agricultural industries as well as determinants of rural income inequality such as economic development, foreign trade, and inflation rate.

4.1 Income Distribution System in Chinese Rural Area Before and After System Reform and Change of Income Inequality of Rural Residents

This section is mainly devoted to making a contrasted analysis of rural income distribution before and after system reform and giving a detailed examination on the change of rural income inequality.

4.1.1 Forms of Production and System of Income Distribution and Their Impact on Income Inequality of Rural Resident Before System Reform

After 1949 and the land reform, according to the general ideology and general mission, the rural production organization well proportionate to China's rural productivity level is community production based on household operation and mainly in the form of cooperative group. By 1952 when the land reform came to

Y. Zhou and Y. Qin, *Empirical Analysis on Income Inequality of Chinese Residents*, Gu Shutang Acad Fund Econ, DOI 10.1007/978-3-642-24952-5_4,

an end, rural household joining cooperative groups only took 39.9% of the total rural household, those in agricultural cooperatives took just 0.1%, and the rest in primary communes. By 1955 cooperative group was still the main agricultural production organization, and rural households joining cooperative groups took 50.7% and 14.2% rural households were in primary agricultural communes. Later with the thrust of heavy industry priority policy and the step-up of agricultural collectivization in 1955, percentage of rural households in cooperatives reached up to 80.3% that year and by the end of 1956 grew to 96.3%. At the same time, senior agricultural communes developed rapidly and its rural households grew from 30.7% in early 1956 to 87.8% at the end of the year. In 1958 the Great Leap in economic construction gave birth to people's commune which pervaded the whole country in the first 3 months, and households joining the commune numbered 127 million, amounting to 99.1% of the whole rural households. In the end, a new form of production and organization based on three-level ownerships, which means that all means of production including the land are owned by people's commune, production brigade, and production team. The last one was the basic unit of production, accounting, and distribution, which was capable of independent accounting, took full responsibility for its own profits and losses, and organized production and proceeds distribution all by its own.

Due to collectivized production and organization and means of production being collectively owned, farmers were deprived of any chance of agricultural and non-agricultural operation as well as private income. Furthermore, the government adopted a household registration system of urban–rural divide governance, which virtually prevented rural labors from entering cities to make a living. The only means of living for them was to join collective production. What corresponded to the collectivized form of production and organization was work-point distribution regime, which meant that the annual income of each rural labor was measured by his total work-points of the year multiplied by the currency value of each work-point, as shown in the following formula:

$$Y_i = T_i \times V. \qquad (4.1.1)$$

Herein Y_i stands for yearly income of number i^{th} labor, T_i stands for his total yearly work-points, which is calculated by his daily work-point multiplied by his total work days of the year, and V stands for the currency value of each work-point calculated by yearly disposable income of the production team divided by yearly aggregate work-points of the team's total labors. The disposable income refers to the remaining income after taxes and production expenditures are recouped from the yearly total income. At the first sight, farmer's income seems to be closely linked with his work (namely, work-point T_i) and the production team's economic efficiency (V), a seemingly realization of more pay for more work. But further analysis reveals many problems.

From (4.1.1), it can be seen that given a fixed currency value of each work-point, a farmer's yearly income depends on the number of his accumulated work-points.

Only when each farmer's work-point is evaluated objectively and correctively can the distribution regime be an incentive, namely, to evaluate his work-point according to his real work. However, this incentive mechanism does not work well on account of farming characteristics. First, farming features decentrality and it cannot afford a complete supervision over each farmer. Short of complete supervision, goldbricking is farmer's first choice. Second, farming has a much longer cycle than industry and the time span from input to output is very large, making it impossible to assess farmer's work and effort by testing the output. As a result, the final assessment is doomed for egalitarianism. In practice, the production team will assign the same work-point standard[1] for farmers of similar age and sexuality, separating the pay from the real work.

Given a fixed work-point, the second factor determining farmer's yearly income is the currency value of each work-point (V). Further expanding to (4.1.1), we have (4.1.2):

$$Y_i = T_i \times \frac{Y}{\sum_{i=1}^{N} T_i} = \frac{T_i}{\sum_{i=1}^{N} T_i} \times Y. \tag{4.1.2}$$

Herein Y stands for the aggregate yearly disposable income of the production team, and N stands for the number of the team's total farmers. The formula shows that the currency value of each work-point is dependent on two factors: the aggregate yearly disposable income of the production team and the aggregate work-points of the team's total farmers. Suppose the aggregate yearly disposable income of the team is fixed, then the yearly income of each labor is determined by his work-point share in the team's aggregate work-points. This greatly loosens the link between a farmer's income and his real output. Take an example. If a farmer's work-point share is 1% but he earns 1,000 yuan for his team, he may only have 10 yuan at the end of the year. In effect, it is distributional egalitarianism.

Since taking part in collective work and accumulating work-points is the major income source for farmers, rural income inequality is very slight. According to many studies (Li Changdui 1986; Ren Caifang and Cheng Xuebin 1996; Adelman and Sunding 1987), by 1978, Gini coefficient of China's rural income fell between 0.21 and 0.22 or so, much lower than other Asian countries (see Table 4.1.1).

Among other Asian countries listed in the table, Indonesia had the largest rural income inequality, its Gini coefficient being up to 0.4, 81.81% higher than that of China. South Korea had the smallest rural income inequality, its Gini coefficient being 0.325, 47.73% higher than that of China.

[1] For instance, in some production teams, the work-point standard for each male adult farmer is 10 points, and that for the female counterpart is 8 points.

Table 4.1.1 Comparison of rural income inequality between China and other Asian countries

Country and year	Gini of rural income
India (1975/1976)	0.34
Bengal (1985/1986)	0.36
Indonesia (1976)	0.40
Thailand (1975/1976)	0.39
Philippines (1985)	0.37
South Korea (1971)	0.325
China (1978)	0.22

Source: Zhao Renwei et al. (1999: 44), Table 1.1 and Table 1.2

4.1.2 The Change of Production Forms and Industrial Structure in Rural Areas After System Reform

In the late 1970s, an extensive economic system reform took off for eliminating the inefficiency in agriculture production. Because the rural population had suffered most during the traditional economic system, the problems in the rural area is rather serious, so the breakthrough of system reform was made in rural areas. System reform effectuated a huge change to forms of agricultural production and organization, economic structure, and rural labor's employment structure. Among others, the following measures were mainly responsible for the change of income inequality of rural residents.

1. *Household Responsibility*. In the end of 1970s of last century, the implementation of household responsibility was the greatest change to rural economic system, which was innovated by the farmers themselves. The implementation of the new system marked a transformation of agricultural production from collective work to household work. By the new system, each farmer was allotted a certain number of land in the form of signing contract with the production team. After turning over a certain amount of agricultural products demanded by the contract, farmers were able to dispose the leftover. In this way, farmers became the basic unit of production, accounting, and distribution. By introducing market mechanism into agricultural production and operation, the new system endowed farmers with rights to retrieve the remaining products, provided working incentive and effective supervision, overcame the original problems with distributional egalitarianism, and created great economic benefit. Statistics show that during the years 1978–1984 when household responsibility was widespread, agricultural total output grew by 42.2% and 6.5% per year at fixed price, the fastest agricultural growth ever since 1949. Thanks to its huge driving force, the household responsibility was soon put into force nationwide. By the end of 1981, 94.5% farming households, 175 million, that is, had been covered by the regime, and by 1984 that figure increased to 99% (see Fig. 4.1.1.).

The household responsibility is a significant reform of agricultural production during the history of agricultural development in China. It changes income distribution of rural residents mainly by making farmers, who now have agricultural production elements including production means and labor to their disposition, become the basic unit of production and distribution. On the one hand, farmers have

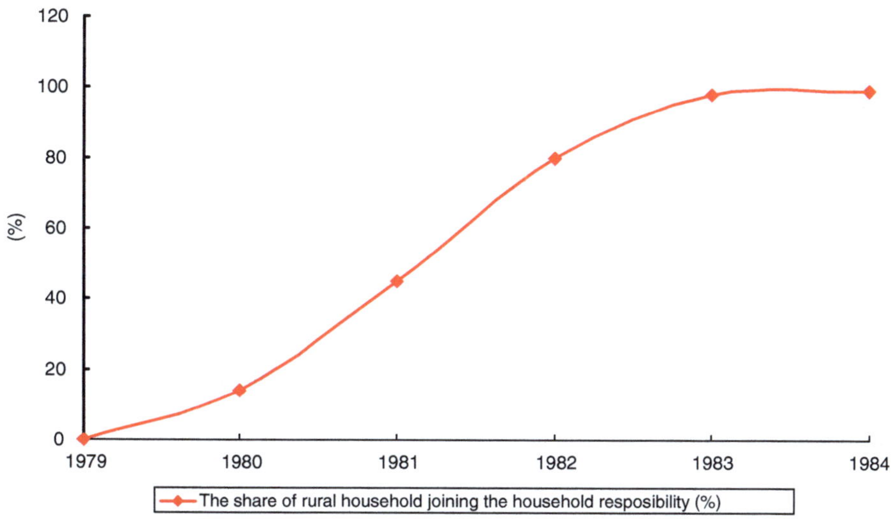

Fig. 4.1.1 Share of rural households in household responsibility 1979–1984. Source: *China's Yearbook of Statistics 1985*

diversified income sources, including family agricultural and non-agricultural operation and outside employment other than regular labor income. On the other hand, farmers' income is dependent not only on local environment and regional economic development, but on their own qualities like amount of labor, employment, and education, as well as status of agricultural and non-agricultural productive investment, possession of arable land, and adoption of agricultural technology. All these elements grow to be main drivers of income inequality of rural residents, which will be discussed in detail later.

2. *Development of non-agricultural industry represented by township enterprises.* Another achievement in rural economic system reform is the rapid development of non-agricultural industry represented by township enterprises which draw more and more rural surplus labors into non-agricultural industry. Statistics show that in 1978 there were 28.27 million rural surplus labors in township enterprises, more than 9% of total rural labors. In 2006, the figure grew to be 146.80 million, more than 30% of total rural labor. Non-agricultural industry has become the pillar industry for developing rural economy and increasing farmers' income. After later years of 1980s, the agriculture sector developed slowly, and even stagnated, so the non-agricultural business income became the main source of the farmer's income growth. According to some studies (Zhang Ping 1992; Zhu Ling 1992; Tsui Kaiyuen 1993; Rozelle 1994; Wei Houkai 1996; Li Shi 1999), since development of non-agricultural industry, especially of township enterprises, has become the main driver of rural regional income inequality, naturally it has become an important determinant of rural income inequality. According to the decomposition made by one of the authors of this book, the contribution of non-agricultural

industry to farmers' total income inequality is above 40% (Chen Zongsheng and Zhou Yunbo 2002).

3. *Outside employment.* With decompression of mass migration control after system reform, more and more rural surplus labors enter cities for employment. For lack of techniques, we have no access to exact statistics on outside employment of rural labors. Some rough estimations show that in the mid-twentieth century, about 90 million rural labors were out for employment, among them 45–50 million were outside of their counties, and 17.5 million were out on mid- and long term (Knight and Song 1996; Li Shi et al. 1999). In 2001 rural labor's migration across counties and provinces reached 63.61 million and 39.33 million, respectively (Wang Xiyu 2000; Fan Xiaoyu 2002). Though, no final conclusion on the impact of outside employment on rural income inequality is available, some studies still indicate that remittance from outside labors helps enlarge rural income inequality (Tsui Kai-yuen 1998a, b).

4.1.3 Gradual Enlargement of Income Inequality of Rural Resident

After the reform, change of agricultural production form, economic structure, and rural labor's employment structure leads to farmers' income rise, which in turn widens income inequality. In 1978 farmer's net per capita income was 134 yuan and in 2010 it grew to 5,919 yuan, a growth of 9.54 times at comparable prices. The growth rate per year was 7.3%. In parallel, the Gini coefficient of farmers' income rose from 0.2122 in 1978 to 0.42616 in 2008, increasing by 100.83% (see Fig. 4.1.2.).

The figures indicate that the change of income inequality of rural residents presented some features. First, totally different from other developing countries and what has been described by dual economic theory, rural income inequality remained always higher than urban income inequality, especially in the mid-1990s. Due to a vast territory, extremely complicated geography and different regional climate and soil conditions which determine to a large degree agricultural production, regional inequality wielded more influence on rural income inequality than on urban income inequality, and ultimately the former was bigger than the latter. Second, in light of growth rate, the year of 1985 was a watershed. Before that year, rural income inequality increased faster than urban one, and after that, it was the other way round. It can be explained from two aspects. For one, since China was through huge throes of institutional transformation, change of urban and rural income inequality was particularly dependent on change of economic system. Before the mid-1980s, China's reform priority was given to the rural areas, with few significant moves in evidence in cities. After 1980s, the priority shifted to cities, and no new breakthrough was made in rural reform. The change of reform priority impacts the change of income inequality of rural and urban residents. For the other, after 1988 the development of non-agricultural industry began to slow

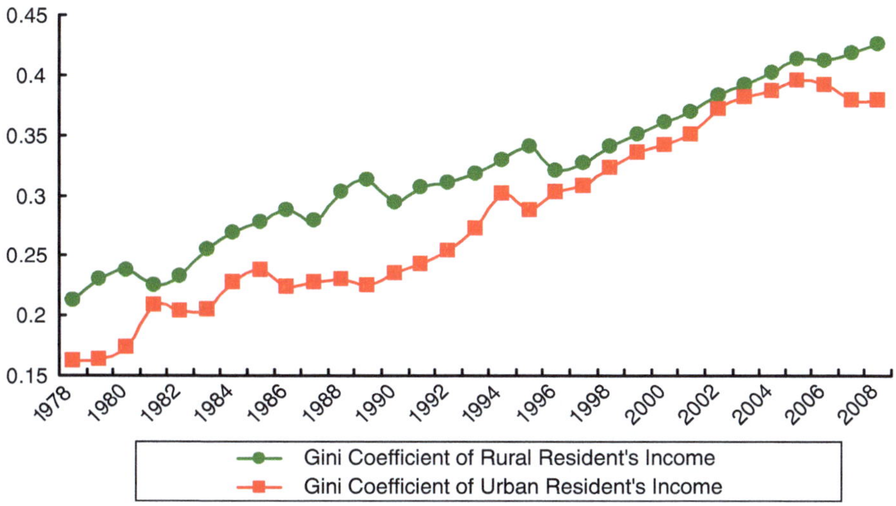

Fig. 4.1.2 Gini coefficient of urban and rural resident's income 1978–2008. Source: (1) Data of 1978–1999 are from *More Remarks on Income Distribution During China's Reform and Development* by Chen Zongsheng and Zhou Yunbo, see Table 2.2.1 (p. 3), Table 2.3.1 (p. 41), and Table 1 and Table 2 in Appendix on pages 32, 41, 49, and 52, respectively. (2) Data of 2000–2008 are author's calculation from *China's Yearbook of Statistics*. For the estimation method on relative data, see Chen Zongsheng and Zhou Yunbo (2002: 37–40)

down. Many studies (Chen Zongsheng 1991; Zhao Renwei et al. 1999) agreed that income from non-agricultural industry was a key driver of rural income inequality, so it was quite reasonable that the slowdown of the non-agricultural industry would reduce the enlargement of rural income inequality. Finally, the change curve of rural income inequality was smoother than urban one, indicating that rural income inequality was influenced more by rural economic development than by the periodical advance of institutional reform.

4.2 Main Factors that Impact Inequality of Total Income Inequality of Rural Resident and Its Change

This section will analyze in detail the main drivers of rural income inequality by rural income structure with the same method as that in Sect. 3.2. The major data source is from Rural Household Survey in Tianjin rural area.[2] The total income of

[2] The time span of data includes 2000 and 2003. In 2000, 750 households are sampled from Tianjin's 12 suburb counties of Tanggu, Hangu, Dagang, Dongli, Xiqing, Jinnan, Beichen, Ninghe, Wuqing, Jinghai, Baodi, and Jixian. In 2003, 600 households are sampled from 7 suburb counties. Survey after 2002 is slightly different from 2000 by including such items as outside employment and transfer to non-agricultural industry.

rural resident is net income, namely, the balance after productive expenditures and taxes are subtracted from farmer's total income. The total income here is composed mostly of cash including that in kind, but not the income from properties like house and production tools converted at current prices. Thanks to an underdeveloped renting market in rural areas, farmer's rents are also not included. Moreover, since data about the wage rate and work time are not easily available, farmer's wage from his family work is not contained in production cost. Finally, the income for calculation is mainly per capita income, namely, equally dividing farmer's net income according to average population of households, not a sexuality- and age-based conversion on equivalence scales. This section uses household as the basic analytical unit, in that we need not split those incomes from fuzzy sources, though it would lead to underestimation on family welfare level. In effect, one of the authors undertook a similar analysis using data of Tianjin 1994–2000. Here we will use data of 2000 and 2003 to examine drivers of rural income inequality by income structure since the new century.

4.2.1 Main Factors Impacting Income Inequality of Rural Resident: Analyzing by Income Components

Since the opening up and system reform, income structure of rural resident is becoming more intricate, including business income from agricultural and non-agricultural operations as well as wage income from local township enterprise and urban employment. As a product of rural reform and economic development, change of the income structure of rural residents crystallizes the direction and dynamics of reform and development. A careful dissection of income structure change will show how much rural reform drives rural income inequality. Meanwhile, by measuring each income source's contribution to total income inequality and its change, we hope it would be of policy implication to put rural income distribution right. In Sect. 3.2, the method of decomposing income inequality from income structure was introduced. The following part will continue to use this method for the purpose of investigating rural income sources and their percentage in total income, as well as their contribution to total income inequality and its change.

1. *Income structure of rural resident.* A general probe into rural income source is given in Table 4.2.1. In light of absolute number, from 2000 to 2003, all income sources except those given by relatives and friends increased. Agricultural income grew from 1,279.47 yuan to 1,529.92 yuan per capita, increasing by 17.23% after allowing for inflation. Non-agricultural income rose from 2,546.13 yuan to 3,065.36 yuan, increasing by 18.03% at comparable prices. One of the largest growth is the wage from outside employment, growing from 241.98 yuan to 418.86 yuan, up 69.70% as compared with the same period of the previous year. Coming next is the wage from local enterprise employment, growing from 1,302.84

Table 4.2.1 Means of income sources of rural resident and their share in total income

	2000		2003	
	Mean (yuan)	Share (%)	Mean (yuan)	Share (%)
Agricultural income	1,279.47 (2,072.46)	31.22	1,529.92 (4,075.61)	31.28
Non-agricultural income	2,546.13 (2,721.72)	62.12	3,065.36 (3,804.94)	62.67
Wage from local non-entrepreneurial employment	406.31 (1,002.37)	9.91	412.11 (1,130.21)	8.43
Wage from local entrepreneurial employment	1,302.84 (2,199.23)	31.79	1,547.49 (3,310.24)	31.64
Wage from outside employment	241.98 (700.73)	5.90	418.86 (1,158.33)	8.56
Income from non-agricultural business	595.00 (1,618.80)	14.52	686.90 (2,876.86)	14.04
Property income	68.7 (471.26)	1.68	157.5 (741.66)	3.22
Interests	12.08 (139.95)	0.29	7.69 (106.84)	0.16
Stock dividend	8.46 (163.64)	0.21	2.55 (41.36)	0.05
Rents	10.26 (108.8)	0.25	19.81 (211.28)	0.40
Others	37.9 (396.1)	0.93	127.45 (708.05)	2.61
Transfers	77.2 (494.85)	1.88	90.94 (726.12)	1.86
Old age pension	48.16 (461.74)	1.17	49.73 (369.72)	1.02
Relief and compensation	1.04 (12.75)	0.03	5.85 (84.32)	0.12
Others	28 (184.77)	0.68	35.36 (615.43)	0.72
Income given by relatives and friends	127.34 (560.66)	3.10	47.78 (320.30)	0.97
Total	4,098.84 (3,043.45)	100	4,891.50 (5,278.48)	100

Source: Household surveying data in Tianjin rural area (2000 and 2003)
Note: The number in brackets is standard deviation

yuan to 1,547.49 yuan, up 16.45% as compared with the same period of the previous year. The third is income from non-agricultural family business, growing from 595 yuan to 686.9 yuan, up 13.18% as compared with the same period of the previous year, and the wage from local non-entrepreneurial employment had the least growth rate, from 406.31 yuan to 412.11 yuan, down 0.6% at comparable prices. Property income increased from 68.7 yuan to 157.5 yuan, up 124.76% as compared with the same period of the previous year, of which interests and stock dividend dropped from 12.08 yuan and 8.46 yuan per capita to 7.69 yuan and 2.55

yuan, respectively, down 37.59% and 70.45% in that order. Rent income from land and machines and other income rose from 10.26 yuan and 37.9 yuan to 19.81 yuan and 127.45 yuan, up 89.29% and 229.69%. Transfers from government rose from 77.2 yuan to 90.94 yuan, up 15.49%, of which old age pension, relief and compensation money, and other income rose from 48.16 yuan, 1.04 yuan, and 28 yuan to 49.73 yuan, 5.85 yuan, and 35.36 yuan, up 1.23%, 451.47%, and 23.81%, respectively. Income given by relatives and friends reduced from 127.34 yuan to 47.78 yuan, dropping by 63.21%.

In terms of the relative share of income sources to total income, in Tianjin rural area non-agricultural income of rural resident became dominant,[3] its shares in 2000 and 2003 being 62.12% and 62.67%, whereas agricultural income dropped to the second, its shares in 2000 and 2003 being, respectively, 31.22% and 31.28%, somewhat different from the general picture of the whole country. In 2000 and 2003, as to income structure of rural resident in the whole country, non-agricultural income took 46.10% and 48.20%, while agricultural income took 48.4% and 45.6%, broadly equal in percentage. In the 2 years, the net income of Tianjin rural households from non-agricultural was 16.02%, 14.47% higher than national average, and that from agricultural was 17.18%, 14.32% lower than national average. It is mainly because Tianjin, as a developed coastal region, has a much more advanced rural economy, non-agricultural industry, and rural urbanization than national average. In particular, most of the surveyed areas are on the outskirts of Tianjin. With convenient transportation, more information, well-developed labor market and dense township, and foreign enterprises, rural labors found more opportunities of non-agricultural employment which contributed to a higher percentage of non-agricultural income than national average.

Within non-agricultural income, wage from local enterprises had the leading share, being 31.79% and 31.64% in 2000 and 2003, respectively, income from non-agricultural family business came next, taking 14.52% and 14.04% in the 2 years, and wage from local non-entrepreneurial employment came third in 2000, taking 9.91%, but dropped to fourth in 2003, taking 8.43%. By contrast, wage from outside employment was fourth in 2000, taking 5.90%, but rose to third in 2003, taking 8.56%. To sum up, within non-agricultural income, wage income made up the major body and its shares in the 2 years were 47.60% and 48.63%, nearly half of total income, broadly in line with general picture of the whole country. Statistics show that in 2000 and 2003, in income structure of rural household of the whole country, wage income took 31.16% and 35.02%, slightly lower than in Tianjin, and non-agricultural business income took 14.94% and 13.18%, almost the same with that in Tianjin. It proves that a higher non-agricultural income than national average was mainly ascribed to its well-developed non-agricultural industry which provided

[3] Since non-agricultural income is getting more and more share in rural household income structure, we will further analyze later on in terms of its distribution and contribution to total rural income inequality.

more employment opportunities for rural labors instead of to farmer's own non-agricultural family business.

Property income inclusive of interests, stock dividend, and rents had a very small share, being 1.68% and 3.22% in the 2 years, old age pension and relief and compensation by government took less than 2%, and income given by relatives and friends was 3.1% and 0.97% in the 2 years.

For the 2 years alone, no great change occurred in the percentage of agricultural and non-agricultural income in total income. Within non-agricultural income, wage from local enterprises and income from non-agricultural family business saw little change of share, while the share of wage from local non-entrepreneurial employment was slightly down 1.48%, and the share of wage from outside employment was up 2.66%. Property income saw a marked change of share, growing by 1.64%. Share of transfers was slightly down, but income given by relatives and friends was down about 2%.

2. *Correlation between each income component and total income.* We just described the absolute number of each income source and its contribution to total income. Next, we will study the correlation between each income component and total income by using correlation coefficient and Pseudo Gini Coefficient. See Table 4.2.2.

Table 4.2.2 Correlation coefficient between each income component and total income of rural residents and their Pseudo Gini

	2000		2003	
	Correlation coefficient	Pseudo Gini	Correlation coefficient	Psedudo Gini
Agricultural income	0.40553	0.34837	0.66356	0.47032
Non-agricultural income	0.70330	0.34566	0.60875	0.37864
Wage from local non-entrepreneurial employment	0.26040	0.38331	0.10595	0.33363
Wage from local entrepreneurial employment	0.50373	0.35563	0.39163	0.38797
Wage from outside employment	0.00922	0.07032	0.06949	0.17976
Income from non-agricultural business	0.33290	0.41008	0.28624	0.50588
Property income	0.26468	0.52584	0.21968	0.26650
Interests	0.34329	0.73903	0.08484	0.58576
Stock dividend	0.08246	0.72502	0.02442	0.56162
Rents	−0.01762	−0.04619	0.08190	0.36411
Others	0.16438	0.56831	0.19144	0.22616
Transfers	0.11598	0.39046	0.12404	0.50573
Old age pension	0.08811	0.37703	0.07929	0.37396
Relief and compensation	0.00160	0.00186	0.01170	0.16593
Others	0.09033	0.42806	0.09711	0.74726
Income given by relatives and friends	0.19029	0.48696	0.00319	0.12867
Total	–	0.35476	–	0.40363

Source: Household surveying data in Tianjin rural area (2000 and 2003)

The correlation coefficient indicates a close correlation of agricultural and non-agricultural income to total income. In 2000, the correlation coefficients of these two income sources to total income were 0.40533 and 0.7033; in 2003 they were 0.66356 and 0.60875. The correlation degree of agricultural income to total income was a little up, while that of non-agricultural income to total income was a little down. Within non-agricultural income, wage from local entrepreneurial employment was mostly correlated to total income, and its correlation coefficients in the 2 years were 0.50373 and 0.39163. The second was family non-agricultural business income, its correlation coefficients being 0.3329 and 0.28624. Wage from local non-entrepreneurial employment came third with correlation coefficients being 0.2604 and 0.10595. The least correlated was wage from outside employment, its correlation coefficients being only 0.00922 and 0.06949. For the 2 years alone, except the wage from outside employment, all the other three income components saw correlation reduction in one way or another. The correlation coefficients of property income were 0.26468 and 0.21968 in the 2 years. Under this category, interests saw the greatest reduction of correlation coefficient, from 0.26468 down to 0.21968.

Correlation coefficient provides us a tool to measure the magnitude of income component's correlation to total income. Next we will investigate in detail the distribution of each income component and their relation with total income by using Pseudo Gini coefficient. The Pseudo Gini coefficient in the table suggests that (1) concerning agricultural income, its Pseudo Gini coefficient in 2000 was slightly smaller than that of total income, implying that this income component, though procured more by high-income group than by low-income group, was tolerably equalizing relative to total income. But in 2003 things were different. The Pseudo Gini coefficient of agricultural income was ostensibly higher than that of total income, indicating an evident tilt toward high-income group, namely, more agricultural income went to high-income group. It is well known that agricultural income comes from grain-growing and cash crops, as well as fishery and husbandry. With a view to disclosing the driving force of agricultural income inequality, we calculate the Pseudo Gini coefficient of per household arable land areas, grain and cash crop-plantation areas, and the usable areas of agricultural film and greenhouse. See Table 4.2.3.

From 2000 to 2003, the Pseudo Gini coefficient of usable areas of agricultural film and greenhouse rose from 0.05420 and 0.21022 to 0.19276 and 0.32715,

Table 4.2.3 Pseudo Gini coefficient of per household arable land areas and grain plantation areas

Household feature	2000	2003
Per household arable land	−0.03857	−0.00925
Grain-plantation areas	−0.04192	−0.19729
Therein: Which high quality grain plantation	−0.06586	−0.32648
Cash crop-plantation areas	0.17234	−0.09023
Usable areas of agricultural film	0.05420	0.19276
Usable areas of greenhouse	0.21022	0.32715

Source: Household surveying data in Tianjin rural area (2000 and 2003)

respectively, up 255.65% and 55.62% correspondingly. It points out that the tilt of agricultural income toward high-income group was probably because these households used agricultural biotechnology like agricultural film and greenhouse, which yielded more farm produce with higher added value and increased agricultural income.

Concerning non-agricultural income, its Pseudo Gini coefficient of the 2 years was slightly smaller than that of total income, indicating that its distribution pattern was a little equalizing than that of total income. Within non-agricultural income, the Pseudo Gini coefficient of wage from local entrepreneurial employment and income from non-agricultural family business were consistently larger than that of total income for the years under review. Comparing the 2 years alone, the Pseudo Gini coefficient of the two components showed an upward trend, suggesting that only those rich households were able to invest in non-agricultural industry, took up non-agricultural business, or went to local township and private enterprises for employment, making the two income components more leaning toward high-income households. The relation between the wage from local non-entrepreneurial employment and total income inequality was unstable. In 2000 the former's inequality was larger than the latter, but in 2003 it was the other way round. Compared with total income inequality, the wage inequality from outside employment was much smaller, suggesting that in Tianjin, most of the labors seeking outside employment were from mid-income households and this part of source played a balancing role. This is different from the previous study (Tsui Kai-yuen 1998a, b).

The relation of property income to total income was not a stable one. In 2000 the former's Pseudo Gini coefficient was much higher than that of the latter, namely, the distributional inequality of property income was much larger than total income inequality. In 2003 its Pseudo Gini coefficient saw a great fall. Why? Further decomposing it indicates that the Pseudo Gini coefficient of interests and stock dividend were all the time larger than that of total income, an evidence of this income going to high-income households, for only they had the surplus capital for investment and bank savings. In 2000, Pseudo Gini coefficient of the recipients of rents from land and machines was negative, it means that the recipients of rents from land and machines virtually got more by low-income households, but in 2003 they got more by high-income households, though in general showing a smaller inequality than total income inequality. As opposed to rents, other property income had a higher Pseudo Gini coefficient than the Gini coefficient of total income, that is to say, this income source tilted absolutely toward high-income households, but in 2003 its inequality was greatly reduced, for its Pseudo Gini coefficient was much lower than the Gini of total income. Because this income component took 50–80% of property income, it played a decisive role in twitching the distributional relation between property income and total income. For lack of further data on this income component, we cannot give a reasonable explanation.

The Pseudo Gini coefficient of transfer income was persistently higher than the Gini coefficient of total income, indicating that the largest recipients were high-income households, a phenomenon quite at odds with the meaning of transfer income. According to economic theory, transfers, as a subsidy offered by government for low-income group or the poor, should have a distributional pattern as opposed to that of total income. That is, most of it should go to low-income group and its Pseudo Gini coefficient should be negative. However, our measurement contravened the theory. After further decomposing, it shows that distribution of old age pension remained stable, its Pseudo Gini coefficient being slightly higher in 2000 and slightly lower in 2003 relative to the Gini coefficient of total income. But in general, this income component went more to high-income households than to low-income households. Relief and compensation by government, though much more equally distributed, did not completely go to the low-income households or the poor. Obviously, its distribution mechanism needs further improvement so as to subsidize those in real need. Others under the category had a higher Pseudo Gini coefficient than the Gini coefficient of total income, that is to say, it helped stimulating income inequality. For lack of data on its structure, we cannot take further analysis, but as a part of transfer income aiming to subsidize the poor, its distribution mechanism also needs improvement.

As to income given by relatives and friends, it went completely to high-income households in 2000, but in 2003 it saw an improved distribution.

3. *Contribution of each income component to the inequality of total income and their marginal effect.* Correlation Coefficient and Pseudo Gini coefficient can only reflect the relation of each income component to total income. Here we will examine the contribution of each income component to total inequality and their marginal effect. See Table 4.2.4.

Agricultural income contributed 30.65% to total income inequality in 2000, and its marginal effect was −0.49%, meaning with other income components unchanged, each growth of 1% of this income will reduce total income inequality by 0.49%. In other words, increasing agricultural income can reduce rural income inequality, a conclusion which agrees with previous studies (Rozelle 1994). In 2003, due to a sudden enlargement of inequality on the part of agricultural income, its contribution increased to 36.44%, and its marginal effect rose to 5.17%, meaning that every 1% of growth will lead to 5.17% of increase of rural income inequality. In other words, the growth of agricultural income will widen rural income inequality.

Non-agricultural income contributed 60% or so to total income inequality, mainly because it was the major body of total income. For the years under review, its contribution dropped slightly by 1.73 points from 60.52% in 2000 to 58.79% in 2003. Its marginal effect was −1.40% in 2000, indicating that every 1% of growth will help reduce 1.4% of total income inequality, and in 2003 it became −3.88%, indicating that every growth of 1% will help reduce 3.88% of total income inequality. Obviously, for the period under review, non-agricultural income was a persistent contributor of inequality reduction, somewhat different from previous studies (Knight and Song 1993; Rozelle 1994; Zhang Ping 1996; Cheng 1996). Several facts may be held accountable for the deviation. First, the samples in previous studies cover a full range of regions from well-developed provinces like Guangdong (Yuk-shing Cheng 1996) to underdeveloped provinces like Sichuan

Table 4.2.4 Contribution of each income component to the inequality of total income and elasticity

	2000		2003	
	Contribution (%)	Elasticity (%)	Contribution (%)	Elasticity (%)
Agricultural income	30.65	−0.49	36.44	5.17
Non-agricultural income	60.52	−1.40	58.79	−3.88
Wage from local non-entrepreneurial employment	10.71	0.70	6.96	−1.46
Wage from local entrepreneurial employment	31.86	0.07	30.41	−1.23
Wage from outside employment	1.17	−4.16	3.81	−4.75
Income from non-agricultural business	16.78	1.99	17.61	3.56
Property income	2.48	0.71	2.13	−1.09
Interests	0.61	0.28	0.23	0.07
Dividend	0.42	0.19	0.07	0.02
Rents	−0.03	−0.25	0.37	−0.04
Others	1.48	0.49	1.46	−1.14
Transfers	2.08	0.16	2.33	0.47
Old age pension	1.25	0.06	0.94	−0.08
Relief and compensation	0.01	−0.02	0.05	−0.07
Others	0.82	0.12	1.34	0.62
Income given by relatives and friends	4.27	1.02	0.31	−0.67
Total	100	0	100	0

Source: Household surveying data in Tianjin rural area (2000 and 2003)

and Jiangxi (Rozelle 1994; Yuk-shing Cheng 1996), whereas samples in this study are only limited to Tianjin, a coastal metropolis which typifies metropolitan agriculture rather than a national average. Second, the time span of previous studies is from the late 1980s to the early 1990s, whereas this study is extended to early twenty-first century. Less than a decade's time has seen a huge change in China's rural areas which may draw different conclusions. Third, previous studies are usually village-based or on higher levels (Rozelle 1994), while this study is household-based. Fourth, non-agricultural income in previous studies mainly amounts to farmer's income from employment in township enterprise, but in this study it covers a variety of sources, including income from local non-entrepreneurial employment,[4] wage from local entrepreneurial employment (township enterprises and private enterprises), income from outside employment (outside of the town), and net income from family non-agricultural business. Different coverage may lead to opposite conclusions.

There have long been two views on relation between non-agricultural income and total income inequality. One argues that non-agricultural income benefits for the most part the poor, so it serves to cushion inequality. The other thinks quite

[4] Like wage from employment in local primary and secondary school, or township government.

differently, assuming non-agricultural income enlarges inequality. The contraction lies in the difference of objects under research. Some studies point out that in countries and regions rich in labor forces but short of land, some Asian countries and regions for instance, the poor are more likely to be edged out of the land and into non-agricultural business. By contrast, in countries rich in land but short of labors, some African countries for instance, most farmers are tied to the vast land and only a few rich can enter non-agricultural industry. This theory is flawed by ignoring the impact of land distribution system on non-agricultural employment and non-agricultural income.

Further analysis on non-agricultural income finds that the biggest contributor to total income inequality is farmer's wage from local entrepreneurial employment. Its contribution dropped slightly from 31.86% in 2000 to 30.41% in 2003, and its marginal effect fell from 0.7% to −1.46%, suggesting that the growth of this income underwent a change, from enlarging inequality in 2000 to reducing inequality in 2003. More likely, for explanation, since the rapid development of non-agricultural industry created more opportunities for more farmers, its marginal effect reversed accordingly.[5] Coming next is income from family non-agricultural business with 16% to 18% contribution. Its marginal effect was kept positive and had the potential of growth, increasing by 1.57% from 2% in 2000 to 3.56% in 2003. Considering that only mid-and high-income households can afford family non-agricultural business in rural area, income in this line tends to be concentrated in their pockets. Moreover, business income has accumulative effect to some degree. It is reasonable that it gains increasing contribution to total income inequality and growing marginal effect. Coming third is income from local non-entrepreneurial employment, contributing 10.71% in 2000 and 6.96% in 2003, down 3.75%. Its marginal effect fell also from 0.70% to −1.46%, suggesting that increase of this income component helped enlarge inequality in 2000, but in 2003 began to help reduce inequality. Further explanation will be given later. Least contribution was made by farmer's income from outside employment, with 1.17% in 2000 and 3.81% in 2003. Its marginal effects, being −4.16% and −4.75% in the 2 years, were kept negative, indicating that in rural areas of well-developed coastal cities like Tianjin with a mature labor market, outside employment on the part of rural labors may offset to some degree the income inequality, possibly a contrast to that in underdeveloped mid- and western regions of China.

Property income contributed 2.48% in 2000 and 2.13% in 2003, with small reduction, a little different from that in developed and other developing countries, also unlike the dynamics of urban income inequality in China. In general, with economic growth and raise of resident's income, property income will take a larger share in resident's total income and make accordingly larger contribution to total income inequality, which is substantiated by analysis on urban income inequality by one of the authors (Chen Zongsheng 1997; Chen Zongsheng and Zhou Yunbo

[5] Whether it is true in reality, we will present detailed analysis later.

2001a, b, c, 2002). The exception with rural areas may be considered as temporary and influenced by macroscopic fluctuation. The marginal effect of property income reversed from 0.71% in 2000 to −1.09% in 2003. As to the 2–2.5% of contribution made by property income, others were responsible for 1.5% or so, taking more than 60% share; its marginal effect was 0.49% in 2000 and −1.14% in 2003. Because of the small share in total income, interests and dividend together were responsible for 1% odd in 2000 and 0.3% in 2003. Rents were responsible for −0.03% in 2000 and reduced the inequality of total income; in 2003 its contribution was 0.37%, and its marginal effect was always positive, though.

Transfer income by government had almost the same contribution as property income, about 2% on average, growing from 2.08% in 2000 to 2.33% in 2003, and its marginal effect remained positive, indicating that based on current distribution pattern, increasing subsidy on this income component could not help reduce inequality but backfire. After further decomposition, it can be inferred that old age pension and relief and compensation, though having a positive contribution, had for the most time negative marginal effect, except in 2000 when the marginal effect of old age pension was 0.06%. If government increases subsidy on the two income components, it will reduce rural income inequality. Others in the category contributed 0.8%–1.4% and had a positive marginal effect. For lack of detailed data on this source, we choose to put it aside.

The contribution and marginal effect of income given by relatives and friends was 4.27%, 1.02% in 2000, and 0.31−0.67% in 2003. For it has not defining policy implication. This income will not be discussed here.

To sum up, in developed coastal cities like Tianjin, non-agricultural income is the main contributor to rural total income inequality, and next comes the agricultural income. Property income and transfer income, having small share in total income, make slight contribution.

4.2.2 Main Drivers that Impact Change of Income Inequality of Rural Residents: Analysis by Income Components

The previous subsection examined the contribution of income components of rural household to total income inequality of rural resident and their marginal effects. From 2000 to 2003, the Gini coefficient of rural resident's income grew by 13.78%, from 0.35476 to 0.40363. Next, we will analyze the impact of each income component on the dynamics of total income inequality by using the method given in Sect. 3.2. Before proceeding further, we first take a rough look into the impact of structural effect and distribution effect on added value of total income inequality by using cross multiplication, namely, to multiply the share of all income components in 2000 with their Pseudo Gini coefficient in 2003 and find the sum, then to multiply the Pseudo Gini of coefficient income component in 2000 with their share in 2003

Table 4.2.5 Outcome of cross multiplying shares of income sources and their Pseudo Gini coefficient

	Distribution effect	Structural effect
Farming income	0.14681	0.10896
Non-farming income	0.23521	0.21662
Property income	0.00447	0.01693
Transfer income	0.00954	0.00726
Income from relatives and friends	0.00400	0.00476
Total	$G_2 = 0.40003$	$G_1 = 0.35452$

Source: Household surveying data in Tianjin rural area (2000 and 2003)

and find the sum, and finally to compare the outcomes of the two calculations. The computation formula is

$$G_1 = \sum_{i=1}^{N} G_i(2000) \times Y_i(2003),$$

$$G_2 = \sum_{i=1}^{N} G_i(2003) \times Y_i(2000).$$

The dummy result of cross multiplication is seen in Table 4.2.5.

If the share of income component in 2000 is replaced with that in 2003 and the distribution pattern remains the same as in 2000, namely, multiplying share of income components in 2003 with their Pseudo Gini coefficient in 2000, and finding the sum, we have $G_1$to be 0.35452, and its difference from the actual Gini coefficient in 2003, 0.40363, is 0.04911, while its difference from the real Gini coefficient in 2000, 0.35476, is 0.00024. If we replace the Pseudo Gini coefficient of income components in 2000 with that in 2003 and their share in total income remains the same as that in 2000, we have G_2 to be 0.40003. The difference between G_2 and the actual Gini coefficient in 2003, namely 0.40363, is 0.0036, while that between G_2 and the actual Gini coefficient in 2000, namely 0.35476, is 0.04527. The observation tells us two things. For one, the change of rural total income inequality in Tianjin is mainly attributed to the change of internal distribution pattern of each income component rather than to the change of its share in total income, an observation contravening what we have concluded in previous parts on urban income inequality. For the other, if compare G_1(0.35452) with the actual Gini coefficient in 2000, 0.35476, that is, we find that the former is smaller than the latter, implying that if the internal distribution pattern of each income component remains fixed, the change of its share in total income will bring about reduction in total income inequality. Put in another way, structural effect, in a sense, plays an equalizing role in total income distribution. For further measurement of their impact, see Table 4.2.6 calculated by (3.2.16).

According to the data, distribution effect, contributing up to 92%, was the major driver of the enlargement of total income inequality, while structural effect

Table 4.2.6 Decomposing enlarged rural income inequality

	Distribution effect		Structural effect		Interaction effect		Total	
	Num. value	Share (%)	Num. value	Share (%)	Num. value	Share (%)	Num. value	Share (%)
Farming income	0.03807	77.88	0.00022	0.45	0.00008	0.16	0.03837	78.49
Non-farming income	0.02049	41.92	0.00190	3.89	0.00018	0.37	0.02257	46.18
Property income	−0.00435	−8.90	0.00812	16.61	−0.00400	−8.18	−0.00023	−0.47
Transfer income	0.00217	4.44	−0.00010	−0.20	−0.00003	−0.06	0.00204	4.18
Income from relatives and friends	−0.01113	−22.77	−0.01037	−21.22	0.00763	15.61	−0.01387	−28.38
Total	0.04525	92.57	−0.00023	−0.47	0.00386	7.90	0.04888	100

Source: Household surveying data in Tianjin rural area (2000 and 2003)

contributed −0.47%, in line with what was observed in previous parts, or in other words, change of share of income components in total income helped reduce total income inequality to certain extent. Interaction effect contributed 7.9% to total income inequality. After further decomposing, we find that for distribution effect, the change of agricultural income inequality was mostly responsible for total income inequality, contributing almost 78%, the contribution of non-agricultural income approaches 42%, that of transfer income 4% or more, which means that the distribution of this income needs improvement, and that of property income and income from relatives and friends were all negative, being −8.9% and −22.77% correspondingly, suggesting that their internal change of distribution offsets total income inequality. For structural effect, property income, non-agricultural income and agricultural income contributed 16.61%, 3.89%, and 0.45, respectively, to total income inequality. That is to say, change of the share of the three income components in total income widened total income inequality. The other two sources, income from relatives and friends and transfer income, had negative contributions of −21.22% and −0.20%, respectively, suggesting that change of their share countervail total income inequality. For interaction effect, the largest contributor was the income from relatives and friends, as high as 15.61%, while agricultural income and non-agricultural income had very slight contributions, as little as 0.16% and 0.37%, respectively. Property income and transfer income had negative contributions of −8.18% and −0.06%, helping reduce total income inequality. Combining the three effects, we find that change of internal distribution of agricultural income and its share in total income, with a contribution of as large as 78.49%, was mostly responsible for the change of total income inequality which rose from 0.35476 in 2000 to 0.40363 in 2003. Non-agricultural income comes next, contributing 46.18%, somewhat different from previous observation (Chen Zongsheng and Zhou Yunbo 2002). Transfer income, though contributing less than 5%, helped to widen inequality up to a point, supporting our previous study (Zongsheng and Zhou Yunbo 2002). Income from relatives and friends helped to cushion income inequality, contributing −28.38%, and property income contributed very little, less than 5%.

In total, the change of internal distribution pattern of income components was the major driving force behind the enlarged rural income inequality, namely, for the enlargement of total income inequality from 2000 to 2003; distribution effect took the largest responsibility. The change of each income component's share in total income offsets the enlargement of total income inequality, but to limited effect. Within income component, agricultural income was the largest contributor to the enlargement of total income inequality, while income from relatives and friends played a countervailing role to some extent.

4.3 Main Factors that Impact Non-agricultural Income Inequality of Rural Resident and Its Change

The past section presents main drivers of rural total income inequality by income structure of rural resident. The rapid rural economic growth has brought about great change to income structure of rural residents with non-agricultural income taking more share in total income and playing a significant role in rural income inequality, as proved by many studies (Knight and Song 1993; Rozelle 1994; Zhang Ping 1996; Cheng 1996; Chen Zongsheng and Zhou Yunbo 2002). According to the measurement in the past section, for total income of Tianjin rural resident, 60% came from non-agricultural. This section will present a detailed analysis on the distribution inequality and its change of non-agricultural income.

4.3.1 *Main Factors Impacting Non-agricultural Income Inequality of Rural Resident*

1. *Correlation between each income component to total non-agricultural income.* First we work out the correlation coefficient between each income component and non-agricultural income in Table 4.3.1. The outcome shows that wage from local entrepreneurial employment of rural resident and his income from family non-agricultural business were more correlated to non-agricultural income, their correlation coefficients in 2000 reaching up to 0.70833 and 0.48746, respectively, and in 2003 up to 0.54969 and 0.62881. Coming third is wage from local non-entrepreneurial employment, whose correlation coefficient grew by 37.79% from 0.32168 in 2000 to 0.44324 in 2003. Wage from outside employment had the least correlation coefficient, but with a striking growth rate of 136.02%, from 0.07477 in 2000 to 0.17647 in 2003.

Wage from local entrepreneurial employment and income from family non-agricultural business had a higher Pseudo Gini coefficient than total non-agricultural income for the years under review and had enlargement trend. It indicates that the two income components were more unequally distributed than total non-agricultural

Table 4.3.1 Correlation coefficient between each non-agricultural income component and total non-agricultural income of rural residents and their Pseudo Gini coefficient

	2000		2003	
	Correlation coefficient	Pseudo Gini coefficient	Correlation coefficient	Pseudo Gini coefficient
Wage from local non-entrepreneurial employment	0.32168	0.45532	0.17458	0.44324
Wage from local entrepreneurial employment	0.70833	0.53662	0.61727	0.54969
Wage from outside employment	0.07477	0.24056	0.17647	0.35400
Net income from family non-agricultural business	0.48746	0.59362	0.47270	0.62991
Total non-farming income	–	0.50883	–	0.52662

Source: Household surveying data in Tianjin rural area (2000 and 2003)

Table 4.3.2 Contribution of each non-agricultural income component to the inequality of total income and elasticity

	2000		2003	
	Contribution (%)	Elasticity (%)	Contribution (%)	Elasticity (%)
Wage from local non-entrepreneurial employment	14.28	−1.68	11.31	−2.13
Wage from local entrepreneurial employment	53.97	2.80	52.70	2.21
Wage from outside employment	4.49	−5.01	9.19	−4.48
Net income from family non-agricultural business	27.26	3.89	26.80	4.40
Total non-farming income	100	0	100	0

Source: Household surveying data in Tianjin rural area (2000 and 2003)

income. Wage from non-entrepreneurial employment and wage from outside employment had a smaller Pseudo Gini coefficient than total non-agricultural income, implying that the income components were more equally distributed relative to total non-agricultural income.

2. *Contribution of each income component to the inequality of total non-agricultural income and their marginal effect.* Correlation coefficient and Pseudo Gini coefficient are only indicative of the correlation between each income component and total non-agricultural income. For the actual contribution of income components to total non-agricultural income and their marginal effect, see Table 4.3.2.

From the data, we observe that wage from local entrepreneurial employment made the largest contribution, 53.97% in 2000 and 52.70% in 2003, and its marginal effect was kept positive, 2.8% in 2000 and 2.21% in 2003, indicating that growth of this income source would lead to the enlargement of non-agricultural income inequality. Coming next is income from family non-agricultural business, contributing 27.26% and 26.86% in the 2 years, and its marginal effect was kept positive and indicative of 0.51% of growth rate, from 3.89% in 2000 to 4.40% in 2003. The third is wage from non-entrepreneurial employment, contributing 14.28% in 2000 and 11.31% in 2003, down about 3% and its marginal effect remained to be negative, −1.68% in 2000 and −2.13% in 2003, suggesting that growth of this source would lead to reduction of total non-agricultural income inequality. Income from outside employment made the least contribution, but growing from 4.49% in 2000 and 9.19% in 2003. Part of it is because this income component gained more percentage in total non-agricultural income and further inequality of itself. Its marginal effect remained to be negative, being −5.01% and −4.48% in the 2 years.

4.3.2 Main Factors Impacting Change of the Non-agricultural Income Inequality of Rural Resident

In the following part, we will examine in detail the contributions made by distribution effect, structural effect, and interaction effect to the Gini coefficient growth of non-agricultural income inequality from 2000 to 2003, an added value of 0.01779, that is. Which makes the largest contribution? Likewise, before further decomposing, we will first take a preliminary look into the impact of structural effect and distribution effect on total income inequality by using cross multiplication as done before. The dummy result is given in Table 4.3.3.

If the shares of income components in 2000 are substituted with that in 2003 and the distribution inequality remains the same as in 2000, namely, multiplying their shares in 2003 with their Pseudo Gini coefficient in 2000 and finding the sum, we have G_1 to be 0.49801. The difference between G_1 and the actual Gini coefficient in 2003, namely 0.52662, is 0.02861, and the difference between $G_1$and the actual Gini in 2000 is 0.01082. If doing the other way round, multiplying the Pseudo Gini coefficient of income components in 2003 with their shares in 2000 and finding the sum, we have G_2, namely 0.53285. The difference between G_2 and the actual Gini coefficient in 2003 is 0.00623, but the difference between G_2 and the actual Gini coefficient in 2000, namely 0.50883, is 0.02402. The observation reveals that first, the change of non-agricultural income inequality of Tianjin rural resident from 2000 to 2003 was mainly attributed not so much to the change of each income

Table 4.3.3 Outcome of cross multiplying shares of income components with their Pseudo Gini coefficient

	Distribution effect	Structural effect
Wage from local non-entrepreneurial employment	0.07073	0.06121
Wage from local entrepreneurial employment	0.28127	0.27090
Wage from outside employment	0.03364	0.03287
Net income from family non-agricultural business	0.14720	0.13302
Total non-farming income	$G_2 = 0.53285$	$G_1 = 0.49801$

Source: Household surveying data in Tianjin rural area (2000 and 2003)

Table 4.3.4 Decomposing the enlarged non-agricultural income inequality of rural resident

	Distribution effect		Structural effect		Interaction effect		Total	
	Num. value	Share (%)	Num. value	Share (%)	Num. value	Share (%)	Num. value	Share (%)
Wage from local non-entrepreneurial employment	−0.00193	−10.84	−0.01145	−64.35	0.00031	1.71	−0.01307	−73.48
Wage from local entrepreneurial employment	0.00669	37.60	−0.00368	−20.70	−0.00009	−0.50	0.00292	16.39
Wage from outside employment	0.01078	60.61	0.01001	56.27	0.00472	26.53	0.02551	143.42
Net income from family non-agricultural business	0.00848	47.68	−0.00570	−32.05	−0.00035	−1.96	0.00243	13.67
Total non-farming income	0.02402	135.05	−0.01082	−60.83	0.00459	25.78	0.01779	100

Source: Household surveying data in Tianjin rural area (2000 and 2003)

component's share as to its internal distribution pattern. Second, by comparison, we find that $G_1(0.49801)$ was smaller than the actual Gini coefficient in 2000, 0.50883, revealing that if the internal distribution pattern of each income component remained unaltered, the variation of its share in total non-agricultural income would lead to slight reduction of total non-agricultural income inequality, or put another way, structural effect somewhat played an equalizing role in total non-agricultural income inequality. The two observations support what we have decomposed on the growth of rural total income inequality. Next, we continue to measure the impact of distribution effect, structural effect, and interaction effect in Table 4.3.4.

Distribution effect took the main responsibility for the enlarged non-agricultural income inequality, which contributed as high as more than 135%, while structural effect contributed expectedly −60.83%, indicating that the change of each income component's share in total non-agricultural income was responsible for the reduction of total non-agricultural income inequality to a point. The interaction effect contributed 25.78%. After further examination, we find that for distribution effect, the change of distribution pattern of wage from outside employment was the main contributor to enlarged non-agricultural income inequality, taking almost 61%, income from non-agricultural business contributed about 48%, wage from local entrepreneurial employment 37.60%, and wage from local non-entrepreneurial employment was a negative −10.84%, which indicates that its internal distribution variation offsets the inequality of total non-agricultural income. For structural effect, the contribution of all income components were negative except wage from outside employment, which contributed 56.27%, suggesting that its change of share helped to widen total non-agricultural income inequality. The other three income components with their contributions of −64.35%, −32.05%, and −20.70%, respectively, helped to reduce inequality. For interaction effect, wage from outside employment took the lead in widening the inequality, contributing up to 26.53%, wage from local non-entrepreneurial employment contributed as little as 1.71%, and wage from local entrepreneurial employment and income from family non-agricultural business made negative contributions, −0.50% and −1.96%. Combining the three effects, we find that for the enlargement of non-agricultural income inequality from 2000 to 2003, the change of internal distribution pattern of wage from outside employment and its share in total non-agricultural income took the leading responsibility, contributing up to 143.42%. wage from local entrepreneurial employment contributed 16.39%, non-agricultural business income contributed 13.67%, and wage from non-entrepreneurial employment had a notable function to cushion the inequality, contributing −73.48%.

In conclusion, the variation of internal distribution pattern of each income component was the main driver of enlarged non-agricultural income inequality, that is to say, distribution effect mainly answered for the added value of non-agricultural income inequality from 2000 to 2003. Coming next is interaction effect. The change of each income component's share in total non-agricultural income notably countervailed the widening inequality of total non-agricultural income. For income components themselves, wage from outside employment contributed the most to the enlarged inequality, and wage from local entrepreneurial employment and non-agricultural business income came next, while wage from local non-entrepreneurial employment somewhat reduced the inequality.

4.4 Impact of Non-agricultural Sector Employment of Rural Labors on Income Inequality of Rural Resident

We have analyzed the main drivers of the inequality of total income and total non-agricultural income of rural resident from a microscopic perspective by using rural household data. This section goes on to examine how the labor transfer to non-agricultural industry influences income inequality of rural resident, or to be exact, the internal and external factors behind the labor transfer, its historical setting, main ways, general scenario, and their impact on income inequality of rural resident.

4.4.1 Internal and External Factors Behind the Labor Transfer to Non-agricultural Sector

To explain the rural labor transfer to non-agricultural industry, we may borrow the "push-and-pull" theory, namely, the driving force behind the labor transfer comes from the push power from agricultural sections and pull power from non-agricultural sections. The push power of agricultural section is mainly from the growing rise of

Table 4.4.1 Change of China's total arable land and per capita arable land

Year	Year end actual arable land square (million *mu*)	Net reduction of arable land square (million *mu*)	Total population (billion)	Per capita arable land square (mu)
1997	1,948.5465	2.0415	1.23626	1.58
1998	1,944.6315	3.9150	1.24761	1.56
1999	1,938.0825	6.5490	1.25786	1.54
2000	1,923.6465	14.4360	1.26743	1.52
2001	1,914.2370	9.4095	1.27627	1.50
2002	1,888.9440	25.2930	1.28453	1.47
2003	1,850.8830	38.0610	1.29227	1.43
2004	1,836.6645	12.0045	1.29988	1.41
2005	1,831.2405	5.4240	1.30756	1.40
2006	1,827.0000	4.6020	1.31448	1.39
2007	1,826.0280	0.972	1.32129	1.38
2008	1,825.7385	0.2895	1.32802	1.37

Source: Land resources announcement by Ministry of Land and Resources 1998–2009

rural surplus labor forces[6] due to improved agricultural productivity, intensified tension between labors and land resource, and advanced level of agricultural mechanization.

First, the progress of agricultural mechanization and biotechnology is effectively associated with an improvement of agricultural productivity, which in turn results in a conflict between a shrinking demand for production labor and a spiraling supply of labor forces. In 1978, the total motive power of agricultural machinery was 11.7496 million kw, and the quantity of chemical fertilizers used for farming was 8.84 million tons. In 2009, the two rose to 874.961 million kw and 54.044 million tons, 74.47 times and 6.11 times of those in 1978 in that order. At the same time, rural labor forces were increasing at the pace of 1.38% per year. By the end of 2009, the net growth of labor forces was 162.37 million and the total amount of rural labor forces reached 468.75 million.[7] A conflict between the falling demand for labors and the increasing supply of labors emerged. Second, because of the shrinking total arable land square and per capita arable land square, relation between farmers and land resource was even more stressed, which can be seen in Table 4.4.1. From 1997 to 2008 China's total arable land shrank from 1948.54 million *mu* to 1825.74 million *mu* and per capita arable land shrank from 1.58 *mu* to 1.37 *mu*. The increasingly stressed man–land relation led to more rural labor surplus, which inevitably exerted pressure and emergency for rural labors' transfer to non-agricultural industry.

[6] Zhao Yaohui (2006) held scarcity of arable land and rural household labor surplus as the leading two factors of most importance behind labor transfer to non-agricultural sections.

[7] Cited from China Agricultural Development Report 2005 (Agricultural Economic Information Web).

Table 4.4.2 Surplus labor in rural area and agricultural sector (10,000 people)

Year	Rural labor surplus (1)	Rural labor surplus (2)	Rural labor surplus (3)
1985		11,896	5,452
1990		15,785	11,581
1995		19,263	16,667
1996		19,205	15,365
1997	15,207	19,873	15,509
1998	15,180	20,375	15,903
1999	16,884	21,117	17,249
2000	17,032	21,512	22,324
2001		22,170	
2002		22,880	
2003		23,467	
2004		24,491	

Source: (1) Measurement by Cai Fang (2002:72). (2) Measurement by Li Ruifen et al. (2006: 40). (3)Measurement by Han Jijiang (2003)

Thanks to the combined forces, a great number of surplus labors were produced in agricultural sector. Table 4.4.2 lists the rural surplus labor measured by different scholars. In spite of varied measurement methods and outcomes, they all point to a large number of rural surplus labors and a trend of growth, which constitutes a push power for labor transfer to non-agricultural.

In addition, pull power from non-agricultural sector is another vital driving force behind rural labor transfer to non-agricultural industry. In general, agricultural sector has a lower productivity than non-agricultural sector on account of technology and forms of production. High productivity in non-agricultural means more income, so non-agricultural sector attracts more and more rural labors. Meanwhile, urban–rural income gap constitutes the major pull power for rural labor transfer to urban area.[8] We may well say labor transfer to urban area may take place for all intents and purposes, but the cardinal one is to earn more income. China's urban–rural income gap has been in existence as early as in the beginning of system reform. For example, the ratio of urban per capita disposable income to rural one was 2.57 in 1978, and in 2010 it rose to 3.2. However, it is only a statistical gap, and the actual figure, if benefits and allowances enjoyed by urban residents were taken into account, would be much larger, to be fourfold, fivefold, and even sixfold, according to some scholar's estimation (Li Shi 2004).[9] The huge gap draws many rural labors to cities and towns for employment.

To sum up, it is under the combined force of push from agricultural sector and pull power from non-agricultural sector that a great amount of rural surplus labors transfer to non-agricultural industry both in rural areas and in cities.

[8] For studies on decisive drivers of labor transfer, see Zhao Zhong (2006).

[9] See Li Shi (2004).

4.4.2 *Background of Rural Labor Transfer to Non-agricultural Sector*

It is well known that from the foundation of New China to the eve of System Reform and Opening-up, a dual urban–rural divide administration system was pervading, which had produced a great number of surplus labor in agricultural sector. Since 1978 apace with the advance of institutional reform, rural labors began to transfer to non-agricultural sector. Generally speaking, rural labor transfer came to the stage against the following backdrops.

Firstly, the takeoff of household responsibility system in 1978 provided the premise for rural labor transfer. Household, having family labor force to their own disposition, became the basic subject for production and operation which created the condition for rural labor transfer.

Secondly, development of township enterprises and private economy in urban area made labor transfer possible. For one, township enterprises were a great brainchild of Chinese farmers who are now able to leave the field without leaving their villages and go to the factory without necessarily going to cities, a mode of labor transfer in Chinese characteristics. For the other, deep urban reform gave birth to a plural economic pattern with various ownerships and operation forms in coexistence. Self-employed enterprises, private economy, and foreign enterprises emerged rapidly, which were mainly labor-intensive industries in great demand for rural labors.

Finally, the decompression of the dual urban–rural divide administration created a loosening social environment for labor transfer. As to the large-scaled rural labor transfer into non-agricultural sector and farmer's going out for urban employment, government shifted policies from rigorous curbing to active instructing. Take examples. The State Council issued "Opinions on Better Approach to Agriculture and Rural Work in 2002", where a policy on urban rural workers was for the first time laid down, namely, fair treatment, proper guide, better administration, and improving services. In January 2003, the General Office of the State Council issued a "Circular on Administration of Urban Rural Workers and Their Services", demanding that unreasonable bans on urban rural workers be lifted, arrears of wages and wage deduction of urban–rural migrant workers be solved effectively, their working and living conditions be upgraded, and their children's schooling be well arranged. In 2004 No. 1 Document by Central Government reckoned that urban–rural migrant workers had made up a substantial part of industrial workers, and they created huge wealth for cities and tax income for government. The statement not only raised urban rural workers' social status, but acknowledged their great contribution to economic growth.

At the same time, many departments and local governments formulated some policies and regulations benefiting labor transfer, providing first-rate services and supports for its organization, training, and rights safeguarding. For instance, in November 2001 State Development & Planning Commission and Ministry of Finance jointly issued an "Announcement on Complete Revamping of Charging

Migrant Workers", stipulating in explicit terms that all charges except certificate cost fees on migrant workers should be eliminated and any illegal charges should be refunded. In September 2003, a "2003–2010 Training Project for Migrant Workers" was formulated jointly by Labor and Social Security Department, Ministry of Agriculture, Ministry of Education, and Ministry of Finance, where they required central administration and local administration to earmark funds for training migrant workers. Meanwhile, the Ministry of Agriculture put in motion the so-called Sunshine Project, offering training programs for migrant workers to improve their quality and technique. In February 2004, the General Office of State Council forwarded an announcement of Opinions on Improving Work on Offering Schooling for Migrant Workers' Children originally issued by Ministry of Education, asking local governments to take over the education of migrant workers' children and stipulating that their children enjoy the same rights as local native children do. With a view to incorporating migrant workers into urban social security system and reduce their emergency expenditure, Labor and Social Security Department issued "Opinions on Involving Employees in Mixed Ownership Enterprises and Non-public Economy in Medical Insurance", clearly demanding that employers include migrant workers in urban medical insurance system.

4.4.3 Major Ways of Rural Labor Transfer to Non-agricultural Sector

There are three major ways for rural labors to join non-agricultural industry: joining local township enterprises, self-employed and private enterprises, entering cities for employment, and taking up family non-agricultural business. Among the three, the first two take the lead.

Statistics show that from 1978 to 2002 the number of township enterprises of sundry kinds rose from 1.5243 million to 21.3269 million, increasing by 13 times during 25 years. By the end of 2009 rural labors working in township enterprises and self-employed and private enterprises had reached up to 209.92 million, taking 44.78% of the total rural labors that year. Township enterprises, by providing enormous employment opportunities for rural surplus labors and alleviating urban stress from labor migration, had become the most important venue for labor transfer. Quantitative analysis shows that the correlation coefficient between the number of township enterprises and the number of rural labor's non-agricultural employment was 0.93 from 1978 to 2006. It is due to development of the former that China's rural labor force began to see its first decline in 1992 since the foundation of new China. Also it is due to township enterprises that China has mapped out a unique way out for rural surplus labors, that is, leaving the field without leaving the village. China, before knowing it, is stepping on decentralized industrialization in western modern economic development theory.

Table 4.4.3 Rural labor's outside employment (10,000 people)

Year	Outside County	Outside Province
1989	–	700
1993	4,300	2,050
1995	5,400	2,500
1996	4,487	2,364
2001	6,361	3,933

Source: Wang Xiyu (2000), Fan Xiaoyu (2002:3)

Outside employment in cities is the second important way for labor transfer. Because of technical difficulties, no exact statistics on the size of labor transfer have been available. Some rough estimation can be made, though. In 1994, Ministry of Labor made a sampling survey in eight provinces and found that about 20% of rural labors were working outside, of which 40% were working in their native counties (Knight and Song 1996). Based on this survey, it may be inferred that about 90 million rural labors were working outside their villages, and 45–50 million outside their native counties. Another survey on resident's income by Economic Institute of China Academy of Social Science found that rural labors working outside took 9.9% of total labor force that year, amounting to 45 million. Li Shi et al. (1999) made an estimation of the size of migrant workers according to a sample survey of 1% of the nation's total population in 1995, and found that the long-term rural migrant workers were 17.5 million, and the more developed the region was, the more migrant workers it drew. Studies by Wang Xiyu (2000) and Fan Xiaoyu (2002) showed that in 1993 rural labors working outside their counties were 43 million, outside their provinces were 20.5 million, and in 2001 the two groups increased to 63.61 million and 39.33 million correspondingly, up 47.93% and 91.85%, respectively (Table 4.4.3).

Non-agricultural business is the third way of labor transfer. Not having data on the number of rural labors doing non-agricultural business, we can only approach it from the structure of farmer's non-agricultural productive capital. Official statistics show that in 2009 the initial value of non-agricultural productive fixed assets of rural households were 2,978.72 yuan, to which the first three contributors were transport, 1,214.21 yuan, industry, 698.3 yuan, and wholesale and retail and catering, 490.63 yuan, totaling 2,403.14 yuan. They took 40.76%, 23.44%, and 16.47% in that order, totaling 80.67%. It is obvious that rural labors tended to take up non-agricultural business mainly in transport, industry and wholesale and retail, and catering which require less initial investment, comparatively lower technology, and smaller entry barrier. Part of it is because, first, low income on the part of rural residents makes it difficult for them to invest in sectors requiring huge initial investment; next, financial repression is pervading in rural areas of developing countries, and China is no exception. Under financial repression, rural households do not have easy access to capital from the country's financial system; furthermore, because of lower levels of education received, farmers are barred away from high-tech industries like education, culture, and health; finally, administrative monopoly is still reigning in some sectors, and institutional barriers prevent rural household from investing therein.

4.4.4 Phasic Change of Labor Transfer to Non-agricultural Sector

In 1978 China had 306.38 million rural labors in total, of which 7.12% were non-agricultural labors, amounting to 21.82 million. In 2009 the total rural labors increased to 468.75 million, of which 47.78% were non-agricultural labors, amounting to 209.19 million, 9.59 times that in 1978 with its annual growth up to 8.26%. As to the change course, the labor transfer is phasic, not stable, closely linked with the phasic moves of institutional reform as shown in Fig. 4.4.1.

Stage one is from 1978 to 1983 when rural areas became the focus of reform where household responsibility system was put into effect. Rural household, becoming the basic unit of production, accounting, and income distribution, began to find unprecedented enthusiasm for production. At the same time, township and private enterprises were spotty, which decreased from 1.524 million in 1978 to 1.3464 million in 1983 (see Fig. 4.4.2), and to top it all, various restraints were imposed on outside employment. No surprise that in this stage, not many rural labors entered non-agricultural sector and the number of migrant workers rose from 21.82 million only to 30.45 million, with an annual growth of 6.89%. Share of non-agricultural labors in total rural labors rose from 7.12% in 1978 to 8.78% in 1983 only by 1.66%.

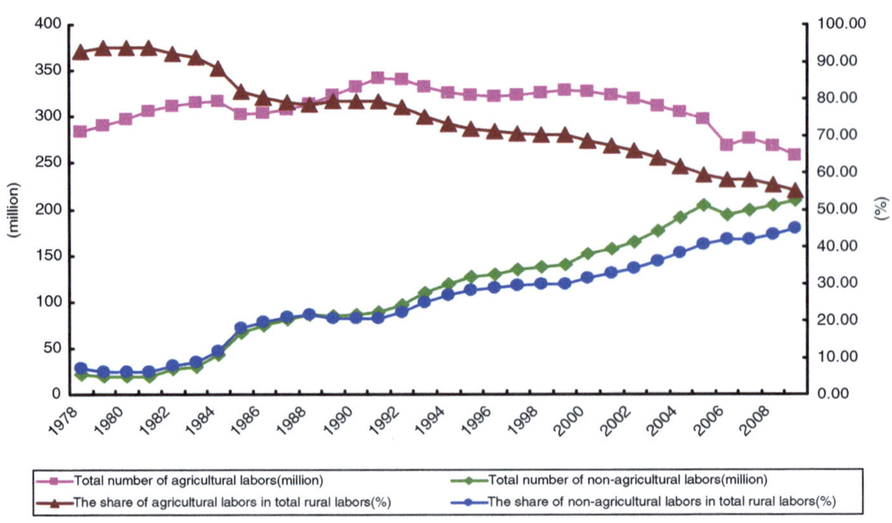

Fig. 4.4.1 Change of employment structure of rural labors 1978–2009. Source: *China Yearbook of Statistics 1979–2010*

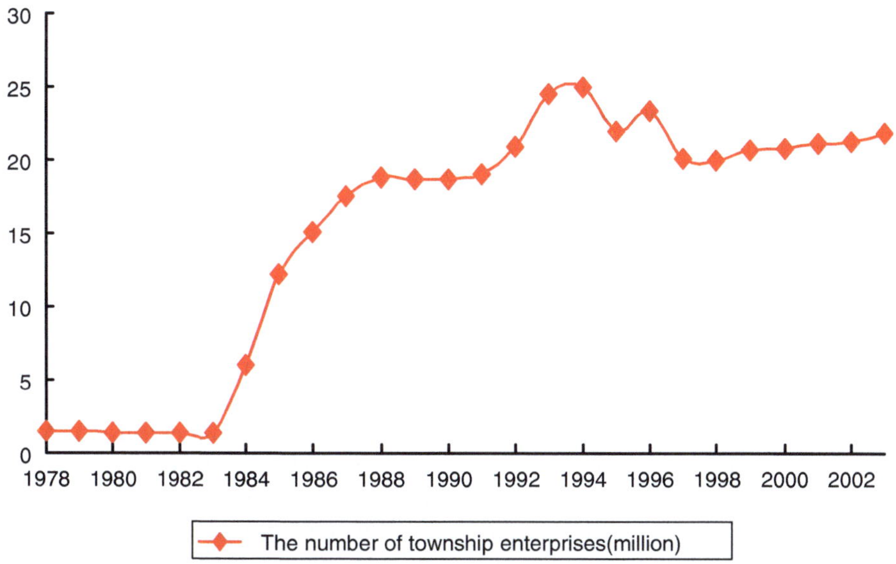

Fig. 4.4.2 Growth of China's township enterprises 1978–2002. Source: *China Yearbook of Statistics 1979–2003*

The second stage is from 1984 to 1988 when labor transfer saw a rapid growth. To answer for it, in this stage township enterprises and private enterprises also saw a rapid development, attracting a good large number of surplus labors. Official statistics show that by 1988 township enterprises of all sorts reached 18.882 million, 14 times that in 1983 and growing by 70% per year. In addition, household registration system and social administration policies aiming to restrain population migrant were greatly loosened, and the boom of urban economy and rapid growth of non-public economy facilitated the demand for more labors. In 1988, the number of rural labors working in non-agricultural sector peaked to 86.11 million, 2.82 times that in 1983 and growing by 23.11% per year. The share of non-agricultural labors in total rural labors rose by 12.71%, from 8.78% in 1983 to 21.49% in 1988.

The third stage is from 1989 to 1991 when China saw the first two-digital inflation since the reform due to economic overheating. Compounding this, the central government began to put brake on the economy as a whole, making development of township and private enterprises stagnant, and even slide in a few years. The aggregate number of township enterprises in 1991 was 19.089 million, rising only by 1.1% relative to 1988. Stagnation of township enterprises notably slowed down the pace of labor transfer. In 1992 non-agricultural labors totaled 89.07 million, rising by 3.44% than in 1988, and their share rose by no more than 1%, from 21.49% in 1988 to 22.29% in 1992.

The fourth stage comes from 1992 to 1995 when Deng Xiaoping's speech during his south China tour in 1992 initiated China's economic system reform anchored on a socialist market economy. China's economic development and system reform stepped into a new period. Because township and private enterprises staged a comeback of booming with the rapid development of urban economy which created the great demand for rural labors, the size of migrant workers doubled and the pace of labor transfer was accelerated. In 1992, 1993, 1994, and 1995 rural non-agricultural labors increased at the speed of 9.63%, 12.63%, 8.78% and 6.21%, respectively. By 1995 the total non-agricultural labors in rural area amounted to 127.07 million, rising by 42.66% relative to 1991, and their share in total rural labors rose by 7.54%, from 20.67% in 1991 to 28.21% in 1995.

1996–1999 is the fifth stage when labor transfer continued at a steady speed. In 1996, 1997, 1998, and 1999 non-agricultural labors increased at the speed of 2.53%, 3.83%, 2.06%, and 1.30%, respectively. Why did the speed of rural labor transfer declined during this stage. Part of it is, first, development of township and private enterprises entered into structural consolidation after early rapid expansion. After 1997 state-owned enterprises began to see more powerful reform and much higher efficiency, posing a challenge to township and private enterprises to the detriment of the latter. The number of township and private enterprises decreased. In 2002 there were 21.3269 million township and private enterprises in total with 132.88 million employees, down 8.72% and 1.63% correspondingly than in 1998. However, the stagnation in this stage was not much the same as that in 1989–1991. The former is a natural result of market competition, while the latter is influenced by government's macro-regulation. Though falling in number, township and private enterprises were upgraded in technology, management, and operation mechanism. Second, further reform in state-owned enterprises produced a large number of layoffs, who exerted huge employment pressure to cities and accordingly reduced the demand for rural labors. The two factors greatly slowed down the pace of labor transfer. From 1996 to 1999, the growth rates of rural non-agricultural labors were 2.53%, 3.83%, 2.06%, and 1.30%. In 1999 rural non-agricultural labors totaled 139.85 million, rising by 10.06% than in 1995 and their share in total rural labors reached 29.82%, up 1.6% only than in 1995 (Fig. 4.4.3).

The sixth stage is from 2000 till 2005 which has seen a sharp growth of labor transfer in terms of both speed and quantity. The annual growth rates of labor transfer from 2000 to 2005 were 8.43%, 4.05%, 4.80%, 7.11%, 7.83%, and 6.87%. In 2005 the aggregate number of rural non-agricultural labors was 204.12 million, up 45.96% compared with 1999, and its share in total rural labors reached 40.67%, up 12.46% compared with 1999. Why the accelerated pace of labor transfer in this stage? Part of it is the new century saw a new boom of township and private enterprises as well as urban non-public economy which created a good deal of employments for rural labors.

The seventh stage is from 2006 till now which has seen a low growth of labor transfer. The annual growth rates of labor transfer from 2006 to 2009 were −4.67%, 2.52%, 2.25%, and 2.91%. In 2005 the aggregate number of rural non-agricultural labors was 209.92 million, up 2.8% compared with 2005, and its share in total rural labors reached 44.78%, up 4.11% compared with 2005.

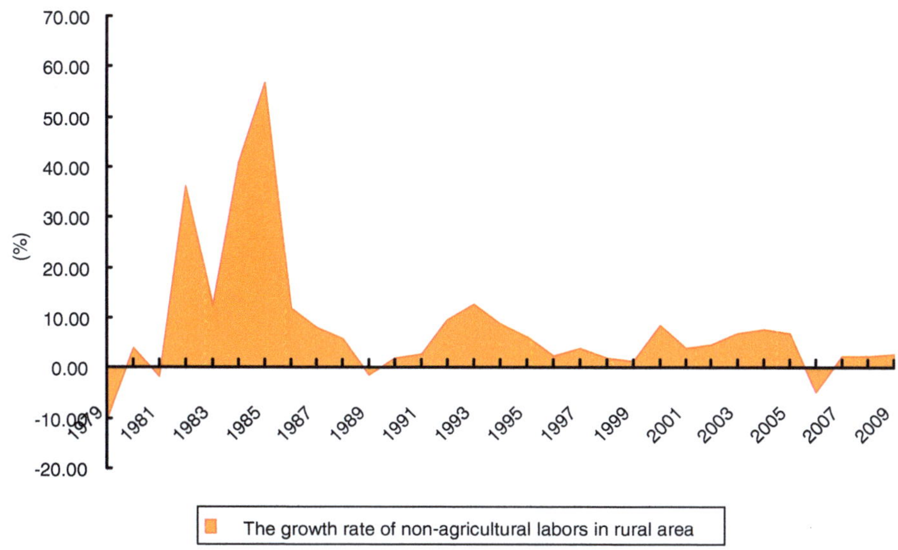

Fig. 4.4.3 Annual growth rate of rural non-agricultural labors 1978–2009. Source: *China Yearbook of Statistics 1979–2010*

4.4.5 Impact of Labor Transfer to Non-agricultural Sector on Income Inequality of Rural Resident

In the following part analysis will be concentrated on the impact of labor transfer on rural income inequality.

1. *Empirical model and selection and test of data.* The empirical model used here is as follows:

$$G_u = C + \alpha_1 L_f + \alpha_2 L_f^2 + \alpha_3 \text{RJGDP} + \alpha_3 \text{RJGDP}^2 + \alpha_5 \text{INE} + \alpha_6 \text{INF} + \mu, \quad (4.4.1)$$

where L_f refers to the share of rural non-agricultural labors in total rural labors. Since labor transfer from agricultural sector to non-agricultural sector tends to have a impact on rural income inequality like an inverted U, that is enlarge the income inequality at first stage, and then decrease the income inequality at later stage, we introduce the square of L_f. Others are all controlled variables, among which RJGDP means GDP per capita at comparable prices, INE means foreign trade dependency, namely, percentage of total imports and exports in GDP, and INF refers to consumer price index which indicates the impact of inflation on rural resident's income inequality. Data on all variables are from *China Yearbook of Statistics* of each year. The Gini coefficient of rural income, aggregate number of rural non-agricultural labors, and its share in total rural labors are given in Table 4.4.4, and their statistics are given in Table 4.4.5.

Table 4.4.4 Gini coefficient of rural resident's income and rural non-agricultural labors

	Gini of rural income	Aggregate number of rural non-agricultural labors (10,000 people)	Share in total rural labors (%)
1978	0.2122	21.82	7.12
1979	0.2308	19.53	6.29
1980	0.2382	20.28	6.37
1981	0.2256	19.94	6.10
1982	0.2333	27.14	8.01
1983	0.2554	30.45	8.78
1984	0.2697	42.83	11.91
1985	0.2785	67.13	18.11
1986	0.2884	75.22	19.80
1987	0.2798	81.30	20.85
1988	0.30285	86.11	21.49
1989	0.31261	84.98	20.76
1990	0.29474	86.73	20.65
1991	0.3074	89.07	20.67
1992	0.31062	97.65	22.29
1993	0.31812	109.98	24.85
1994	0.32996	119.64	26.79
1995	0.3407	127.07	28.21
1996	0.321	130.28	28.77
1997	0.32724	135.27	29.43
1998	0.34097	138.06	29.73
1999	0.3512	139.85	29.82
2000	0.36039	151.64	31.62
2001	0.36986	157.78	32.71
2002	0.38389	165.36	34.08
2003	0.41044	177.12	36.17
2004	0.41202	190.99	38.43
2005	0.41346	204.12	40.67
2006	0.41192	194.59	42.04
2007	0.41903	199.49	41.87
2008	0.42616	203.98	43.15
2009	–	209.92	44.78

Source: *China Yearbook of Statistics 1980–2010*

Note: Gini coefficient of rural resident's income in 1978–1999 is from Chen Zongsheng and Zhou Yunbo (2002). Gini coefficient after 2000 is the authors' calculation by data from *China Yearbook of Statistics*

Table 4.4.5 Statistics of Gini coefficient of rural resident and share of rural non-agricultural labors

Variable	Mean	Standard deviation	Min. value	Max. value
Gini coefficient of rural resident's income	0.32182	0.06324	0.2122	0.42616
Share of rural non-agricultural labors (%)	24.44	11.53	43.15	6.10

Source: The same as Table 4.4.4

Note: Since statistics of per capita GDP, inflation rate, and foreign trade dependency have been given in Table 3.5.2, they are omitted here

Table 4.4.6 Unit root test of Gini coefficient of rural resident and share of rural non-agricultural labors

Variable	Type of test (C, T, K)	T statistic	Critical value at 5% significance level	Result
Gini coefficient of rural resident's income	(0,0,3)	3.36936	−1.95247	Unstable
	(C,0,3)	−0.63163	−2.96397	Unstable
	(C,T,3)	−2.85811	−3.56838	Unstable
Share of rural non-agricultural labors in total rural labors (%)	(0,0,3)	1.62877	−1.95291	Unstable
	(C,0,3)	−0.82398	−2.96777	Unstable
	(C,T,3)	−3.44172	−3.57424	Unstable

Source: Authors' calculation by data from Table 4.4.4

Note: (1) C in test type (C, T, K) means whether the model includes constant, T means whether the model includes tendency variable, and K stands for lag length.(2) Since ADF tests on per capita GDP, inflation rate, and foreign trade dependency have been given in Table 3.5.3, they are omitted here

Table 4.4.7 Unrestricted cointegration rank test (Trace)

Hypothesized no. of CE(s)	Eigenvalue	Trace statistic	0.05 Critical value	Prob.
None*	0.820222	132.2277	69.81889	0.0000
At most 1*	0.745932	82.46268	47.85613	0.0000
At most 2*	0.592339	42.72820	29.79707	0.0010
At most 3*	0.410045	16.70590	15.49471	0.0327
At most 4	0.047206	1.402327	3.841466	0.2363

* rejecting the hypothesis in 5%(1%) significant level

Source: Authors' calculation by data from Tables 4.4.4 and 3.5.1

Note: Trace test indicates 4 cointegrating eqn(s) at the 0.05 level

Table 4.4.8 Unrestricted cointegration rank test (Maximum Eigenvalue)

Hypothesized no. of CE(s)	Eigenvalue	Max-Eigen statistic	0.05 Critical value	Prob.
None*	0.820222	49.76497	33.87687	0.0003
At most 1*	0.745932	39.73448	27.58434	0.0009
At most 2*	0.592339	26.02229	21.13162	0.0094
At most 3*	0.410045	15.30358	14.26460	0.0341
At most 4	0.047206	1.402327	3.841466	0.2363

* rejecting the hypothesis in 5%(1%) significant level

Source: Authors' calculation by data from Tables 4.4.4 and 3.5.1

Note: Max-eigenvalue test indicates 4 cointegrating eqn(s) at the 0.05 level

Because we use time-series data, we first have to do stability test for all variables in model (4.4.1), the outcome of which can be seen in Table 4.4.6.

From the table, we learn that the Gini coefficient of rural income and the share of rural non-agricultural labors are unstable times series at 5% significance level. Judging from the test results in Table 3.5.3 of Sect. 3.5, we may conclude that the regression among these variables is more likely to be spurious regression, but some combination of these unstable time variables may be stable. In this case, cointegration test is needed to examine whether there is a long-standing equilibrium between these variables. Outcome of the cointegration test is given in Table 4.4.7.

The results in Tables 4.4.7 and 4.4.8 show that at 5% significant level, there are at least two CEs between the Gini coefficient of rural resident's income on the one hand, and share of rural non-agricultural labors, per capita GDP, foreign trade dependency, and inflation rate on the other. A long-standing equilibrium between the two parties can also be inferred and an OLS estimation can be made on model (4.4.1).

2. *Outcome of empirical test.* If we feed the data in Tables 4.4.4 and 3.5.1 into (4.4.1), we have the outcome in Table 4.4.9.

Table 4.4.9 OLS estimation of the impact of share of rural non-agricultural labors and some macroeconomic variables on rural income inequality

Variable and equation test	Model I	Model II	Model III	Model IV	Model V	Model VI
Constant	0.08275 (1.69)	0.08984* (1.73)	0.21228	0.00661 (0.21)	0.06285 (1.60)	0.22805
Share of rural non-agricultural labors	0.00233** (2.21)	0.00200 (1.61)	0.00598	–	–	–
Square of rural non-agricultural labors	–	−0.00002 (0.52)	–	–	–	–
Per capita GDP	–	–	–	0.01369 (1.33)	0.04489** (2.57)	0.16302
Square of per capita GDP	–	–	–	–	−0.00442** (−2.13)	0.01605
Foreign trade dependency	−0.00003 (−0.05)	−0.00014 (−0.21)	0.00036	−0.00036 (−0.56)	−0.00017 (−0.29)	0.00062
First-order lag term of foreign trade dependency	0.00018 (0.26)	0.00012 (0.16)	–	0.00018 (0.23)	0.00026 (0.37)	–
Second-order lag term of foreign trade dependency	−0.00038 (−0.70)	−0.00056 (−0.86)	–	−0.00104 (−1.35)	−0.00100 (−1.41)	–
Inflation rate	0.00047 (0.94)	0.00060 (1.06)	0.00154	0.00135** (2.58)	0.00131** (2.72)	0.00476
First-order lag term of inflation rate	−0.00062 (−1.02)	−0.00067 (−1.07)	–	−0.00128** (−2.21)	−0.00090 (−1.6)	–
Second-order lag term of inflation rate	−0.00046 (−1.03)	−0.00030 (−0.54)	–	0.00039 (0.70)	0.00019 (0.37)	–
First-order lag term of Gini of rural income inequality	0.61020** (2.39)	0.60552** (2.32)	–	1.04194*** (6.91)	0.72464*** (3.56)	–
General assessment of equation	$R^2 = 0.98$ $F = 144.69$ DW = 1.98	$R^2 = 0.98$ $F = 123.98$ DW = 1.95	–	$R^2 = 0.98$ $F = 126.27$ DW = 2.17	$R^2 = 0.98$ $F = 132.61$ DW = 1.87	–
ADF test of the residue	$T = -4.92046$	$T = -4.90411$	–	$T = -5.75141$	$T = -5.00766$	–

Source: Authors' calculation

*Suggests 10% significance level, **suggests 5% significance level, ***suggests 1% significance level

The residues of model I and model II are stable at 5% significance level, and the residues of model III and model IV are stable at 1% significance level

Considering that there is a strong correlation between the share of rural non-agricultural labors and per capita GDP, the correlation coefficient being up to 0.92, we separately introduce the two variables into model (4.4.1). At the same time, we introduce the first-order lag term of dependent variable in order to eliminate au-correlation. For detailed estimation outcome, see model I, model II, model IV, and model V in Table 4.4.9, and for further estimation result, see model III and model VI.

First, from model I we observe that the regressive coefficient of the share of rural non-agricultural labors is positive and very significant, while the regressive coefficient of its square is negative but not significant. It suggests that by far labor transfer from agricultural sector to non-agricultural sector is still in a stage of widening income inequality of rural resident, far from one of reducing the inequality. Next, in model V the regressive coefficient of per capita GDP is positive, suggesting that economic development helps in a sense to enlarge rural income inequality, and coefficient of its square is negative and pass the significance test, indicating that just like the dynamics of urban income inequality, the inverted U hypothesis is supported by the dynamics of rural income inequality too. In addition, foreign trade does not have significant impact on rural income inequality possibly because of two factors. For one, foreign trade department holds a slight position in rural areas, and naturally the income gap between foreign trade department and non-foreign trade department is slightly related to income inequality of rural resident. For the other, the income gap between foreign trade department and non-foreign trade department has been taken into account in labor transfer. Finally, inflation rate helps to widen rural income inequality. Chances are that inflation tends to work on income inequality via affecting residents' business income and asset income; with economic development, Chinese rural residents have more and more business income and asset income, which, by the end of 2009, amounted to no more than 4,400 yuan and 167 yuan per capita and their share in the total income of rural resident is more than 63. Therefore, inflation has a significant impact on income inequality of rural resident.

Chapter 5
Income Inequality of China's Total Resident and the Factors Which Impact It

In Chaps. 3 and 4, we analyzed income inequality of China's urban and rurala residents and their drivers in succession. This chapter, by combining urban inequality and rural inequality, will try to investigate the dynamics of income inequality of China's total resident and its drivers.

5.1 Status Quo of Income Inequality of China's Total Resident

First we introduce the method of calculating income inequality of China's total resident and the result.

5.1.1 Method and Data of Calculating Income Inequality of Total Resident

In a strict sense, there is not much consecutive measurement of income inequality of total resident due to limited method and data, except for some measurements on the Gini coefficient of total resident's income in a few years by some scholars and organizations (Zhao Renwei and Griffin 1994; Zhao Renwei et al. 1999) and some estimations on income inequality of total resident according to the degree of urban inequality and urban–rural inequality by some scholars. One of the authors of this book once measured the Gini coefficient of income inequality of total resident from 1988 to 1999 using hierarchical weighted method and urban/rural weighted method combined.

Presently there are quite a few methods for measuring the Gini coefficient of total resident's income, of which two are often used. One is hierarchical weighted method proposed by Chen Zongsheng (1991). With this method, shares of all-income groups of urban and rural residents, and their income shares are mixed and

Y. Zhou and Y. Qin, *Empirical Analysis on Income Inequality of Chinese Residents*, Gu Shutang Acad Fund Econ, DOI 10.1007/978-3-642-24952-5_5,

rearranged by calculating the new shares of all-income groups population and their income shares. The Gini coefficient of total resident's income can be worked out by the new data.[1] Since the method has a high demand for data and cannot be put into general practice, we adopt another method called urban/rural weighted method, which was originally proposed by Sundrum (1990) and later adopted by some Chinese scholars (Xiang Shujian 1998a, b; Chen Zongsheng and Zhou Yunbo 2002). The computation formula is:

$$G = P_{\mathrm{u}}^2 \frac{y_{\mathrm{u}}}{y} G_{\mathrm{u}} + P_{\mathrm{r}}^2 \frac{y_r}{y} G_{\mathrm{r}} + P_{\mathrm{u}} P_{\mathrm{r}} \left| \frac{y_{\mathrm{u}} - y_{\mathrm{r}}}{y} \right|. \quad (5.1.1)$$

Herein G stands for the Gini coefficient of total resident's income, G_{u} and G_{r} stand for the Gini coefficient of urban resident's income and Gini coefficient of rural resident's income, respectively, P_{u} and P_{r} are the percentage of urban population and percentage of rural population in total population, respectively, y_{u} and y_{r} are the urban per capita income and rural per capita income, respectively, and y is national per capita income which can be calculated by the following formula:

$$y = P_{\mathrm{u}} \times y_{\mathrm{u}} + P_{\mathrm{r}} \times y_{\mathrm{r}}. \quad (5.1.2)$$

The first part in the formula may be considered as contribution of urban income inequality to income inequality of total resident, and the second part may be considered as contribution of urban–rural inequality to income inequality of total resident. With a small variation to the formula, we can have the computation formulas of the relative contributions of urban income inequality, rural income inequality, and urban–rural inequality to income inequality of total resident as follows:

$$T_{\mathrm{u}} = \frac{P_{\mathrm{u}}^2 \frac{y_{\mathrm{u}}}{y} G_{\mathrm{u}}}{G} \times 100\%, \quad (5.1.3)$$

$$T_{\mathrm{r}} = \frac{P_{\mathrm{r}}^2 \frac{y_{\mathrm{r}}}{y} G_{\mathrm{r}}}{G} \times 100\%, \quad (5.1.4)$$

$$T_{\mathrm{ur}} = \frac{P_{\mathrm{u}} P_{\mathrm{r}} \left| \frac{y_{\mathrm{u}} - y_{\mathrm{r}}}{y} \right|}{G} \times 100\%. \quad (5.1.5)$$

Herein T_{u}, T_{r}, and T_{ur} refer to the relative contributions of urban income inequality, rural income inequality, and urban–rural inequality to income inequality of total resident. Compared with the hierarchical weighted method, the urban/rural

[1] For detailed calculation procedure, see Chen Zongsheng and Zhou Yunbo (2002: 26–27).

weighted method is more direct in calculating and does not have a strict requirement for data and therefore is used in this book to calculate the Gini coefficient of total resident's income.

5.1.2 *Status Quo of Income Inequality of China's Total Resident*

From (5.1.1), we know that in order to work out the Gini coefficient of total resident by the urban/rural weighted method, we need to know the per capita income, population share, and the Gini coefficient of urban residents and rural residents and national per capita income, the last of which can be calculated through (5.1.2). Data are given in Table 5.1.1, and calculated Gini coefficient of total resident's income can be seen in Figs. 5.1.1 and 5.1.2.

In Figs. 5.1.1 and 5.1.2, we observe the following facts:

1. From 1978 to 2006, the Gini coefficient of total resident' income in general rose regardless of a few drop-years. In 1978, the Gini coefficient of total resident' income was 0.30227, and it rose to 0.46809 by 54.86% in 2008, suggesting that current income inequality of total resident was enlarging, as shown in the first half of inverted U curve proposed by Chen Zongsheng (1991).
2. Thanks to huge urban–rural gap, the Gini coefficient of total resident in most of the years under review was bigger than the Gini coefficient of urban and rural resident's income. In other words, except for a few years, the Gini coefficient of total resident was located above the Gini coefficient of urban and rural resident income.
3. From Fig. 5.1.1, we see that income inequality of total resident was undergoing phasic development. Each step corresponded to different stage of economic system reform. For instance, the rapid rise of income inequality of total resident in 1985 corresponded to the initiation of urban entrepreneurial reform and the increase in income inequality of total resident in 1993 benefited from the confirmation of market economy and the take-off of full-blown reform, another proof for the interesting hypothesis by Chen Zongsheng (1994, 1997), that is, the synchronous advance of institutional reform and change of economic development pattern will cause China's income inequality to take on phasic form in the expected ascending phase of inverted U curve.
4. It can be seen from Fig. 5.1.2 that the change in income inequality of total resident was in tandem with that of urban–rural income inequality. Take examples. The urban–rural income ratio fell from 2.57 in 1978 to 1.70 in 1983, and the Gini coefficient of total resident's income underwent a similar fall from 0.30227 to 0.25310. Again, from 1983 to 1989, the urban–rural income ratio rose from 1.70 to 2.28, and the Gini coefficient of total resident's income rose from 0.25310 to 0.33969. Then in 1990 the urban–rural income ratio dropped to 2.20, and the Gini coefficient of total resident's income was also down to 0.32578. From 1990 to 1994, the urban–rural income ratio grew from

Table 5.1.1 Data needed for calculating the Gini coefficient of total resident's income with urban/rural weighted method

Year	P_u (%)	P_r (%)	y_u (yuan)	y_r (yuan)	y (yuan)	G_u	G_r
1978	17.92	82.08	343.40	133.60	171.1962	0.16214	0.2122
1979	18.96	81.04	410.50	160.17	207.6326	0.16431	0.2308
1980	19.39	80.61	477.60	191.33	246.8378	0.17326	0.2382
1981	20.16	79.84	488.80	223.44	276.9366	0.20916	0.2256
1982	21.13	78.87	500.00	266.00	315.4442	0.20454	0.2333
1983	21.62	78.38	526.00	310.00	356.6992	0.20496	0.2554
1984	23.01	76.99	608.00	355.00	413.2153	0.2275	0.2697
1985	23.71	76.29	739.10	397.60	478.5697	0.23764	0.2785
1986	24.52	75.48	899.60	423.80	540.4662	0.224	0.2884
1987	25.32	74.68	1,002.20	462.60	599.2267	0.22778	0.2798
1988	25.81	74.19	1,181.40	544.90	709.1807	0.23068	0.30285
1989	26.21	73.79	1,373.90	601.50	803.946	0.22592	0.31261
1990	26.41	73.59	1,510.20	686.30	903.892	0.23543	0.29474
1991	26.94	73.06	1,700.60	708.60	975.8448	0.24246	0.3074
1992	27.46	72.54	2,026.60	784.00	1,125.218	0.25363	0.31062
1993	27.99	72.01	2,577.40	921.60	1,385.058	0.27244	0.31812
1994	28.51	71.49	3,496.20	1,221.00	1,869.66	0.30175	0.32996
1995	29.04	70.96	4,283.00	1,577.70	2,363.319	0.28804	0.3407
1996	30.48	69.52	4,838.90	1,926.10	2,813.921	0.30341	0.321
1997	31.91	68.09	5,160.30	2,090.10	3,069.801	0.30794	0.32724
1998	33.35	66.65	5,425.10	2,162.00	3,250.244	0.32303	0.34097
1999	34.78	65.22	5,854.00	2,210.30	3,477.579	0.3361	0.3512
2000	36.22	63.78	6,280.00	2,253.40	3,711.835	0.34165	0.36039
2001	37.66	62.34	6,859.60	2,366.40	4,058.539	0.35121	0.36986
2002	39.09	60.91	7,702.80	2,475.60	4,518.912	0.37263	0.38389
2003	40.53	59.47	8,472.20	2,622.20	4,993.205	0.38196	0.39267
2004	41.76	58.24	9,421.61	2,936.40	5,644.624	0.38754	0.40285
2005	42.99	57.01	10,493.03	3,254.93	6,366.59	0.39563	0.41346
2006	43.90	56.10	11,759.45	3,587.04	7,174.73	0.3918	0.41192
2007	44.94	55.06	13,785.81	4,140.36	8,475.02	0.3793	0.41903
2008	45.68	54.32	15,780.76	4,760.62	9,794.62	0.3801	0.42616

Source: *China Yearbook of Statistics (1979–2009)*

2.20 to 2.86, and the Gini coefficient of total resident's income grew from 0.32578 to 0.40402. Again the urban–rural income ratio fell to 2.47 in 1997 with the Gini coefficient of total resident's income falling to 0.37331. After 1997 the urban–rural income ratio winded up to 3.31 in 2008 and the Gini coefficient of total resident's income to 0.46809. The correlation coefficient of the urban–rural income ratio to the Gini coefficient of total resident's income, according to our calculation, was as high as 0.94. This heavy correlation between the two implies that the urban–rural income inequality played a very important role and even a decisive role in income inequality of total resident, as has been supported by many studies (Chen Zongsheng 1991; Khan and Riskin 2001; Lu 2002; Fang et al. 2002; Chen Zongsheng and Zhou Yunbo 2002). In the

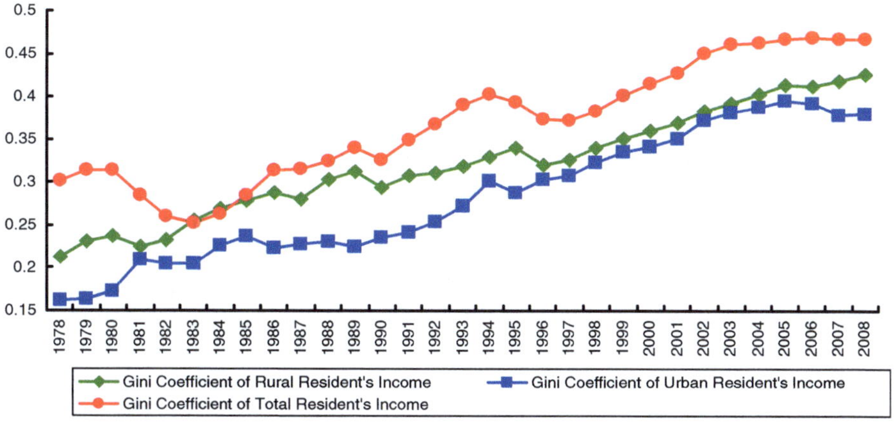

Fig. 5.1.1 Gini coefficient of urban, rural, and total resident's income 1978–2008. Source: Authors' calculation by data from Table 5.1.1

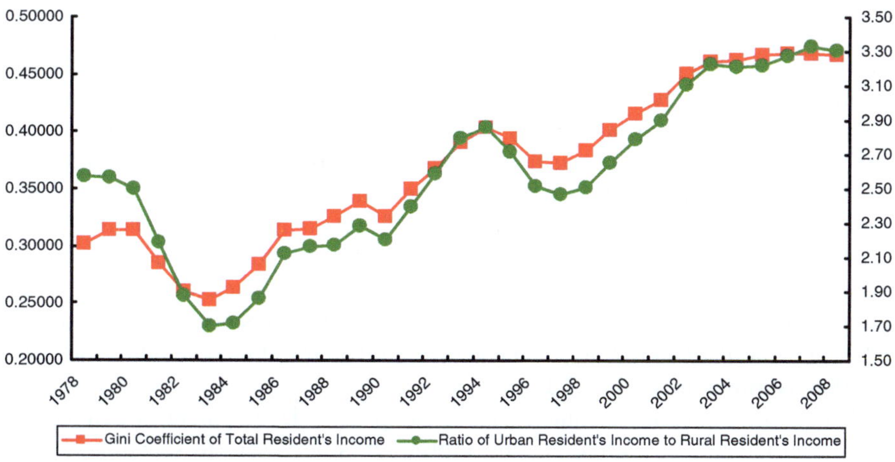

Fig. 5.1.2 Ratio of urban income to rural income and Gini coefficient of total resident's income 1978–2008. Source: Author's calculation by data from Table 5.1.1

following part, we will measure the impact of urban–rural inequality on China's income inequality of total resident in real terms.

5.2 Urban–Rural Inequality and Its Impact on Income Inequality of Total Resident

The method used for measurement of the impact of urban–rural income inequality on income inequality of total resident is the same with that in Sect. 5.1, viz., from (5.1.1) and (5.1.5). But at first this section will review the change in urban–rural income inequality since the reform.

5.2.1 Urban–Rural Income Inequality Since the Reform

Before proceeding further, we first review the change in urban–rural income inequality since the reform. The criterion and scope of urban–rural population divide conform with the official one, or rather, with *China Yearbook of Statistics*. Data of urban and rural household income in *China Yearbook of Statistics* all come from surveys on urban and rural households. After 2002 the urban households under survey changed from the original non-agricultural population to urban population, and the rural households under survey refer to households dwelling for a long time within township administration and villagers under township administration.

The urban–rural income ratio is used as the main index for measuring urban–rural income inequality, the calculation formula of which is:

$$\mathrm{URG} = \frac{y_\mathrm{u}}{y_\mathrm{r}}. \tag{5.2.1}$$

Herein URG refers to urban–rural income ratio, y_u urban yearly per capita disposable income, and y_r rural household's yearly per capita disposable net income. y_u is the yearly income for consumption and other expenditures and savings, which can be disposed freely by urban dwellers. It is what is remained after the income tax, social security expenditure, and subsidy for keeping accounts have been deducted from total family income and is averaged by the number of permanent residents. y_r refers to the yearly income for rural household's reproduction and consumption, savings, and all sorts of non-compulsory expenditures. It is what is remained after taxes, expenditure on family business, depreciation of productive fixed assets, and gifts to relatives have been deducted from total family income and is averaged by the number of permanent residents. Using the data in *China Yearbook of Statistics*, we calculate the urban–rural income ratio from 1978 to 2006 as shown in Table 5.2.1.

Urban–rural income inequality takes on phasic development which is also evident in China's economic system reform.[2] It is necessary to spend some time studying the relation between the change in urban–rural gap and advance of reform at different stages. From 1978 till now, the reform has been through six stages, i.e., 1978–1983, 1984–1988, 1989–1991, 1992–1994, 1995–2002, 2003 and beyond. Table 5.2.2 displays a close link between the change in urban–rural income inequality and economic reform, economic growth, and policy priority at each stage.

The first stage witnessed a rural-centered reform of economic system when the implementation of rural household responsibility system and the government's decompression on prices of agricultural products and by-products greatly

[2] One of the authors covered the relation between phasic institutional reform and urban–rural income inequality from 1978 to 1999 in his previous study. Here we will continue the study by extending the time span to the beginning of the new century.

Table 5.2.1 Urban–rural income ratio 1978–2009

Year	1978	1979	1980	1981	1982	1983	1984	1985
Urban–rural income ratio	2.57	2.56	2.50	2.19	1.88	1.70	1.71	1.86
Year	1986	1987	1988	1989	1990	1991	1992	1993
Urban–rural income ratio	2.12	2.17	2.17	2.28	2.20	2.24	2.58	2.80
Year	1994	1995	1996	1997	1998	1999	2000	2001
Urban–rural income ratio	2.86	2.71	2.51	2.47	2.51	2.65	2.79	2.90
Year	2002	2003	2004	2005	2006	2007	2008	2009
Urban–rural income ratio	3.11	3.23	3.21	3.22	3.28	3.33	3.31	3.33

Source: *China Yearbook of Statistics 1979–2010*

stimulated farmer's enthusiasm and farming began to see a rapid growth of agricultural production. As the first nationwide breakaway from traditional planning economy, the reform supplied farmers with comparatively equal development opportunity and benefited most of the farmers with growing income. As opposed to rural areas, no significant changes in economic system occurred in cities and towns where traditional wage system and income distribution mechanism remained intact. Correspondingly, urban per capita income increased at a lower speed than rural one, the former being 11% and the latter 18%. That is why urban–rural income inequality was reduced and urban–rural income ratio decreased by 33.85%, from 2.57 in 1978 to 1.70 in 1983, with annual reduction of 7.93%.

In stage two (1984–1988) the reform priority of economic system moved to cities and towns. Two measures accounted for urban income growth, one enterprise contract system, the incentive effect of contract system greatly spurred productivity and increased employees' income accordingly. On the other hand, the development of non-state sectors including self-employed and private economies, apart from creating employments, increased urban dweller's income sources besides wage. This stage saw a growth rate of 5.67% in per capita income of urban resident. At the same time farmers' income rose by only 3.30% per year, since the household responsibility system was lending a decreasing incentive to agricultural production and the government's procurement prices for farm products kept steady. That is why from 1984 to 1988 the urban–rural income gap enlarged. By 1988 the urban-to-rural income ratio rose to 2.17, increasing by 26.9% than in 1984, almost the same as in 1981.

The 3 years from 1989 to 1991 was a period of economic revamping. Suffering from political impact, economic reform was slowed down. There was virtually no new measures coming out. The recession of economic growth in the 3 years directly effectuated the fall of urban and rural resident's real income in 1989. The growth rates of GDP in the 3 years were 4.1%, 3.8%, and 9.2%, respectively, and the urban–rural income inequality was slightly reduced.

After 1992 China began its full-blown March toward market economy. Economic reform went along hand in hand with economic growth. Urban employment was increased and resident's income sources were broadened because of the development of non-state sectors. Capital market represented by stock market and property market was taking shape. Apart from personal labor income, urban

Table 5.2.2 Relation between China's economic system reform and urban–rural income inequality

Stage of reform	Main reform measures	Reform of distribution system	Growth rate of annual GDP	Change of urban–rural income inequality	Change of urban–rural income ratio
First stage: 1978–1983	(1) Household responsibility system (2) Increasing procurement prices for farm products	(1) Single collective distribution was broken (2) Piece rate and premium were introduced into urban enterprises	8.38%	Rapid reduction	−7.93% per year
Second stage: 1984–1988	(1) Urban enterprise contract system (2) Development of non-state sectors (3) Farmer's independent operation	(1) Wage was linked to efficiency in urban enterprises (2) Production factors became drivers of farmer's income	11.32%	Enlargement	6.14% per year
Third stage: 1989–1991	Economic revamping	(Non)	5.70%	Slight reduction	−0.88% per year
Fourth stage: 1992–1994	(1) Reform in state enterprises (2) Surge of non-state sectors (3) Building market system	(1) Plural distributions centered on "to each according to his work" (2) Wage decided by labor market	13.40%	Rapid enlargement	5.29% per year
Fifth stage: 1995–2002	(1) Improving efficiency by downsizing staffs in state enterprises (2) Reform of financial system (3) Reform of grain circulating system (4) Reform in government departments (5) Reform of housing system	Compatibility of distribution by factors and distribution by work	7.98%	Spiral enlargement	1.99% per year
Sixth stage: 2003–	(1) Reform of taxation in rural areas (2) Constructing socialist new countryside (3) Coordinated reform in cities and rural areas (4) Increase the central government's fiscal spending on agriculture, rural areas and farmers	(1) Broaden the coverage of urban social security and upgrading its standard (2) Set up rural social security system	9.75%	Little enlargement	0.51%

Source: Data from stage one to stage five come from Chen Zongsheng and Zhou Yunbo (2002:68). Data about stage six are the authors' calculation

residents could obtain other incomes from stock dividend, rent, and revenue from investment in capital market. Another significant measure is the reform of urban housing system which from its very root made resident's invisible income under planning economy public and transformed his welfare into personal income or properties. Although urban unemployment and poverty became noticeable, urban resident's income as a whole rose by a large scale, 7.93% per year to be exact. Naturally the surge of urban economy attracted many rural labors to the cities for employment, and the labor transfer not only relieved the rural pressure from surplus labors, but also increased rural per capita income. Meanwhile, the growth of township enterprises accelerated the process of rural industrialization which helped to reduce the urban–rural inequality. All these offset the urban–rural gap to some extent. However, with market mechanism playing an increasing role in China's economy, fierce competition forced enterprises to adopt capital and technology intensive development which in turn demanded highly qualified labors (Zhang Ping 1998). Rural workers, with low education and inadequate working experience, could only offer crude labor requiring no expertise and consequently earned a much lower wage as enjoyed by their urban counterparts. No wonder in the fourth stage of reform, the urban–rural inequality was further widened and the urban-to-rural income ratio rose by 10.85% from 2.58 in 1992 to 2.86 in 1994.

From 1995 to 2002, the institutional framework for China's economic reform had been basically established. In the process of promoting socialist market economy, how to crack the nutshell of what had been left by command economy came to be the leading problem in this period and even several years beyond. Measures of improving efficiency by downsizing staffs on the part of state enterprises and reform in government administrations spewed out a large stock of laid-offs. Since employment was a key determinant of income, rising unemployment would undoubtedly lead to reduction in urban resident's income. Compounding this, the Asian financial crisis in 1997 was still playing havoc to the point that economic and income growth were contained. By contrast, rural economy, though under the same impact, had stayed strong thanks to successive harvests (the grain output in 1997 amounted to 0.49 billion tons). Rural income rose within a context of fall of total income growth and the urban–rural income inequality was somewhat alleviated. However, low prices of farm products and the stimulus package of issuing national debts to initiate domestic demand contributed to enlarging the urban–rural income inequality since 1998. Taken as a whole, the urban–rural inequality in this stage went along a U-form course, contracting at first and then expanding.

Since 2003, the new government was more concerned with the poor, especially the rural poor, apart from economic growth. Main measures to this effect included making a better urban social security system and broadening its coverage and upgrading its standard. In 2002 the government signed into law the reform of taxation in rural areas with a view to alleviating farmer's burden, and in 2006 it announced that farming tax be eliminated for good, which drew a line at the 2,600-year history of farmers paying taxes. At the same time, a wide range of subsidies for farming production means were put into force, including direct subsidy, high-quality seed subsidy, and farming machines purchase subsidy. The government continued to offer the lowest procurement prices for key grain species in key areas and increase the transfer payments to big grain producing counties and towns with financial difficulties. In addition, the construction of socialist new countryside was under way, and a growing investment was put in such infrastructural construction projects as rural roads, water conservancy, and electricity. In 2009 the central government's fiscal spending on agriculture, rural areas, and farmers reached 725.3 billion yuan, increasing by 21.8% than the previous year. In 2010 the central government's fiscal spending on agriculture, rural areas, and farmers reached 857.97 billion yuan, 132.67 more billion yuan than the previous year. In 2011 the central government's fiscal capital on agriculture, rural areas, and farmers was 988.45 billion yuan, with additional 130.48 billion yuan compared with the previous year. All these measures contributed to farmer's income growth. Meanwhile, with the recovery of domestic economic growth, urban income also saw a rapid rise. On account of the synchronized growth of urban and rural income, the urban–rural income inequality ground to a virtual halt.

In general, the urban–rural income inequality since system reform has been up and down. In the early period of reform, it was quickly reduced, but from the mid- and late-1980s to the beginning of the new century it was expanded for a long time until in recent years when the expansion was curbed to some degree. But in 2006 the inequality began to see further enlargement, which should alert the government and all walks of life. In the following a quantitative measurement is carried out, which proves that the urban–rural income inequality will remain the main driver of income inequality of total resident all the time.

5.2.2 *Impact of the Urban–Rural Income Inequality on Income Inequality of Total Resident and Its Change*

To analyze the relation between the urban–rural inequality and income inequality of total resident, we have to first tell how much of the latter is related to the former. The income inequality of total resident can be decomposed into urban income inequality, rural income inequality, and urban–rural income inequality. One of the authors of the book once measured the contribution of urban–rural income inequality to income inequality of total resident from 1988 to 1999 by using the method of decomposing Gini coefficient step by step and urban/rural weighted method (Chen Zongsheng and Zhou Yunbo 2002). We are to measure contributions made by urban income inequality, rural income inequality, and urban–rural inequality to income inequality of total resident by using urban/rural weighted method combined with data from Tables 5.1.1 and 5.2.3.

From 1978 to 2008, income inequality of rural resident made its largest contribution to income inequality of total resident in 1983, amounting to 53.88%, and made its smallest contribution in 2008, 13.06%. Income inequality of urban resident made its largest contribution in 2008, 27.30%, that is, and made its smallest

Table 5.2.3 Decomposition on income inequality of total resident by using urban/rural weighted method

Year	Contribution of income inequality of rural resident (%)	Contribution of income inequality of urban resident (%)	Contribution of urban–rural income inequality (%)
1978	36.91	3.46	59.63
1979	37.26	3.72	59.02
1980	38.23	4.02	57.76
1981	40.67	5.26	54.07
1982	46.98	5.56	47.46
1983	53.88	5.58	40.54
1984	52.12	6.73	41.16
1985	47.35	7.26	45.39
1986	41.01	7.13	51.86
1987	38.22	7.75	54.03
1988	39.34	7.86	52.79
1989	37.49	7.81	54.70
1990	37.20	8.42	54.38
1991	34.06	8.76	57.18
1992	30.92	9.35	59.73
1993	28.12	10.17	61.71
1994	27.26	11.35	61.39
1995	29.04	11.16	59.80
1996	28.39	12.96	58.65
1997	27.67	14.12	58.21
1998	26.25	15.62	58.13
1999	23.67	17.06	59.27
2000	21.42	18.25	60.33
2001	19.59	19.67	60.74
2002	17.32	21.54	61.14
2003	15.79	23.06	61.15
2004	15.34	24.35	60.31
2005	14.68	25.76	59.56
2006	13.82	26.38	59.80
2007	13.25	26.61	60.14
2008	13.06	27.30	59.64
Average contribution rate from 1978 to 2008	30.53	13.03	56.44
Increment from 1978 to 2008	−30.42	70.76	59.66

Source: Authors' calculation from Table 5.1.1.

contribution in 1978, as little as 3.46%. Urban–rural income inequality contributed as high as 61.71% in 1993 and as little as 40.54% in 1983. By comparison, we can see that urban–rural income inequality contributed the most to income inequality of total resident, averaging 56.44%, the second was income inequality of rural resident, which contributed 30.63% on average, and the third was income inequality of urban resident, which contributed 13.03% on average. With regard to the change, income inequality of rural resident was seeing a declining contribution rate from 36.91% in 1978 to 13.06% in 2008, down more than 23%, while urban income inequality was seeing a growing contribution rate from 3.46% in 1978 to 27.30% in 2008, up almost 24%. Urban–rural income inequality presented a volatile nature considering its full course of development, contributing 59.63% in 1978 and 59.64% in 2008 (Fig. 5.2.1).

From the figure, we see the change in the contribution made by urban–rural income inequality to income inequality of total resident was in proportion to urban-to-rural income ratio. For instance, the urban-to-rural income ratio fell from 2.57 in 1978 to 1.70 in 1983, and its contribution to income inequality of total resident during this period also fell from 59.63% to 40.54%. Likewise the urban-to-rural income ratio rose from 1.70 to 2.28 from 1983 to 1989, and again dropped to 2.20 in 1990, and its contribution also rose from 40.54% to 54.70%, and then dropped to 54.38% in the same time span. Again the urban-to-rural income ratio grew from 2.20 in 1990 to 2.86 in 1994, and then dropped to 2.47 in 1997, and its contribution rose accordingly from 54.38% to 61.39% and then dropped to 58.21%. Beyond that time, the urban-to-rural income ratio wound up with 3.31 in 2008, and its contribution also rose to 59.64%. The correlation coefficient between the urban-to-rural income ratio and income inequality of total resident was, based on our calculation, as high as 0.95.

The decomposition on the increment of the Gini coefficient of income inequality of total resident from 1978 to 2008 shows that urban income inequality made the largest contribution, amounting to about 70.76%. There are two reasons: the fast growing income inequality of urban resident and the rapid growth of urban

Fig. 5.2.1 Contribution of urban–rural inequality to the income inequality of total resident (1978–2008). Source: Authors' calculation from Table 5.1.1

population percentage caused by urbanization. Urban–rural inequality came the next, contributing 60% odd, and the least contribution was made by rural income inequality, about −28% or so, because of the tumbling rural population percentage.

In conclusion, by decomposing income inequality of total resident and its change, we find that the urban–rural income inequality and its change are the most important drivers in that the latter directly determines where the former should go. The biggest problem with income distribution in today's China is the urban–rural income inequality. If policies are not targeted at the urban–rural income inequality, it is really hard to imagine they will work.

5.3 Impact of Urbanization on China's Income Inequality of Total Resident

Analysis above proves that the urban–rural income inequality remains the biggest problem in China's income distribution pattern. The fundamental way to solve it is to accelerate urbanization by transferring the multitudinous rural population to cities and surplus rural labors to non-agricultural industry. In the process of economic development in countries and regions, urbanization is a vital driver of income inequality. Kuznets (1995) once regarded urbanization one of the most important factors to expand income inequality in early stage of economic development. This section will review China's urbanization since system reform with emphasis put on the impact of urbanization on income inequality of total resident.

5.3.1 Concept, Process, and Measurement of Urbanization

Urbanization is a process of rural population and non-agricultural activities moving toward spatial concentration and that of urban internal structure gradually getting advanced. Urbanization has two stages, one is centralized urbanization, a process of population and all production factors moving toward big cities, and the other decentralized urbanization, a process of population and production factors moving toward suburbs and middle and small cites. The evolution from concentrated urbanization to decentralized urbanization crystallizes a course of urbanization in developed countries. In the early stage of industrialization, enormous rural population kept moving to cities and towns whose population share in total population rocketed as a result. The transfer of rural population did not stop until World War II when a movement of anti-urbanization came in. First reason, centralized urbanization brought about such problems as breakneck land price, highly densed population and building, traffic jam, and deteriorating environment. In addition, after World War II western countries began to attach importance to city planning, developing transport system both within and across cities, and regional economic construction as well, which shook themselves off spatial constraints of market,

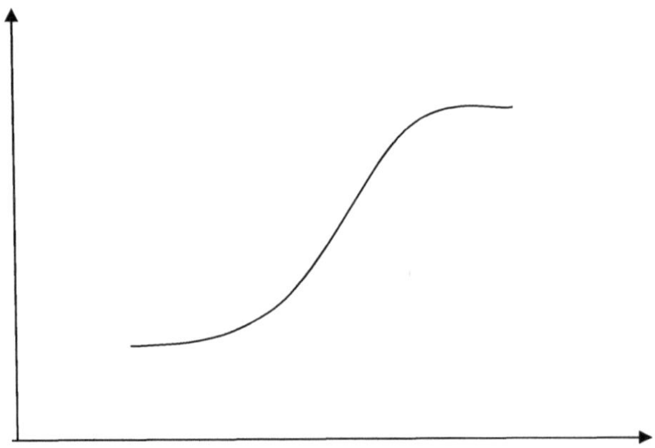

Fig. 5.3.1 "S" curve of urbanization process. Source: Authors' own design

production, and dwelling. Urban economy and population expanded to a larger scale, so did the function of cities, which is called as "anti-urbanization."

Certain laws can be derived from the growth of urbanization. The first one is the law of stage-like progression, viz., in the beginning, urbanization is slow, but with the growth of domestic economy and at some level (generally 20–25%), it will gain much more speed, and at some other level (generally 65–85%), it will be steady. The process is like a "S" curve, as shown in Fig. 5.3.1.

In the figure, the vertical line represents the share of urban population in total population, and the horizontal line represents level of economic development. The degree of urbanization can be measured by the size of urban population and the scale of urban land. The degree of urbanization in its common sense refers to the share of urban population in total population. Level of urbanization is closely associated with economic development and their positive correlation coefficient reaches 0.75 or so.

5.3.2 *Situation of China's Urbanization Since Reform*

From the foundation of new China to the early reform, its urbanization unfolded at a very low speed on account of the command economy, though its industrialization was developing fast. According to official statistics, by 1978 the percentage of urban population had been just 17.92% in total population.

After 1978, China's urbanization process speeds up and its level rises steadily owing to institutional decompression. The first evidence is that cities grow fast in number. By the end of 2009, there had been 287 cities over prefecture level of which 124 cities had more than one million population, 14 were megacities with over four million population, 28 cities had two to four million population, and 82 cities had one to two million population. Second, big cities grow spectacularly.

Shanghai and Beijing have been listed in the world's top ten. Third, there come into being several greater metropolitan areas, the emergence of which is a vital feature of China's urbanization. For instance, in the Pearl River Delta, Yangtze River Delta, Beijing–Tianjin–Hebei region, and the Mid- and South Liaoning Province, four greater metropolitan areas have taken shape, surrounding megacities and connecting small cities and towns. Greater metropolitan areas play to their economic strength and influence for numerous enterprises and huge population are concentrated there, producing enormous economic benefit. Finally, a synchronized growth pattern of industrialization and urbanization have been basically in shape.

By the measurement index of urbanization, official statistics show that by the end of 2010 the aggregate number of China's urban population was over 665.5 million, and its percentage in domestic population amounted to 49.9%, up almost 32% compared with that in 1978 (see Fig. 5.3.2). At first blush the speed of urbanization was not fast, but taking the huge population base into account, it was a miracle.

The figure suggests that since reform, China's urban population has been increasing, so has been its share in total population, particularly after the mid-1990s then control of household registration system was loosened. We believe that with the further advance of economic institutional reform and the gradual removal of the dual urban–rural divide administration, China's urbanization will reach a higher level.

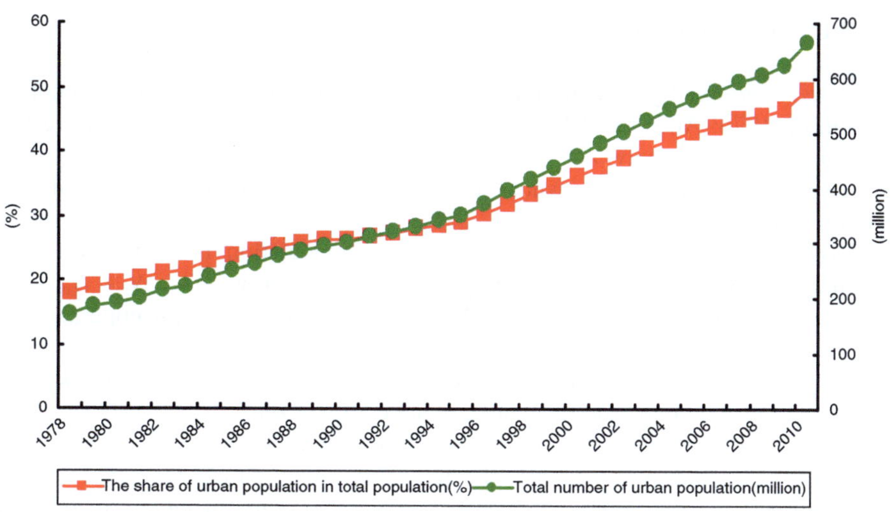

Fig. 5.3.2 Aggregate number of urban population and its share in total population 1978–2010. Source: *China Yearbook of Statistics 1979–2011*

5.3.3 *Theoretical Analysis on Urbanization's Impact on Income Inequality of Total Resident*

As for urbanization's impact on income inequality, Kuznets (1955) has discussed it in his seminal paper. The income inequality of total resident, according to him, may be derived from a combination of income inequality of urban and rural resident. Since income inequality of urban resident is always larger than rural one, demographic flow from rural areas to cities makes the population with larger income inequality have a greater share in total population, thus enlarging total income inequality. Since then, in theoretical analysis of inverted U hypothesis, many researches have been done on the urbanization process and demographic flow between cities and rural areas in developing countries to prove the existence of inverted U curve (Robinson 1976; Glomm and Ravikumar 1992; Anand and Kanbur 1993; Chen Zongsheng 1994, 2000a, b). However, Kuznets put aside one point that as long as there is urban–rural inequality, the urban–rural population flow itself will affect the change in income inequality. Some scholars (Anand and Kanbur 1993; Chen Zongsheng 1994, 2000a, b) actually illustrated this, but without giving strict proof. Other studies indicate that by more generalizing the index of income inequality, if the urban–rural inequality stands and urban income inequality is larger than rural one, then whether the inverted U hypothesis is tenable depends (Anand and Kanbur 1993). Here, we will offer strict mathematical proof for the inverted U relation between urbanization and the change in income inequality of total resident. Meanwhile, the urban–rural inequality will be analyzed on a variable in terms of its impact on the shape and position of inverted U curve.

5.3.3.1 Proof of Theoretical Model

Basic assumptions. By revising the previous assumptions made by some scholars (Robinson 1976; Anand and Kanbur 1993; Chen Zongsheng 1994), we have the assumptions for our study.

Assumption 1: suppose the whole society is divided into two systems, rural area and urban area;

Assumption 2: suppose the number of total population is N, that of rural population is N_r, and that of urban population is N_u, then we have $N_r + N_u = N$, the share of urban population is $P = N_u/N$, and the share of rural population is $1 - P$;

Assumption 3: suppose there is an equal income distribution pattern both in urban and in rural areas, and their income inequality is zero, i.e., $G_r = G_u = 0$;

Assumption 4: unlike the previous studies, we consider the urban–rural inequality a variable. Without losing the generality, suppose rural per capita income is 1, and urban per capita income is x, then the share of urban income is $Y = \dfrac{x \times N_u}{x \times N_u + N_r}$. If the right part to the equal mark is divided by N, we have

$Y = \dfrac{x \times P}{x \times P + (1 - P)}$, and the percentage of income in agricultural sector is $1 - Y$.

On the basis of the above assumptions, we have the Lorenz curve as shown in Fig. 5.3.3.

Relation between urbanization and urbanization-caused income inequality. Under the above four conditions and according to the definition of Gini coefficient, we have:

$$G = 2 \times S_1. \tag{5.3.1}$$

Herein, $S_1 = \frac{1}{2} - (S_2 + S_3 + S_4)$, $S_2 = \frac{1}{2} P \times Y, S_3 = \frac{1}{2} \times (1 - Y) \times (1 - P)$, $S_4 = (1 - Y) \times P$. Now if we substitute S_2, S_3, S_4 into (5.3.1), since $G \geq= 0$, so if $x > 1$, i.e., urban average income is larger than rural one, then,

$$G = Y - P. \tag{5.3.2}$$

Because $x > 1$, and according to assumption 4, $Y = \dfrac{x \times P}{x \times P + (1 - P)}$, so,

$$G = \frac{P \times (1 - P) \times (x - 1)}{x \times P + (1 - P)}. \tag{5.3.3}$$

To find the first derivative with respect to P in (5.3.3), we have:

$$\frac{\mathrm{d}G}{\mathrm{d}P} = \frac{(x - 1) \times [(1 - x) \times P^2 - 2 \times P + 1]}{[x \times P + (1 - P)]^2}. \tag{5.3.4}$$

Since $x - 1 > 0, [x \times P + (1 - P)]^2 > 0$, to solve $\dfrac{\mathrm{d}G}{\mathrm{d}P} = 0$ means to solve

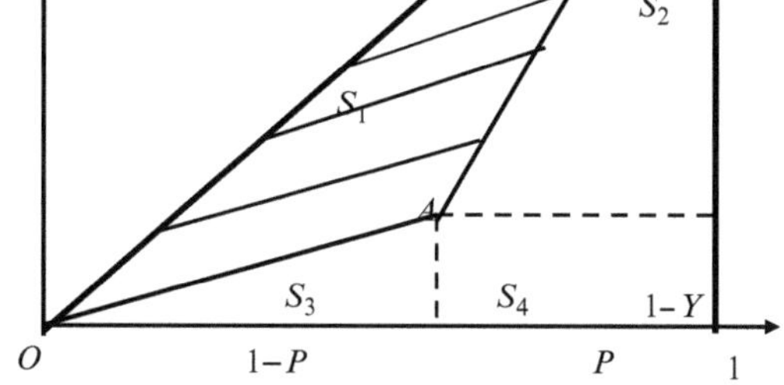

Fig. 5.3.3 Lorenz curve derived from the assumptions

$$(1-x) \times P^2 - 2 \times P + 1 = 0. \tag{5.3.5}$$

Since $(1-x) < 0$, so (5.3.5) amounts to a downward parabola with $P' = \frac{1}{1-x}$ as the symmetry axis, as shown in Fig. 5.3.4. Solving (5.3.5), we have

$$P_1^* = -\frac{x^{\frac{1}{2}} + 1}{x - 1} = \frac{-1}{x^{\frac{1}{2}} - 1}, \quad P_2^* = \frac{x^{\frac{1}{2}} - 1}{x - 1} = \frac{1}{x^{\frac{1}{2}} + 1}. \tag{5.3.6}$$

Since $x > 1$, we have $P_1^* < 0$ and $P_2^* > 0$.

Because P_1^* contravenes the second assumption, it is cut out, while P_2^* is kept for it is in accordance with the assumptions. Thus, in $P \in [0, 1]$, when $P < P_2^*$, $\frac{dG}{dp} > 0$, that is, G is P's increasing function, and when $P > P_2^*$, $\frac{dG}{dp} < 0$, that is, G is P's decreasing function. In this way, we prove that when the urban–rural income inequality is fixed, the urbanization-caused income inequality will present an inverted U dynamics along with the gradual rise of urban population share, that is to say, it will expand first, then reduce. In the process, P_2^* serves as a turning point from expansion to reduction on the part of income inequality.

If we substitute $P_2^* = \frac{1}{x^{\frac{1}{2}}+1}$ into (5.3.3), we have

$$G^* = \frac{x^{\frac{1}{2}} - 1}{x^{\frac{1}{2}} + 1}. \tag{5.3.7}$$

From the formula, we learn that G^* is the maximum value of income inequality caused by share flow between cities and rural areas, and P_2^* represents the percentage of urban population in total population when income inequality reaches its maximum value, which may be also called the critical value of population share when population shifts from expansion to reduction due to the change in income

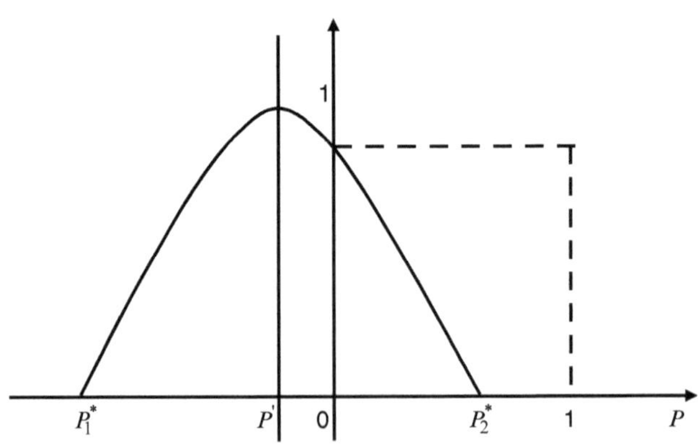

Fig. 5.3.4 Graph of parabola indicated in (5.3.5)

inequality. Formulas (5.3.6) and (5.3.7) show that the actual numerical values of P_2^* and G^* depend on the urban–rural inequality itself, i.e., the size of x.

Impact of the change of urban–rural income inequality on the shape and position of inverted U curve. In the following we will discuss how the change in urban–rural inequality (x) affects G and P_2^*. At first, we find the first derivative of G with respect to x, and then we have

$$\frac{\mathrm{d}G}{\mathrm{d}x} = \frac{P \times (1 - P)}{(x \times P + 1 - P)^2} > 0. \tag{5.3.8}$$

Since $\frac{\mathrm{d}G}{\mathrm{d}x} > 0$, so G is x's increasing function, viz., a growing urban–rural inequality will lead to the growth of urbanization-caused income inequality. In other words, a growing urban–rural inequality causes the inverted U curve to move upward in general. At the same time, we find the first derivative of P_2^* with respect to x, and we have:

$$\frac{\mathrm{d}P_2^*}{\mathrm{d}x} = \frac{-1}{2 \times x^{\frac{1}{2}} \times (1 + x^{\frac{1}{2}})^2} < 0. \tag{5.3.9}$$

From (5.3.9), we can see that P_2^* is x's decreasing function, or, a growing urban–rural inequality will lead to a falling share of urban population when income inequality reaches its maximum. To find the limit value of P_2^* when x approaches 1 and $+\infty$ separately, we have

$$\lim_{x \to 1} P_2^* = \lim_{x \to 1} \frac{1}{1 + x^{\frac{1}{2}}} = 0.5, \quad \lim_{x \to +\infty} P_2^* = \lim_{x \to +\infty} \frac{1}{1 + x^{\frac{1}{2}}} = 0.$$

It means that when the urban–rural income inequality approaches zero gradually, the share of urban population when the income inequality reaches its maximum will approach 50%, while when the urban–rural income inequality approaches the infinite, the share of urban population when the income inequality reaches its maximum will approach 0. In other words, when the urban–rural inequality grows gradually, the whole inverted U curve will move toward upper left.

In summary, with a fixed urban–rural inequality, the urbanization-caused income inequality will rise first, then fall, just like an inverted U curve. At the same time, with the widening of urban–rural inequality, the whole inverted U curve will move upward, but the share of urban population at the maximum income inequality will decrease, that is to say, the whole inverted U curve will move toward the upper left.

5.3.3.2 Simulation Test of the Model

Now we use some data to make simulation test of some conclusions from the theoretical analysis. First, we work out the corresponding relation between the share of urban population and income inequality when the urban–rural inequality is 1.5, 2, 2.5, 3, 3.5, 4, 5, and 10 by turns, the result of which is shown in Fig. 5.3.5.

Figure 5.3.5 shows clearly that on the condition of a fixed urban–rural inequality and with the increasing share of urban population, the urbanization-caused income inequality is through an inverted U change course, expanding first and then shrinking. At the same time, when urban–rural inequality increases, the whole inverted U curve moves to the upper left. We further calculate the maximum value of urbanization-caused income inequality and the corresponding share of urban population, outcomes of which are shown in Table 5.3.1.

The data show that the maximum value of income inequality caused by population transfer from rural area to urban area grows in direct proportion to urban–rural income inequality, whereas the critical value of the share of urban population is in inverse proportion to urban–rural income inequality, a strong proof for the conclusion from our theoretical analysis. We then calculate the share of urban population when the income inequality caused by urbanization reaches its maximum value from 1978 to 2010 separately and compare it with its contemporary actual share by using (5.3.6) and taking the ratio of urban per capita disposable income to rural per capita net income as the urban–rural income inequality. The result is given in Fig. 5.3.6.

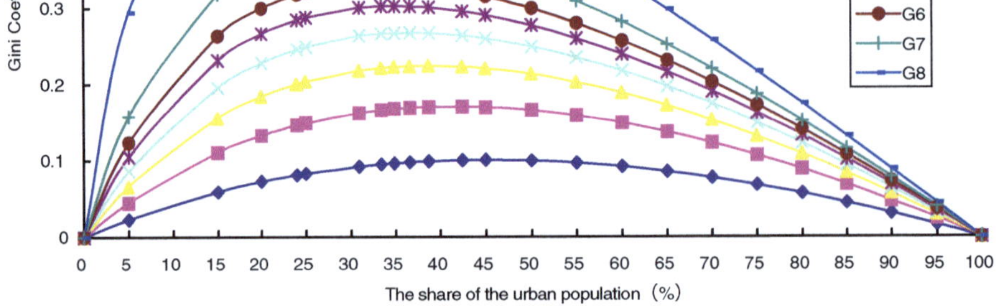

Fig. 5.3.5 Graph of the relation between share of urban population and urban–rural inequality and urbanization-caused income inequality. Note: G_1 is the Gini curve when urban–rural income ratio is 1.5, G_2 is the Gini curve when urban–rural income ratio is 2, G_3 is the Gini curve when urban–rural income ratio is 2.5, G_4 is the Gini curve when urban–rural income ratio is 3, G_5 is the Gini curve when urban–rural income ratio is 3.5, G_6 is the Gini curve when urban–rural income ratio is 4, G_7 is the Gini curve when urban–rural income ratio is 5, and G_8 is the Gini curve when urban–rural income ratio is 10

Table 5.3.1 G^* and P_2^* corresponding to urban–rural income ratio

x	G^*	$P_2^*(\%)$
1.00	0.00000	50.00
1.50	0.10102	44.95
2.00	0.17157	41.42
2.50	0.22515	38.74
3.00	0.26795	36.60
3.50	0.30334	34.83
4.00	0.33333	33.33
5.00	0.38197	30.90
10.00	0.51949	24.03

Source: Authors' measurement

The figure indicates that after 2001 the urban population share in China's total population has surpassed the critical value when the urbanization-caused income inequality reaches its maximum. Urban–rural inequality is the main contributor to income inequality of total resident, about 60% according to our measurement in previous chapters. Moreover, urban income inequality has always been smaller than rural one. Plausibly urbanization will suggest a growth of population with smaller income inequality. Combining the two factors, two hypotheses may be given for test.

Hypothesis One. Since the reform, the income inequality within cities and rural areas, though enlarging constantly, does not support the inverted U hypothesis. Nevertheless, the change in income inequality of total resident accounting probably supports the inverted U hypothesis.

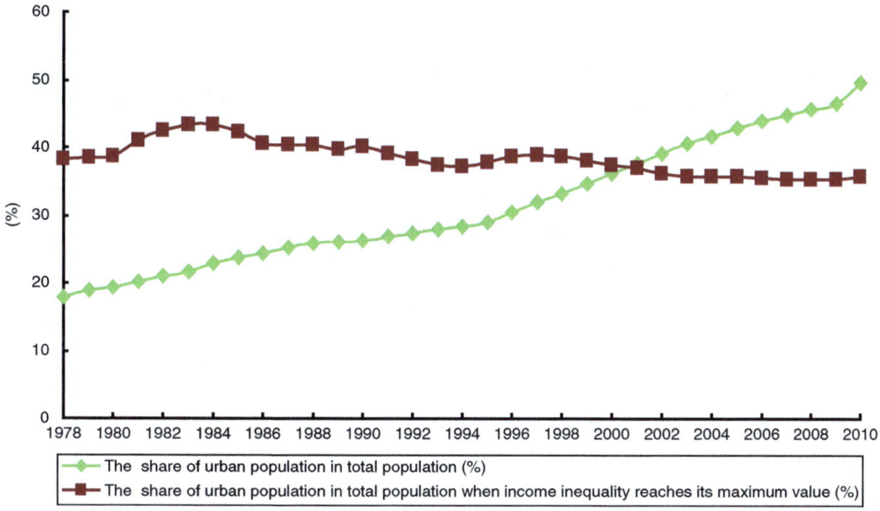

Fig. 5.3.6 Actual share of urban population and its critical value when dynamics of urbanization-caused income inequality shifts 1978–2010. Source: *China Yearbook of Statistics* 1978–2011

Hypothesis Two. If the first hypothesis holds good, the leading element causing income inequality of total resident to undergo an inverted U course is the urbanization-caused population flow from rural areas to urban area.

Next, we will use statistic data to test the two hypotheses.

5.3.4 Empirical Test on the Impact of Urbanization on Income Inequality of Total Resident

5.3.4.1 Empirical Model and the Test of the Main Variables

The following empirical model is designed for the purpose of testing the two hypotheses.

$$G = \beta_0 + \beta_1 \mathrm{RJGDP} + \beta_2 \mathrm{RJGDP}^2 + \beta_3 \mathrm{UPSHARE} + \beta_4 \mathrm{UPSHARE}^2 + \beta_5 \mathrm{URGAP} + \beta_6 X + \mu. \tag{5.3.10}$$

Herein, dependent variable G refers to the Gini coefficient of income of total resident. Independent variables fall into four groups: per capita GDP (RJGDP) and its square as the first group used to test Hypothesis One; Urban population share (UPSHARE) and its square as the second group used to test the impact of urbanization on the change in income inequality of total resident, i.e., to test Hypothesis Two; urban-to-rural ratio (URGAP) as the third group used to measure the impact of urban–rural gap and its change on income inequality of total resident; controlled variable (X) as the fourth group, including one dummy variable, used to examine the impact of reform in urban area after 1984 on income inequality of total resident. In the fourth group, the value of dummy variable from 1978 to 1983 is taken as zero, and after 1984 taken as 1. Inflation rate and foreign trade dependency are also included in the last group to investigate how fluctuation of the whole economy and the opening up policy affect income inequality of total resident.

Most of the data used here come from *China Yearbook of Statistics 1979–2007*. The statistic properties of the above-mentioned variables are shown in Table 5.3.2.

Since all variables are time series, we first undertake stability test on them, result of which is given in Table 5.3.3.

The table shows that the Gini coefficient of income of total resident, the share of urban population in total population, and the urban-to-rural income ratio are unstable time series at 5% significant level. Considering the test results in Table 3.5.3, we may conclude that the regression made between these variables is likely to be a spurious one, the outcome of which is unbelievable. Nevertheless, a combination of one kind or another among these unstable time variables is possibly stable regardless. This is where cointegration test comes in to study whether there is a longstanding equilibrium among the time variables. Table 5.3.4 presents the test results.

Table 5.3.2 Statistic properties of the variables in Model (5.3.10)

Variable	Mean	Standard deviation	Minimum	Maximum
Gini coefficient of income of total resident	0.36867	0.06947	0.25310	0.46910
Urban population share in total population (%)	30.24	8.43	17.92	45.68
Ratio of urban income o rural income	2.57	0.48	1.70	3.33

Source: Authors' measurement based on data from *China Yearbook of Statistics 1979–2007*
Note: Statistic properties of per capita GDP, inflation rate, and foreign trade dependency have been given in Table 3.5.2

Table 5.3.3 Test on unit foot of economic variables in empirical model

Variable	Test type (C, T, K)	T-statistic	Critical value of 5% significant level	Conclusion
Gini coefficient of income of total resident	(0, 0, 3)	0.86845	−1.95291	Unstable
	(C, 0, 3)	−0.59740	−2.96777	Unstable
	(C, T, 3)	−4.76231	−3.57424	Stable
Urban population share (%)	(0, 0, 3)	2.28832	−1.95291	Unstable
	(C, 0, 3)	0.98003	−2.96777	Unstable
	(C, T, 3)	−2.39145	−3.58062	Unstable
Urban-to-rural income ratio (%)	(0, 0, 3)	0.49942	−1.95338	Unstable
	(C, 0, 3)	−1.48005	−2.96777	Unstable
	(C, T, 3)	−4.80363	−3.57424	Stable

Source: Authors' calculation by the data in Table 3.5.1
Note: (1) In the test type (C, T, K), C means whether the model contains constant, T means whether the model contains trend variable, and K refers to lag length
(2) ADF test results of per capita GDP, inflation rate, and foreign trade dependency have been given in Table 3.5.3

Table 5.3.4 Unrestricted cointegration rank test (Trace)

Hypothesized no. of CE(s)	Eigenvalue	Trace statistic	0.05 Critical value	Prob.
None*	0.734732	131.2928	95.75366	0.0000
At most 1*	0.717211	92.80936	69.81889	0.0003
At most 2*	0.635167	56.18075	47.85613	0.0068
At most 3	0.412905	26.93961	29.79707	0.1031
At most 4	0.302867	11.49511	15.49471	0.1828
At most 5	0.034977	1.032505	3.841466	0.3096

* rejecting the hypothesis in 5%(1%) significant level
Source: Authors' calculation by the data from *China Yearbook of Statistics*
Note: Trace test indicates 3 cointegrating eqn(s) at the 0.05 level

From the test results in Tables 5.3.4 and 5.3.5, we learn that at 5% significant level, there exist at least three CEs between the Gini coefficient of the income of total resident on one side, and the share of urban population in total population, per capita GDP, foreign trade dependency, inflation rate, and the urban-to-rural income ratio on the other side, proving a longstanding equilibrium among these variables and that an OLS estimation can be made for model (5.3.10).

Table 5.3.5 Unrestricted cointegration rank test (maximum eigenvalue)

Hypothesized no. of CE(s)	Eigenvalue	Max-eigen statistic	0.05 Critical value	Prob.
None	0.734732	38.48347	40.07757	0.0748
At most 1*	0.717211	36.62861	33.87687	0.0229
At most 2*	0.635167	29.24114	27.58434	0.0304
At most 3	0.412905	15.44450	21.13162	0.2590
At most 4	0.302867	10.46260	14.26460	0.1833
At most 5	0.034977	1.032505	3.841466	0.3096

* rejecting the hypothesis in 5% (1%) significant level
Source: Authors' calculation by the data from *China Yearbook of Statistics*
Note: Max-eigenvalue test indicates 2 cointegration at the 0.05 level

5.3.4.2 Empirical Outcome

When making OLS estimation for model (5.3.10), we find that between per capita GDP and the share of urban population,[3] inflation rate and foreign trade dependency, there is multicollinearity. We then input them separately into the above empirical mode for estimation, the results of which are given in model I, model II, model III, and model IV. Besides, we make ADF test on the residue of each estimation model to check the reliability of the results. The outcomes show that the residues of all models are highly stable, demonstrating the estimation for each model is reliable (Table 5.3.6).

First, in model I, per capita GDP and its square have a highly significant estimation coefficient. A negative coefficient of square of per capita GDP points to an inverted U relation between per capita GDP and the change in income inequality of total resident, proving Hypothesis One to be true. It indicated that income inequality of total resident demonstrates a change of reducing after expanding.

Second, the estimation results of model II show that there is an inverted U relation between income inequality of total resident and the share of urban population, suggesting that the advance of urbanization in China begins to countervail income inequality of total resident and that Hypothesis Two is proved. However, the square of urban population share has a small estimation coefficient, and, therefore, a weak influence.

Third, estimation coefficients of model I, II show that the widening urban–rural inequality helps to expand income inequality of total resident spectacularly. Each growth of 1 in the urban-to-rural income ratio will lead to a growth of at least 0.07–0.09 in the Gini coefficient of income inequality of total resident, showing a great influence of the former on the latter.

[3] According to calculation, the correlation coefficient of per capita GDP to the share of urban population amounts to 0.97. It is because of the strong degree of correlation between the two variables that the share of urban population is used as an important index in judging the development level of an economy by some scholars who thereby derive an inverted U relation between economic development and the change of income inequality.

Table 5.3.6 OLS estimation and test for Model (5.3.10)

Independent variable	Model I	Model II
Constant	0.08904***	−0.12864***
	(14.63)	(−9.20)
Per capita GDP (yuan)	0.05934***	–
	(11.88)	
Square of per capita GDP	−0.00844***	–
	(−11.15)	
Share of urban population in total population (%)	–	0.01390***
		(15.64)
Square of share of urban population	–	−0.00017***
		(−12.31)
Urban-to-rural income ratio	0.07726***	0.09173***
	(24.04)	(44.41)
Foreign trade dependency (%)	0.00016	0.00013
	(0.94)	(1.07)
Inflation rate (%)	0.00033**	0.00026**
	(2.21)	(2.45)
Intercept time variable	0.01422***	0.01316***
	(4.35)	(4.45)
Overall assessment on equation	$A\text{–}R^2 = 0.9973$	$A\text{–}R^2 = 0.9988$
	$F = 1485.73$	$F = 3314.31$
	DW = 1.79	DW = 2.05
ADF test on residue of the model	T-statistic = −5.87	T-statistic = −6.84

Source: Authors' measurement by the data from *China Yearbook of Statistics*
*Suggests 10% significant level, ** suggests 5% significant level, and ***suggests 1% significant level
The critical values of 1%, 5%, and 10% significant levels through ADF test are −3.74, −2.99, and −2.64, respectively

Fourth, the priority of system reform shifting from rural areas to urban area plays a noticeable role in expanding income inequality of total resident. The Gini coefficient of income of total resident increases as a result by 0.013–0.014.

Finally, the opening up policy contributes to some degree to the widening income inequality of total resident, but does not pass the significant test. The fluctuation of the whole economy plays a significant role for increasing income inequality of total resident, but its influence is very small.

To sum up, since the reform and opening the door, an inverted U pattern has come in evidence between economic development and income inequality of total resident, or, the inverted U hypothesis is tenable. The main reason is that the accelerated pace of urbanization in China on the one hand causes the income inequality originating from population flow to enter a period of contraction and on the other hand brings about a larger share of urban population with smaller income inequality. Urbanization, in its essence, has been playing a vital role in slowing and even reducing the income inequality of total resident. It is of critical implication for China's formulation of income distribution policy.

Chapter 6
Impact of Rent-Seeking on Income Inequality

All documents point to one fact that rent-seeking activities represented by tax dodging, smuggling, and corruption have been pervading in China and greatly influenced the income inequality in urban and rural areas, provoking general criticism from all walks of life. This chapter aims to present a general picture of some major rent-seeking activities and make a rough estimation of how they influence income inequality of total resident as well as income inequality of urban and rural resident. Tentative economics explanations for the origin and expansion of rent-seeking in China will be given.

6.1 Some Major Activities of Rent-Seeking in China and Their Impact on Income Inequality

The section will first present the definition of rent-seeking in modern rent-seeking theory and offer a general review on the origin and development of some major forms of rent-seeking in contemporary China. It will also make a rough estimation on the impact of rent-seeking activities on urban, rural, and domestic income inequality.

6.1.1 Economics Definition for Rent-Seeking

In the eyes of economists, the practice of seeking after economic gains may fall into two general categories in light of social welfare: one is productive and conducive to social welfare, like legally fair exchange and other activities in production; the other is unproductive and detrimental to social welfare. We name the first one normal profit-seeking activities, and the second one rent-seeking activities.

Y. Zhou and Y. Qin, *Empirical Analysis on Income Inequality of Chinese Residents*, Gu Shutang Acad Fund Econ, DOI 10.1007/978-3-642-24952-5_6,

Rent-seeking theory was first discussed in detail by Gordon Tullock (1967), one of the leading figures in American public choice theory. However, rent-seeking as a theoretical term was put forward by American economist Anne Krueger who, after analyzing numerous rent-seeking practices arising from restricting imports in developing countries, pointed out that rent-seeking causes huge waste of social resources and hinders economic growth in developing countries. Other scholars like James M. Buchanan also made theoretical analysis on rent-seeking. Though from different perspectives, they ascribed the origin of rent-seeking to government's intervention in market, believing that rent-seeking is practiced just for the purpose of obtaining fabulous "rents" by lobbying the government which is endowed with various privileges.

The "rent" in rent-seeking theory differs from the "rent" in modern economic theory. In modern economics rent is represented as the difference between the total return to a factor of production and its real supply price or cost, or the surplus more than its opportunity cost. The leading reason for some resources capable of producing rent is their lack of supply elasticity. For instance, in farming, the number of arable land is limited and therefore lacks supply elasticity, so with other resources like oil and rare mineral deposits. The "rent" in early rent-seeking theory refers to the super profit from the scarcity of some resources due to government's intervention in and control of market which hinders fair competition. The rent is mainly from government's impertinent intervention in market. And so-called rent-seeking means the practice of economic units managing to obtain economic gains by lobbying the government.

In the 1980s Bhagwati (1982) published in *Journal of Political Economics* a paper titled "Directly Unproductive Profit-seeking (DUP) Activities" in which he classed all rent-seeking activities as directly unproductive profit-seeking. In the *New Palgrave Dictionary Of Economics*, he divided rent-seeking practices into the following categories: (1) when government has strict control of imports and supply of foreign exchange in order to protect domestic economy, fabulous rent and rent-seeking activities will occur; (2) rent-seeking activities of various interest groups who compete with one another for occupying larger share in government's budget; (3) rent-seeking activities with a view to influencing government's tax system advantageous to a special interest group, for instance the setup of tax categories and tax rate which will favor certain group; (4) rent-seeking activities like tax avoidance, dodging, tax evasion, and smuggling undertaken for the purpose of skirting government's restriction.

Modern rent-seeking theory, virtually continuing Bhagwati's definition, defines rent-seeking as economic gains-sought unproductive activities in human society, or as unproductive activities for maintaining economic interests and redistributing them. Rent-seeking may take either legal forms, such as enterprises' asking of government for preferential treatment by making use of special policies to consolidate their monopoly, or illegal forms, such as bribery, tax dodging and evasion, and smuggling. To rent seekers, rent-seeking is a positive sum game since it is an economic practice bringing more returns than cost. Both rent-seeking and normal profit-seeking are all activities of pursuing the maximization of economic returns, and are rational from the perspective of economics. But to the whole society, rent-seeking is a negative sum game, since it brings more loss than gain to the society. To be exact, (1) it causes distorted resource allocation and prevents the implementation of more efficient production mode; (2) resources originally for productive practice are wasted on bootless activities; (3) it leads to other rent-seeking activities or rent-avoidance, and more waste of social resources. To sum up, rent-seeking does not increase social wealth; instead it causes huge waste of social resources. So it is detrimental to social welfare, whereas normal profit-seeking is conducive to the growth of social welfare. This is the cutoff point to distinguish them.

As to the values of rent-seeking theory, first, it offers a brand new perspective for viewing human's economic activities, and by extending its research object from productive profit-seeking to unproductive rent-seeking, it stretches the vision of economic studies. Next, the theory regards government a participant in market economy rather than a "night watcher" in traditional economic theory. Rent-seeking theory believes that the origin of rent-seeking activities is in government's unjustified market interference and control. By viewing government's behavior as endogenous, the theory provides a good theoretical basis and thinking for China's government functions' reform. The last and the most important, rent-seeking theory is not focused on the ethics of rent-seeking activities, but on their social economic and institutional conditions. Why does the same person practice normal profit-seeking in one institutional environment but rent-seeking in another? Why does the same society see radically different levels of rent-seeking activities in different economic institutions? What is the social economic and institutional basis behind the disparity? Answers to these questions will be salutary to China's cracking down on illegal economic crimes like corruption, smuggling, and tax dodging and evasion. To eliminate illegal rent-seeking activities, it is necessary to root out the institution from which they originate. Modern rent-seeking theory that views human economic activities from a new perspective proves very useful to explain various rent-seeking activities in China in light of their origin and expansion.

6.1.2 Origin and Expansion of Rent-Seeking Activities in China Since Reform

Under planning economy, huge economic rent was produced because the government had a direct control of the distribution of various economic resources through administrative means, but rent-seeking activities were rarely seen. Since the reform, a full load of rent-seeking activities have taken place in almost every field. The subject of rent-seeking ranges from government organs, through enterprises and institutions, to individual residents and families. Means and forms of rent-seeking are also diversified, legal or illegal. There are some illegal rent-seeking activities that cause comparatively severe damage to social welfare:

The primary one is tax dodging and evasion which has been virtually established in China's economic life, and can be found in enterprises and individuals.

Table 6.1.1 Total size of tax dodging and evasion (100 million yuan)

Year	That of ground economy				That of underground economy	That of the whole society
	Sum	That of non-agricultural sector	That of imports tariffs	That of personal income tax		
1995	3,623.52	2,616.00	979.52	28.00	850.43	4,473.95
1996	3,354.54	2,601.00	680.54	73.00	744.06	4,099.14
1997	3,683.06	2,717.00	684.06	282.00	675.38	4,358.44
1998	3,830.02	2,816.00	676.02	338.00	694.90	4,524.92
1999	3,542.64	2,720.00	330.64	492.00	897.67	4,440.31
2000	3,717.00	2,524.00	461.00	732.00	721.13	4,438.13
2001	3,743.00	2,665.27	270.27	807.47	577.56	4,320.56
2002	3,776.67	2,665.15	165.97	945.55	215.20	3,991.88
2003	3,873.14	2,718.36	142.13	1,012.65	219.33	4,092.47

Source: Data of 1995–2000 are from Jia Shaohua (2002), data of 2001–2003 are from *China Yearbook of Statistics 2004*

According to estimation by some departments concerned, tax dodging and evasion pervades China's enterprises. About 30% of state-owned enterprises, 60% of joint ventures, 80% of private enterprises, and almost 100% of street peddlers commit tax dodging and evasion. In the early 1980s, when China launched the first tax audit, the case value was only 1.3 billion yuan, in 1991 it rose to 10.2 billion yuan, and in 1994 it was up to 20.4 billion yuan (Chen Zongsheng and Zhou Yunbo 2002). Table 6.1.1 gives the total sum of tax dodging and evasion of all kinds since the 1990s.

From Table 6.1.1, we can see that from 1995 to 2003 the sum of tax dodging and evasion of the whole society was declining from 447.395 billion yuan to 409.247 billion yuan, of which that of ground economy saw a slight growth, from 362.352 billion yuan in 1995 to 377.667 billion yuan in 2003, while that of underground economy tumbled from 85.043 billion yuan in 1995 to 21.933 billion yuan in 2003. There are two reasons for the latter's decline. First, further improved socialist market economy led to less institutional defect and a shrinking size of underground economy. Second, the more concentrated striking force on the part of the government also contributed to its shrinkage to some extent. Concerning the ground economy, non-agricultural sector was found to have a slight growth in tax dodging and evasion, from 261.6 billion yuan in 1995 to 271.836 billion yuan in 2003, because of the strike from China's Customs in imports tariffs there was a sharp decline from 97.952 billion yuan in 1995 to 14.213 billion yuan in 2003, whereas in personal income tax, there was a surge from 2.8 billion to 101.265 billion, 35 times altogether. The surging dynamics of income tax dodging and evasion may be accounted for from the following two aspects. First, since the income tax was just put into force, tax payers had a faint tax awareness due to a thin understanding of the laws and regulations in question. Moreover, lagging imposition administration should also take responsibility. Second, with a rapid economic growth and improvement of residents' living standard, people's incomes were more diversified and concealed. Tax authorities had difficulties in detecting the actual income of the rich

Table 6.1.2 Smuggling cases from Chinese customs

Year	Cases investigated	Case value (100 million yuan)	Sum of tax dodging (100 million yuan)	Cases broken	Case value (100 million yuan)	Sum of tax dodging (100 million yuan)
2000	1,846	355.2	164.8	1,376	348	173.3
2001	1,429	69.8	22.1	1,394	86.2	–
2002	1,228	60.8	16.7	1,378	102.8	33.5
2003	–	–	–	–	–	–
2004	1,068	73.4	–	–	–	–
2005	1,090	85	–	–	–	–

Source: *China Yearbook of Laws 2000–2005*

and those with many income sources. It is true that personal income transformed from corporate tax dodging and evasion could influence residents' income inequality through a series of intermediate transfer, but the loss of personal income tax, that of the high-income group in particular, would directly lead to enlarged income inequality.

As for smuggling, its case value saw a dynamics of growth. According to statistics from the Customs, in 1978 the contraband articles valued 2.27 million yuan, in 1981 it rose to 100 million yuan, in 1992 it was up to 1.3 billion yuan, and in 1996 it was next to 10 billion yuan. In the new century, with the concentrated curbing effort on the part of the Customs, smuggling has been checked. By 2005, 1,090 cases were reported involving 8.5 billion yuan (see Table 6.1.2).[1] At the same time, smuggling subjects and types of contraband articles changed a lot. In the early 1980s, the smuggling subjects were mainly individuals and families, and goods for smuggling were mainly necessities of life including electron watches, household appliances, cigarette, and cloth. In 1990s, the "three-funded" ventures, collective enterprises, and state-owned enterprises were all involved in smuggling and the goods ranged from necessities of life to steel, oil, chemical materials, all productive raw materials of primary concern to the state and people. In the twenty-first century, drugs, historical and cultural relics, endangered animals and plants began to be smuggled by criminal groups to the detriment of the society. The means involved changed also from simple smuggling to high-tech commercial fraud.

The last category is bribery on the part of leaders of party and government organs, enterprises, and institutions at various levels. With advance of system reform, more corruption has been found in party and government cadres,[2] and the most telling is the case value reported each year. In the early 1980s, the case value of bribery on the part of some party and government officials was usually around

[1] The case value in 2000 was 35.52 billion yuan, much bigger than other years, mainly because the notorious Yuanhua smuggling case in Xiamen Province was broken. For this purpose, hundreds of staffs and policemen from the Customs throughout the country were deployed and 30 cases were reported and investigated involving 26.4 billion yuan, of which the sum of tax dodging was 13.19 billion yuan.

[2] For detailed information on such cases, see Li Xueqin and Li Xuehui (1999).

Table 6.1.3 Bribery cases filed for investigation by procuratorial organs

Year	Total money involved (100 million yuan)	Number of cadres investigated and prosecuted at county levels	Number of cadres investigated and prosecuted at prefectural levels	Number of cadres investigated and prosecuted at provincial and above levels
1988	4.24	–	–	–
1989	–	–	–	–
1990	8.1	–	–	–
1991	5.0	–	–	–
1992	5.5	75	6	2
1993	20.0	–	–	–
1994	24.0	202	28	1
1995	32.0	396	35	0
1996	42.5	364	43	1
1997	48.8	403	58	5
1998	39.9	434	54	4
1999	39.5	367	65	2
2000	44.2	350	52	3
2001	41.0	419	89	5
2002	41.0	649	105	5
2003	41.0	458	73	6
2004	42.9	668	98	7
2005	64.0	1,748	178	6

Source: *China Yearbook of Laws 1989–2006*

100,000 yuan, few surpassing one million yuan. However, in the late 1980s and especially in the 1990s the money involved was usually in millions, some even up to 10 million and 100 million.[3] Apart from the increasingly large sum of money, more officials with high ranks were involved (see Table 6.1.3).

In 1992 the case value involved in bribery filed and investigated by procuratorial organs was 550 million yuan, and 75 officials at county levels, 6 officials at prefectural levels, and 2 officials at provincial levels were prosecuted, while in 2005 the case value reached 6.4 billion yuan, and 1,748 officials at county levels, 178 officials at prefectural levels, and 6 officials at provincial levels were prosecuted.

Taken as whole, various rent-seeking activities in forms of tax dodging and evasion, smuggling, and bribery permeate China's economic life and see a growing trend. It suggests that regardless of the efforts of striking economic crimes on the part of the government, the situation remains austere. It is obvious that institutional improvement is the key to curbing rent-seeking activities.

[3] For instance, Yin Guoyuan, former Deputy Director of Shanghai Property and Land Administration, accepted bribes of 36.71 million yuan in his term, and another 8.12 million yuan was of unknown origin. He was reportedly to have 30 sets of houses with each worth more than 3 million yuan, totaling 100 million yuan. It was reported that more properties under his name were not discovered.

6.1.3 *Impact of Rent-Seeking Income on Income Inequality of Urban, Rural, and Total Resident*

In order to make an exact measurement of the impact of rent-seeking income on income inequality of urban, rural, and total resident, we need to know the following facts. (1) What income group do rent seekers belong to? Low-income group, mid-income group, or high-income group? If we know this, we know the direction of rent flowing as well as the direction in which rent-seeking influences income inequality. If rent seekers are low-income group, the flow of rent to them will reduce income inequality; otherwise, if rent seekers are high-income group, the flow of rent to them will widen income inequality. (2) How much is the rent seekers' legal income? (3) What proportion of the revenue from rent-seeking activities is transformed into rent seekers' real income? If the three questions are solved, a measurement of the impact of rent-seeking activities on income inequality can be made.

At present, due to limited data and method, research on rent-seeking income is mostly focused on estimating its total sum. According to an estimation made by Hu Heli (1989) of the rent value in 1988,[4] the total sum of various rents was 400 billion yuan, amounting to 40% of Gross National Income that year. Wan Anpei (1995, 1998) made an estimation of the rent size in 1992 and 1996 with the same method, showing that in 1992 the rents from the distortion of price, interest rate, and foreign exchange were 76.66 billion yuan, 198.3 billion yuan, and 115.71 billion yuan, respectively, rent from import and export license control was 36.7 billion yuan, the loss of taxation 100 billion yuan, rent from public welfare and benefit 11 billion yuan, rent from restructuring share-holding enterprises and real estate development 40 billion yuan, rent from unreasonable fiscal proportion taken away by government 10 billion yuan, industrial rent 5 billion yuan, and rent from railway transport was 11 billion yuan. Added together, the total sum of rents of the year was around 634.37 billion yuan, amounting to 32.3% of current domestic income. In 1996 the total sum of rents was about 622.9 billion yuan, 9.18% of current GDP.

Using the method created by Chen Zongsheng (1991), one of the authors of the book once measured how much the income inequality of urban, rural, and total resident from 1988 to 1999 was influenced by rent-seeking income from tax dodging and evasion on the part of private economy, bribery of the party and government officials, smuggling and fraud, and group spending (Chen Zongsheng and Zhou Yunbo 2001a, b, c, 2002). The research showed that from 1988 to 1999, rent-seeking income was responsible for a rise of 17.82% of income inequality of total resident on average, 31.86% of urban income inequality, and 23.24% of rural income inequality. For detailed information, see Table 6.1.4.

[4] The method he used for estimation can be expressed in the formula of $R = \Delta P \times Q = (PM - PP) \times Q$; herein, R refers to value of some rent, ΔP refers to per unit price spread of some resource, which is equal to the difference between the market equilibrium price PM and posted price PP, and Q refers to the quantity of unified distribution of the resource.

Table 6.1.4 Impact of rent-seeking income on income inequality of urban, rural, and total resident

Year	Domestic			Urban			Rural		
	Gini coefficient of normal income	Gini coefficient of income inclusive of rent-seeking income	Perc. of rising income inequality (%)	Gini coefficient of normal income	Gini coefficient of income inclusive of rent-seeking income	Perc. of rising income inequality (%)	Gini coefficient of normal income	Gini coefficient of income inclusive of rent-seeking income	Perc. of rising income inequality (%)
1988	0.34976	0.41686	19.19	0.23068	0.31358	35.94	0.30285	0.37802	24.82
1989	0.36965	0.42450	14.84	0.22592	0.29557	30.83	0.31261	0.37235	19.11
1990	0.34688	0.40150	15.75	0.23543	0.30509	29.59	0.29474	0.35107	19.11
1991	0.36904	0.41700	13.00	0.24246	0.30513	25.85	0.30740	0.36012	17.15
1992	0.37719	0.42620	12.99	0.25364	0.31369	23.68	0.31062	0.36897	18.79
1993	0.40173	0.45952	14.39	0.27244	0.34608	27.03	0.31812	0.38485	20.98
1994	0.43561	0.51115	17.34	0.30175	0.39623	31.31	0.32996	0.42473	28.72
1995	0.41914	0.51733	23.43	0.28804	0.41528	44.17	0.34070	0.44877	31.72
1996	0.40582	0.49909	22.98	0.30341	0.42071	38.66	0.32100	0.42075	31.07
1997	0.40269	0.49124	21.99	0.30794	0.42200	37.04	0.32724	0.41599	27.12
1998	0.40260	0.49005	21.72	0.32303	0.42576	31.80	0.34097	0.41549	21.85
1999	0.41294	0.48017	16.28	0.33610	0.42495	26.44	0.35120	0.41574	18.38
Average	–	–	17.82	–	–	31.86	–	–	23.24

Source: Chen Zongsheng and Zhou Yunbo 2002: 379–380, 399, 413)

Note: When measuring the impact of rent-seeking income on rural income inequality, group spending is not taken into consideration

Because of the limit of relative data, in the following, a quantitative measurement of the impact of rent-seeking income on urban and rural income inequality and income inequality of total resident from 2000 to 2006 will be made by using previous method (Chen Zongsheng and Zhou Yunbo 2001a, b, c, 2002) combined with data available. In order to achieve a good comparison with previous research, some basic assumptions in previous research will be borrowed: (1) suppose self-employed and private businesses in urban and rural areas belong to the highest income group (a brief information about this group is given in Table A.1); (2) suppose party and government officials belong to the high-income group (their total number is given in Table A.2); (3) suppose 80% of private enterprises and 90% of self-employed enterprises commit tax dodging and evasion (their illegal income per capita is given in Table A.3); (4) suppose crime rate of corrupted party and government officials is 10% (their illegal income per capita is given in Table A.4); (5) suppose 15% of administration fees is transformed to personal income (the transformed per capita income is given in Table A.5); (6) suppose other illegal incomes like smuggling and fraud go to 10% of rich people and increase their normal income by 15%. Given these assumptions, the Gini coefficient of the incomes of urban, rural, and total resident inclusive of various rent-seeking incomes can be figured out (Table 6.1.5).

Data in the table show that given the above assumptions, from 2000 to 2006 various rent-seeking incomes at the most increased the Gini coefficient of the income of total resident to 0.5375 by 15.33% on average, the Gini coefficient of urban residents' income to 0.4873 by 25.05% on average, and the Gini coefficient of rural residents' income to 0.47705 by 16.9%. When the rent-seeking income was taken into account, the urban income inequality was larger than rural one, a quite reasonable conclusion in agreement with previous researches (Human Resources Institute National Planning Commission 1995; Ren Caifang and Cheng Xuebin 1996; Yu Zuyao 1998; Chen Zongsheng and Zhou Yunbo 2001a, b, c, 2002) which demonstrated that those who had access to rent-seeking income mostly belonged to high-income group in cities and towns. In light of the trend, the impact of various rent-seeking incomes on income inequality of total resident, urban, and rural was in decline for the following reasons. First, Tables 6.1.1–6.1.3 show that in the new century, intensified operations against tax dodging, smuggling, and corruption on the part of the government had to some degree curbed rent-seeking activities. Second, since 2000 with further economic reform, improved institution, and a more transparent market operation, people found less opportunity for rent-seeking activities. Third, with the improved economic marketization, fewer resources came to the government's control, leaving less room for bureaucratic corruption. Next, we will present economic explanations for contemporary rent-seeking in terms of a growing motive on the part of economic entities and a growing space for rent-seeking owning to institutional defect in a transitional economy.

Table 6.1.5 Impact of rent-seeking income on income inequality of urban, rural, and total resident

Year	Domestic			Urban			Rural		
	Gini coefficient of normal income	Gini coefficient of income inclusive of rent-seeking income	Perc. of rising income inequality (%)	Gini coefficient of normal income	Gini coefficient of income inclusive of rent-seeking income	Perc. of rising income inequality (%)	Gini coefficient of normal income	Gini coefficient of income inclusive of rent-seeking income	Perc. of rising income inequality (%)
2000	0.41543	0.48825	17.53	0.34165	0.43468	27.23	0.36039	0.43164	19.77
2001	0.42791	0.49471	15.61	0.35121	0.44133	25.66	0.36986	0.43429	17.42
2002	0.45050	0.52277	16.04	0.37263	0.47294	26.92	0.38389	0.44746	16.56
2003	0.46178	0.53220	15.25	0.38196	0.47875	25.34	0.39267	0.46260	17.81
2004	0.46332	0.52911	14.20	0.38754	0.48167	24.29	0.40285	0.46545	15.54
2005	0.46785	0.53751	14.89	0.39563	0.48730	23.17	0.41346	0.47705	15.38
2006	0.46910	0.53365	13.76	0.3918	0.48082	22.72	0.41192	0.47696	15.79
Average	–	–	15.33	–	–	25.05	–	–	16.90

Source: Authors' estimation by data in Table 6.1.5

6.2 Economics Explanation for Rent-Seeking Activities in China

Two factors are responsible for the raging of rent-seeking activities since the reform in China. One is the unequilibrium and unstability of interim institutional arrangement in a transitional economy which invites motive for speculation on the part of economic entities. The other is institutional defect characteristic of transitional economy which provides adequate space for rent-seeking (Chen Zongsheng and Zhou Yunbo 2001a, b, c, 2002).

6.2.1 Unequilibrium of Interim Institutional Arrangement as a Spur to Economic Entities' Motive for Rent-Seeking

In light of institutional approach in rent-seeking theory, the development and spread of various rent-seeking activities in contemporary China are closely associated with its specific historical stage and its specific institutional backdrop. Strictly speaking, any rent-seeking activity has subjective and objective attributions. Its objective attribution lies in the institutional defect (Chen Zongsheng and Zhou Yunbo 2001a, b, c, 2002), while its subjective attribution refers to economic entities' motive for speculation. The following part will focus on speculation motive.

Since the reform, compared to traditional command economy, China has seen an obvious rise in economic entities' speculation motive. There are two reasons: one is the market-oriented reform foregrounds the importance of economic gains in people's daily life, an inevitable but normal consequence of market-oriented reform system reform; the other is the unequilibrium and unstability interim institutional arrangement which leads to an increasing uncertainty and risk on the part of economic entities who tend to invest in a short term and increase speculation motive.

Presently, China is at the stage during which the new system is replacing the old one. In an interim institution full of inadequate information and uncertainty for the future, reformers are rational in a limited way in that each step of reform is a trial and error method. That is to say, each reform is a process of repeated game, which in turn affects interim institutional arrangement. "Interim" means many measures of reform are temporary, unbalanced, and unstable in nature (Zhou Bing 2001), producing much larger uncertainty and risk for the future on the part of economic entities, who as a result will pay more attention to short-term economic gains, or speculation.

For the convenience of analysis, we construct a single economic entity-two periods-income model. (1) Suppose there are periods one and two, and the incomes in the two periods are I_1 and I_2; (2) each income is dependent only on the degree of effort (λ) on the part of economic entity, and the larger the λ, the higher the income; (3) cross period total income effect is optimized through economic entity's effort.

$$\mathrm{Max}U(I). \tag{6.2.1}$$

Herein,

$$I = I_1 + \rho I_2, \rho \in (0,1), \tag{6.2.2}$$

$$I_1 = f(\lambda_1), \tag{6.2.3}$$

$$I_2 = f(\lambda_2), \tag{6.2.4}$$

$$\rho = g(\varepsilon). \tag{6.2.5}$$

I refers to the added income of the two periods, and it is the weighted sum of I_1 and I_2. At the same time $\mathrm{d}U/\mathrm{d}I > 0, \mathrm{d}^2U/\mathrm{d}I^2 < 0$, that is, the more income, the larger effect achieved by economic entity, featuring a decline of marginal growth rate. Income of each period (I_1, I_2) is the function of economic entities' effort (λ_1, λ_2), and $\mathrm{d}I_1/\mathrm{d}\lambda_1 > 0, \mathrm{d}^2I_1/\mathrm{d}{\lambda_1}^2 < 0, \mathrm{d}I_2/\mathrm{d}\lambda_2 > 0, \mathrm{d}^2I_2/\mathrm{d}{\lambda_2}^2 < 0$, namely, the more effort, the more income, featuring a decline of marginal growth rate. ρ is discount factor, it is the function of future uncertainty (ε), and at the same time $\mathrm{d}\rho/\mathrm{d}\varepsilon < 0$, namely, it will decline when (ε) grows.

The above formulas may also be expressed as follows:

$$\mathrm{Max}U(I_1, I_2, \rho), \tag{6.2.6}$$

$$S.T., I_1 = f(\lambda_1), \tag{6.2.7}$$

$$I_2 = f(\lambda_2). \tag{6.2.8}$$

And again,

$$\frac{\mathrm{d}U}{\mathrm{d}I} = \frac{\partial U}{\partial I_1} + \frac{\partial U}{\partial I_2}\rho. \tag{6.2.9}$$

From (6.2.9), we have

$$\frac{\partial U/\partial I_1}{\partial U/\partial I_2} = -\rho. \tag{6.2.10}$$

In transitional economy, the unequilibrium and instability of interim institution increase the future uncertainty, that is, an increased ε leads to a declined ρ, which in turn leads to a declined I as demonstrated in (6.2.2) and a declined U as demonstrated in (6.2.1). To retain the original level of effect, the economic entity has to increase its effort in period one (λ_1) and accordingly its income (I_1). According to (6.2.10), the reduction of ρ will lead to a larger marginal effect of

I_1 than that of I_2, suggesting a declined marginal rate of substitution (MRS) between future income and current income. It is natural that economic entity will increase its effort in period one (λ_1) to obtain a larger income (I_1). Obviously economic entity focuses more on current income.

Besides, the declined discount factor caused by unbalanced interim institutional arrangement will weaken the conditions of Folk theorem in repeated game. Chances are that current noncooperative activity will occur. In other words, the interim institutional arrangement forces various economic transactions among economic entities to be close to one-time game, disinheriting the cooperative mechanism binding economic entity's behaviors originally existent in repeated game. This is another reason for increased motive for rent-seeking.

6.2.2 *Defects of Interim Institutional Arrangement as a Source of Rent-Seeking Income*

We just analyzed subjective drivers of various illegal rent-seeking activities. Apart from subjective drivers, there are objective drivers, or, institutional defects of a transitional economy which provide some space for rent-seeking. In the following part, considering subjective and objective drivers combined, a simple economic model will be used to account for the birth and growth of rent-seeking.

Basic assumptions of the model are (1) suppose economic activities of a society fall into two categories, one of normal profit-seeking, and the other of rent-seeking; (2) when institutional defects are fixed, the possibility frontier of quantity combination of the two kinds of economic activities is fixed too, that is to say, institutional defects determine the possibility of max quantity combination of the two kinds of economic activities; (3) the equilibrium number of the two kinds of activities is contingent upon economic entity's speculation motive (see Fig. 6.2.1).

The horizontal axis in the figure represents the number of rent-seeking activities, and the vertical axis the number of profit-seeking activities. AA' refers to curve of quantity combination possibility of the two kinds of economic activities under command economy. Planning economy provides comparatively small space for rent-seeking due to less institutional defects and a tight economic control which provided small space for rent-seeking activities. Meanwhile, since the Planning economy is relatively stable and economic interests mean less to economic entities in comparison to market economy. Therefore, their speculation motive is not strong, and its indifference curve is shown as U_1. So the equilibrium number of rent-seeking and profit-seeking of the whole society is contingent upon the tangency point E_1 between AA' and U_1. The number of rent-seeking is OR_1, and that of normal profit-seeking is OP_1, suggesting that economic entities invest more resources in regular production and operation for gains.

The system reform gave birth to limited rationality on the part of reformers because of inadequate information and uncertainty of the future, and profound

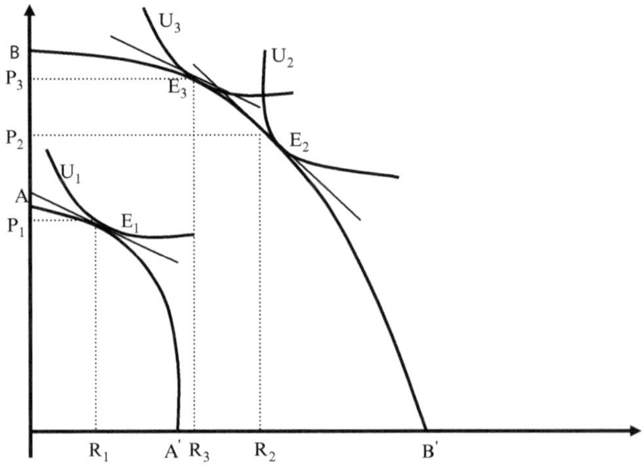

Fig. 6.2.1 Mechanism of birth and growth of rent-seeking in transitional economy

institutional defect came into being. BB' means the curve of quantity combination possibility of the two kinds of economic activities. In comparison to planning economy, market reform has greatly increased the number of various economic activities. That is why BB' is to the upper right of AA'. Meanwhile, the unequilibrium and instability featuring repeated game in system reform as well as the increasingly importance of economic interests fan economic entities' speculation motive. Its indifference curve is shown as U_2. The unequilibrium numbers of the two kinds of economic activities are OR_2 and OP_2, which are determined by the tangency point E_2 between BB' and U_2. Compared to command economy, the number of rent-seeking activities in market economy rises by R_1R_2.

For further decomposition, we set a parallel translation of U_1 to U_3 and tangent with BB' at the point of E_3. The determined unequilibrium numbers of rent-seeking and profit-seeking activities are OR_3 and OP_3, respectively. The increment of rent-seeking activities, R_1R_2, is therefore decomposed into R_1R_3 and R_3R_2, the former being the growth of rent-seeking owning to institutional defects in transitional economy, and the latter being the growth caused by increased speculation motive on the part of economic entities.

We make such a decomposition for expatiating the issue more clearly. However, in real economic life, the reasons for rage of rent-seeking are complicated, with subjective and objective drivers combined. It is hard to tell distinctly subjective drivers from objective drivers.

Chapter 7
Forecast for Chinese Residents' Income Inequality in the Future

Previous chapters examined the urban and rural income inequality and income inequality of total resident and their drivers alongside the impact of a few major rent-seeking activities on income inequality. This chapter will launch a quantitative forecast for the change trend of the income inequality of urban, rural and total resident, and urban–rural income inequality in the future.

7.1 Main Factors Influencing Trend of Income Inequality of Chinese Resident

Prior to forecasting, we first make a brief analysis of the main factors that influence the change trend of Chinese residents' income inequality. In general, they fall into two categories, one contributing to its enlargement, and the other to its reduction.

7.1.1 Main Factors Enlarging Income Inequality

With the economic development and the boost of system reform, some factors that enlarge income inequality still function.

First, nonpublic economy inclusive of self-employed and private economy will be multiplying with Chinese economic system further loosening. At the same time improved market system diversifies residents' investments. Change in these two regards will give rise to a larger share of property income in residents' income. As shown in Chaps. 3 and 4 that the distribution of property income is highly uneven, the increase of its share in total income will undoubtedly lead to larger income inequality.

Second, in rural China, land is virtually equally distributed. However, reasonable land concentration is of necessity for developing intensive scale and modernized

Y. Zhou and Y. Qin, *Empirical Analysis on Income Inequality of Chinese Residents*, Gu Shutang Acad Fund Econ, DOI 10.1007/978-3-642-24952-5_7,

agriculture. With land circulation and transaction market in rural areas being improved, it is more likely that more land will go to capable farmers with production edge, the land concentration that will inevitably help enlarge rural income inequality.

Third, wage reform is under way in institutions and Party and administrative organs in a bid to differentiate wage levels between varied posts and ranks. This move will certainly widen urban income inequality.

Fourth, in the process of economic development, change of industry structure caused by economic cycle and technological progress manifests itself in the decline of some traditional industries and the rise of other emerging ones. This also contributes to the enlargement of income inequality among employees in different industries.

7.1.2 Main Factors Reducing Income Inequality

The factors reducing income inequality are as follows.

First, the central government has already put into effect the strategy of concerted development between regions and the great western development strategy, which, alongside the coming trickling-down effect, will gradually help reduce regional inequality which will reduce the residents' income inequality, especially in rural areas where income inequality of rural resident is more vulnerable to uneven regional development.

Second, with urban–rural overall development strategy on the move and the movement of constructing socialist new countryside ushered in, the urban–rural income inequality will be reduced by degrees, which in turn will contribute to reducing the income inequality of total resident.

Third, the growth of non-agricultural industries in rural areas and the implementation of developing small cities and towns push a large number of rural labor forces into non-agricultural industries. The decrease of dual-economy contrast prevalent in rural internal economic structure will be softened and help reduce rural income inequality.

Fourth, the labor transfer caused by urbanization from rural areas to cities has come to the point of reducing income inequality. With the advance of urbanization, more labor transfer will countervail the income inequality of total resident.

Fifth, economic growth, improved social security system, and poverty-relieving strategy will cut down the number of the poor, improve their income level, and consequently reduce income inequality. At present, the social security system in China is still flawed. Some data show that current social security system in China covers only 5% of population. The vast rural population is virtually out of the system. Of course, in the near future with better social security system and more people coming in, the income level of low-income group will be raised to some extent. With economic development and implementation of poverty-relieving strategy, the poverty population will decrease. All these measures will offset the overall income inequality.

Sixth, a more reasonable taxation system will to some degree cool the too-fast rise of the income level of high-income group, which will in turn help reduce income inequality. The taxation system in present China is seriously flawed, and tax dodging and avoidance remains a headache, though personal income tax is already imposed. Real name deposit system is in force, but interest tax is imposed without differentiation. As to inheritance tax and property tax that are of vital significance to regulate income distribution, they are put into practice on a trial basis. With improved taxation system, the income rise of the rich will be checked up to a point in the service of reducing income inequality.

Seventh, institutional defect will be remedied with further development of socialist market economy. As a result, rent-seeking activities on the part of high-income group will be controlled in the service of reducing income inequality.

Finally, the thousand-year-old Chinese mentality of “fear not of little but of unequal” and the established notion of egalitarianism as equality rooted in socialist planning economy will curb further income inequality ideologically.

7.1.3 Conclusions

Based on the above analysis, we believe that the change of residents’ income inequality in the future depends on the two above-mentioned factors combined. In the coming 5–10 years, factors contributing to the enlargement of income inequality are bound to outweigh factors contributing to its reduction in terms of impact degree. As a result, the income inequality of urban, rural, and total resident will remain on the rise, though slowly. The reason for assuming that drivers of income inequality will take the lead is that many factors are playing their roles in widening residents’ income inequality, such as property income, wage reform in institutions and government departments, and concentration of farming lands, whereas many other factors which should in theory countervail income inequality have not come out, like the taxation policy checking the too-fast rise of income level of the rich; some polices are just on a trial basis, such as the urban–rural overall development strategy, concerted development strategy between regions, and improvement of social security, and their effect will appear in the future (maybe 5–10 years). In the short run, we think that the factors that enlarge income inequality are to be dominant. Next, we will forecast the dynamics of Chinese residents’ income inequality in the future by using empirical analysis.

7.2 Method for Forecast: Exponential Smoothing Model

This section introduces Exponential Smoothing Model as a method for forecasting. The basic principle of the method is to find the mean by introducing a simplified weighted factor, or smoothing coefficient, on the basis of current period actual and current period forecast of certain index. It is a variation of weighted moving average forecast. The Smoothing Coefficient is between 0 and 1, like 0.1, 0.4, 0.6, etc. Five methods for Exponential Smoothing are presented in EViews.

7.2.1 Single Exponential Smoothing Method

Single Exponential Smoothing fits the series which move randomly below and above a constant mean with neither trend nor seasonal patterns. There is a parameter to be estimated in this method, whose calculation formula is

$$G_t^{\mathrm{F}} = G_{t-1}^{\mathrm{F}} + (G_{t-1} - G_{t-1}^{\mathrm{F}}) \times \alpha. \tag{7.2.1}$$

G_t^{F} refers to the forecast figure of current period, G_{t-1} refers to the actual figure of prior period, G_{t-1}^{F} refers to the forecast figure of prior period, and α refers to the Smoothing Coefficient, also called attenuation coefficient. Bowerman O'Connell (1979) argues that under general circumstance, it is ideal for α to have an estimated value between 0.001 and 0.3. The formula implies that the forecast figure of current period can be found by adding to the forecast figure of prior period the difference between the actual figure of prior period and the forecast figure of prior period that is adjusted by Smoothing Coefficient. Usually the forecast figure of current period locates between the actual figure of prior period and the forecast figure of prior period. The size of Smoothing Coefficient may be determined by comparing the forecast figure of prior period with the actual figure of prior period. If the difference is substantial, the Smoothing Coefficient should take a large value; otherwise, it should take a small value. The larger the Smoothing Coefficient, the bigger the impact of recent tendency variation; otherwise, the smaller the impact of recent tendency variation, the smoother.

After further compilation of (7.2.2), we have

$$G_t^{\mathrm{F}} = G_{t-1} \times \alpha + G_{t-1}^{\mathrm{F}} \times (1 - \alpha), \tag{7.2.2}$$

and

$$G_{t-1}^{\mathrm{F}} = G_{t-2} \times \alpha + G_{t-2}^{\mathrm{F}} \times (1 - \alpha). \tag{7.2.3}$$

After repeated replacement, we have in the end

$$G_t^{\mathrm{F}} = \alpha \sum_{s=1}^{t} (1 - \alpha)^s \times G_{t-s}. \tag{7.2.4}$$

Formula (7.2.4) indicates that the estimated value of a time variable (t) is the weighted sum of it's the actual value of prior period, and the weight of $1 - \alpha$ exponentially declines over time. That is why the method is named Exponential

Smoothing. The estimated value of Singe Exponential Smoothing for the future is a constant as given in the following formula:

So long as $k > 0$, the

$$G_{T+k}^{\mathrm{F}} = G_T^{\mathrm{F}} \tag{7.2.5}$$

T is the last period for estimate sample.

7.2.2 Double Exponential Smoothing Method

Double Exponential Smoothing is the double application of Single Exponential Smoothing, which is fit for the time series with linear trend term but without periodic term. The same is with Single Exponential Smoothing: this method has a parameter to be estimated too. The double smoothing sequence G_t is defined by the following recursive formula:

$$S_t = \alpha \times G_t + (1 - \alpha) \times S_{t-1}, \tag{7.2.6}$$

$$D_t = \alpha \times S_t + (1 - \alpha) \times D_{t-1}, \tag{7.2.7}$$

where S_t means single smoothing sequence, and $D_t$double smoothing sequence. The estimated value of G_t can be calculated by the following formula:

$$G_{t+k}^{\mathrm{F}} = \left(2 + \frac{\alpha k}{1-\alpha}\right) \times S_t - \left(1 + \frac{\alpha k}{1-\alpha}\right) \times D_t. \tag{7.2.8}$$

After further compilation, we have

$$G_{t+k}^{\mathrm{F}} = 2S_t - D_t + \frac{\alpha(S_t - D_t)}{1-\alpha} \times k. \tag{7.2.9}$$

Formula (7.2.9) shows that the method Double Exponential Smoothing contains a linear trend term with an intercept of $2S_t - D_t$ and a slope of $\frac{\alpha(S_t - D_t)}{1-\alpha}$.

7.2.3 Holt–Winters-No Seasonal Method

Holt–Winters-No Seasonal fits the time series with linear trend term without periodic term, only that it has two parameters to be estimated. The smoothing sequence G_{t+k}^{F} can be calculated by the following formula:

$$G_{t+k}^{\mathrm{F}} = a + b \times k. \tag{7.2.10}$$

where a is the intercept with impact of long-term factor, and b is the trend term. They are calculated by the following two recursive equations:

$$a(t) = \alpha \times G_t + (1 - \alpha) \times [a(t-1) + b(t-1)], \tag{7.2.11}$$

$$b(t) = \beta \times [a(t-1) + b(t-1)] + 1 - \beta \times b(t-1) \times \alpha. \tag{7.2.12}$$

Herein, $\alpha > 0$ and $\beta < 1$ are attenuation coefficients, whose estimate value can be calculated by the following formula:

$$G_{t+k}^{\mathrm{F}} = a(T) + b(T) \times k. \tag{7.2.13}$$

7.2.4 *Holt–Winters-Additive Method*

Holt–Winters-Additive is fit for the time series with linear time trend term and additive periodic term. Three parameters to be estimated are needed, and the smoothing sequence G_{t+k}^{F} can be calculated by

$$G_{t+k}^{\mathrm{F}} = a + b \times k + c_{t+k}. \tag{7.2.14}$$

Herein, a is the intercept with impact of long-term factor, b is the trend term, and c_{t+k} is the additive periodic factor. They can be calculated by the following three recursive equations:

$$a(t) = \alpha \times [G_t - c_t(t-s)] + (1 - \alpha) \times [a(t-1) + b(t-1)], \tag{7.2.15}$$

$$b(t) = \beta \times [a(t-1) + b(t-1)] + 1 - \beta \times b(t-1), \tag{7.2.16}$$

$$c_t(t) = \gamma \times [G_t - a(t+1)] - \gamma \times c_t(t-s). \tag{7.2.17}$$

Herein, $\alpha > 0$, $\beta < 1$, and $\gamma < 1$are all attenuation coefficients. s is the periodic frequency specified in the Cycle for Seasonal field box. The forecasted value of G_{T+k}^{F} is calculated by the following formula:

$$G_{T+k}^{\mathrm{F}} = a(T) + b(T) \times k + c_{T+k-s}. \tag{7.2.18}$$

Seasonal factor is used for final estimation of s.

7.2.5 Holt–Winters-Multiplicative Method

Holt–Winters-Multiplicative fits the time series with linear time trend term and multiplicative periodic term. Three parameters to be estimated are needed and the smoothing sequence G^{F}_{t+k} may be found out by the following formula:

$$G^{\mathrm{F}}_{t+k} = (a + b \times k) \times c_{t+k}, \tag{7.2.19}$$

a is the intercept containing the impact of long-term factors, b is the trend term, and c_{t+k} is the multiplicative periodic factor. They are calculated by the following recursive equations:

$$a(t) = \frac{\alpha \times G_t}{c_t(t-s)} + (1-\alpha) \times [a(t-1) + b(t-1)], \tag{7.2.20}$$

$$b(t) = \beta \times [a(t-1) + b(t-1)] + 1 - \beta \times b(t-1), \tag{7.2.21}$$

$$c_t(t) = \frac{\gamma \times G_t}{a(t+1)} - \gamma \times c_t(t-s). \tag{7.2.22}$$

Herein, $\alpha > 0$, $\beta < 1$, and $\gamma < 1$ are all attenuation coefficients. s refers to the periodic frequency in the Cycle for Seasonal field box. The forecasted value of G^{F}_{T+k} may be found out by the following formula.

$$G^{\mathrm{F}}_{T+k} = [a(T) + b(T) \times k] \times c_{T+k-s}. \tag{7.2.23}$$

The seasonal factor is used for final estimation of s.

7.3 The Forecast Outcomes for Income Inequality of Urban, Rural and Total Resident, and Urban–Rural Income Inequality

This section aims to make a quantitative forecast for the change trend of the income inequality of urban, rural and total resident, and urban–rural income inequality.

7.3.1 Forecast Outcome of Income Inequality of Urban Resident

A direct forecast is possible by using Double Exponential Smoothing, Holt-Winters-No Seasonal, Holt–Winters-Additive, and Holt–Winters-Multiplicative.

Table 7.3.1 Outcomes of forecast estimation for Gini coefficient of income of urban resident

Estimate coefficient	Double exponential smoothing	Holt–Winters-No Seasonal	Holt–Winters-Additive	Holt–Winters-Multiplicative
α	0.5080	0.94000	0.96000	0.93000
β	–	0.0000	0.0000	0.0000
γ	–	–	0.0000	0.0000
Sum of squares of residue	0.00487	0.00390	0.00384	0.00382

Source: Authors' own measurement by the Gini coefficient of urban resident's income in Table 5.1.1

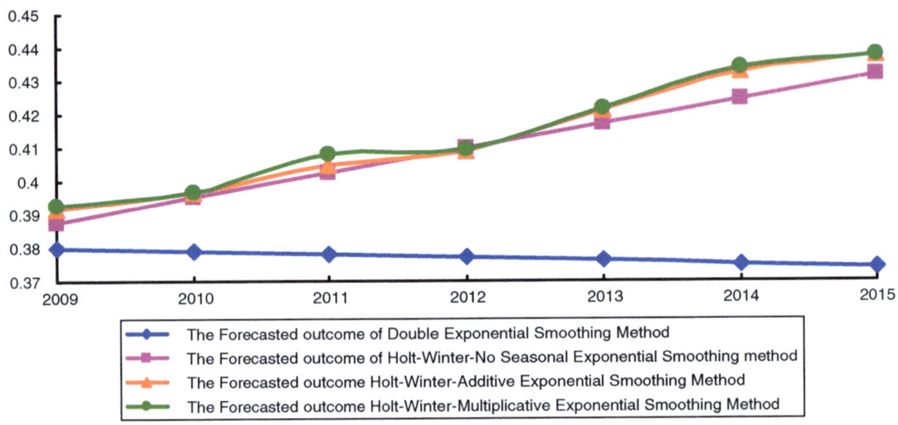

Fig. 7.3.1 Forecast value of Gini coefficient of urban resident's income 2007–2015. Source: Table A.7

The outcomes of estimation are given in Table 7.3.1, and the outcomes of forecasting are given in Table A.7 and Fig. 7.3.1.

From Table A.7 and Fig. 7.3.1, according to Double Exponential Smoothing Method, we may see that Chinese urban income inequality will decrease in the coming years. By the year of 2015, the Gini coefficient of urban income will hit 0.37 or so. But according to the prediction by Holt–Winters-No Seasonal Method, Holt–Winters-Additive Method, and Holt–Winters-Multiplicative Method, Chinese urban income inequality will increase in the coming years. By the year of 2015, the Gini coefficient of urban income will hit 0.43 or so. So we can conclude that in the future the income inequality of urban resident will rise.

7.3.2 *Forecast Outcome of Income Inequality of Rural Resident*

In the same way, rural income inequality will be predicted next. The outcomes of equation are given in Table 7.3.2 and the outcomes of prediction are given in Table A.8 and Fig. 7.3.1.

Table 7.3.2 Outcome of forecast estimation for Gini coefficient of income of rural resident

Estimate coefficient	Double exponential smoothing	Holt–Winters-No Seasonal	Holt–Winters-Additive	Holt–Winters-Multiplicative
α	0.2640	0.6000	0.6300	0.6200
β	–	0.0000	0.0000	0.0000
γ	–	–	0.0000	0.0000
Sum of squares of residue	0.00321	0.00279	0.00189	0.00211

Source: Authors' own measurement by the Gini coefficient of rural income inequality in Table 5.1.1

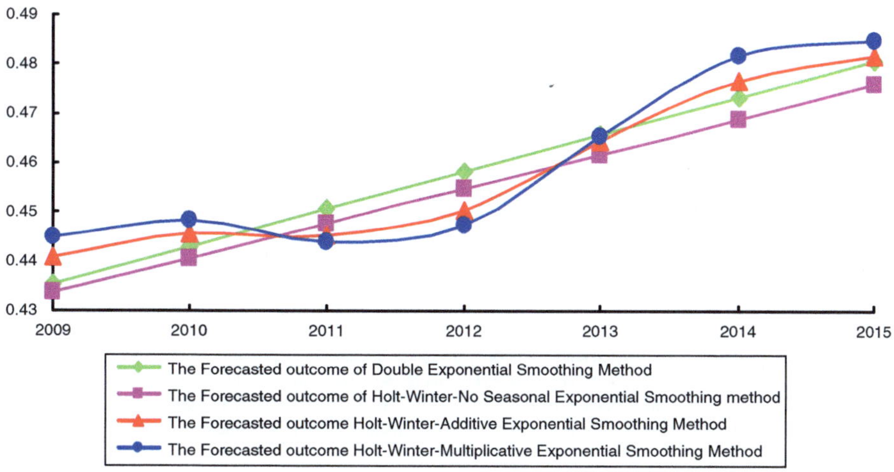

Fig. 7.3.2 Forecast value of Gini coefficient of rural resident's income 2007–2015. Source: Table A.8

From Table A.8 and Fig. 7.3.2, we may see that Chinese rural income inequality will remain on the rise in the coming years. By the year of 2015, the Gini coefficient of rural income will reach around 0.48. To be exact, it will grow from 0.43547 in 2009 to 0.48094 in 2015 based on the prediction by Double Exponential Smoothing Method, from 0.43359 in 2009 to 0.47596 in 2015 based on the prediction by Holt–Winters-No Seasonal Method, from 0.44088 in 2009 to 0.48169 in 2015 based on Holt–Winters-Additive, and it will rise from 0.44497 in 2009 to 0.48477 in 2015 based on Holt–Winters-Multiplicative. So we can conclude that in the future the income inequality of rural resident will rise.

7.3.3 Forecast Outcome of Income Inequality of Total Resident

Similar forecast will be made for income inequality of total resident by using the same four methods. Outcomes of the estimation are given in Table 7.3.3 and results of prediction are given in Fig. 7.3.3.

Table 7.3.3 Outcomes of forecast estimation for Gini coefficient of income of total resident

Estimate coefficient	Double exponential smoothing	Holt–Winters-No Seasonal	Holt–Winters-Additive	Holt–Winters-Multiplicative
α	0.9180	1.0000	1.0000	1.0000
β	–	0.8400	0.0000	0.0000
γ	–	–	0.0000	0.0000
Sum of squares of residue	0.00820	0.00657	0.00645	0.00656

Source: Authors' measurement by the Gini coefficient of total resident's income in Table 5.1.1

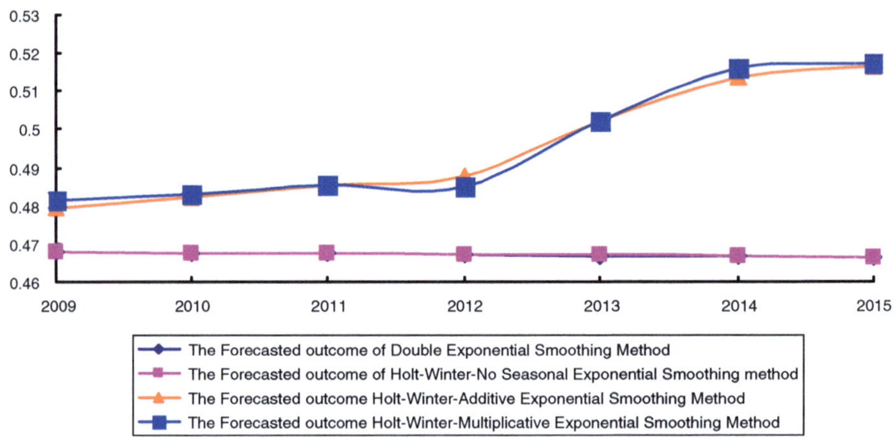

Fig. 7.3.3 Forecast value of Gini coefficient of total resident's income 2007–2015. Source: Table A.9

According to the Double Exponential Smoothing Method and Holt–Winters-No Seasonal Method, the income inequality of total resident will decrease slowly. It will decline from 0.46785 in 2009 to 0.46639 in 2015 based on forecast outcome of Double Exponential Smoothing Method, and will decline from 0.46786 in 2009 to 0.46651 in 2015 based on forecast outcome of Holt–Winters-No Seasonal Method. But according to the Holt–Winters-Additive Method and Holt–Winters-Multiplicative Method, the income inequality of total resident will increase. It will ascend from 0.47950 in 2009 to 0.51639 based on forecast outcome of Holt–Winters-Additive Method, and ascend from 0.48145 in 2009 to 0.51767 based on forecast outcome of Holt–Winters-Multiplicative Method. So we conclude that the change trend of income inequality of total resident is uncertain, it may rise or decline.

7.3.4 *Forecast Outcome of Urban–Rural Income Inequality*

Forecasting urban–rural income inequality is made in the same way. The outcomes of estimation are given in Table 7.3.4 and the results of prediction are illustrated in Fig. 7.3.4.

Table 7.3.4 Outcomes of forecast estimation for urban–rural income inequality

Estimate coefficient	Double exponential smoothing	Holt–Winters-No Seasonal	Holt–Winters-Additive	Holt–Winters-Multiplicative
α	0.9100	1.0000	1.0000	1.0000
β	–	1.0000	0.9000	0.8800
γ	–	–	0.0000	0.0000
Sum of squares of residue	0.87559	0.48674	0.69745	0.70373

Source: Authors' measurement by urban–rural income ratio in Table 5.1.1

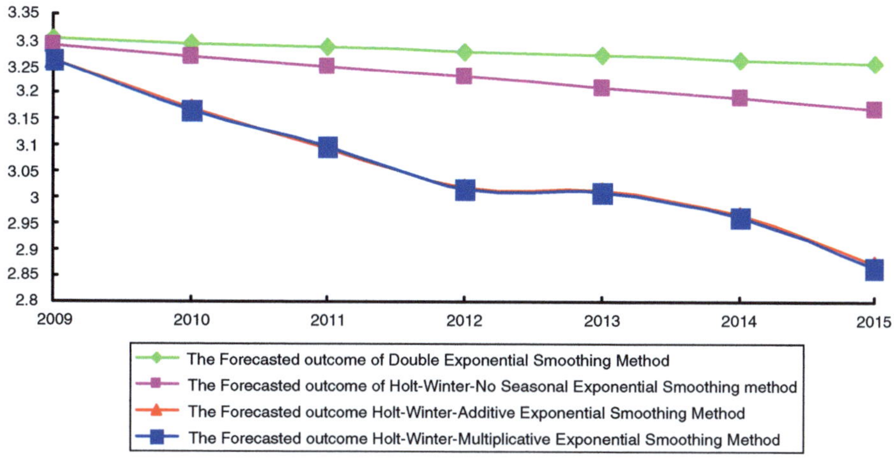

Fig. 7.3.4 Forecast value of urban–rural income ratio 2009–2015. Source: Table A.10

From Table A.10 and Fig. 7.3.4, we may see that Chinese urban–rural income inequality will steadily decrease in the coming years. By the year of 2015, the urban–rural income ratio will reach 2.9–3.2. To be exact, it will decline from 3.30 in 2009 to 3.26 in 2015 based on Double Exponential Smoothing forecast, from 3.29 in 2009 to 3.17 in 2015 based on Holt–Winters-No Seasonal forecast, from 3.26 in 2007 to 2.87 in 2015 based on Holt–Winters-Additive forecast, and it will decrease from 3.26 in 2009 to 2.87 in 2015 based on Holt–Winters-Multiplicative forecast.

In summary, in the coming years, the income inequality of urban and rural resident will rise, but not fast. The change of income inequality of total resident is uncertain, which will lie in many other conditions, especially in the urban–rural income inequality. The urban–rural income inequality will decline in the future which will maybe result in the decline of income inequality of total resident.

Chapter 8
Conclusions and Policy Suggestions

As the concluding part of the book, this chapter will draw main conclusions based on previous theoretical and empirical analysis and look into their policy suggestions as well.

8.1 Main Conclusions

8.1.1 Conclusions for Income Inequality of Urban Resident

1. Since the system reform, income inequality of Chinese urban resident is on the rise as demonstrated in the first half of inverted U curve. Our measurement shows that by 2008 the Gini coefficient of urban resident's income amounted to 0.3801, approximating the cutoff point of 0.4, which is internationally referred to as extreme income inequality, but compared with 0.4262 the cutoff point of Chinese polarization (Chen Zongsheng and Zhou Yunbo 2002), there is still more room for growth. In the coming 7–8 years, the momentum of widening income inequality of urban resident will not be held back.
2. In regard to income sources, wage is still the leading source, but in the future, its share in total income will decline by degrees. The share of credit income comes the next and will increase. Transfer income comes the third, but will see a slight decline. Business net income and property income, though taking a small part in total income, will see growing share.
3. In terms of contribution to total income inequality, credit income is the biggest contributor due to its extreme inequality and will increase greatly. Wage income is the second contributor, but its contribution is on the decline. Transfer income comes the third, of which pension contributes the most, but social relief and insurance has a negative contribution, though unnoticeably. Business income and property income, although making small contribution, have an increasing sway.

Y. Zhou and Y. Qin, *Empirical Analysis on Income Inequality of Chinese Residents*, Gu Shutang Acad Fund Econ, DOI 10.1007/978-3-642-24952-5_8,

4. In light of marginal effect, that of wage income is negative for the years under review, meaning the rise of its share in total income will offset total income inequality. But in the long run, its marginal effect tends to shrink. Credit income has a positive effect due to its highly unequal distribution pattern, suggesting the rise of its share in total income will enlarge total income inequality. Transfer income has a negative marginal effect, and business net income and proper income both have a positive marginal effect which, in the long run, will increase.
5. Decomposing the enlargement of Gini coefficients of urban resident's income from 2002 to 2006 shows that by and large, structural effect is responsible for the enlargement of income inequality, whereas distribution effect and interaction effect play to the contrary, a conclusion quite at odds with our previous study (Chen Zongsheng and Zhou Yunbo 2002). Among all the income sources, structural effect and distribution effect of wage and transfer incomes help countervail the income inequality, considering the three effects blended, while credit, business, and property incomes become the leading force shooting up the income inequality.
6. For the household features, that influencing urban income inequality the most comes from share of wage earners, regional economic development level, householder's education, and householder's industry. Share of wage earner becoming the main driver demonstrates that under current economic framework with public economy playing the leading role, labor income remains the major source for urban households. Therefore, the number of wage earners in a family determines urban income inequality. The driver of regional economic development level suggests that a good part of urban income inequality is accounted for by regional inequality. The driver of householder's education indicates an increasingly better urban labor market. And finally the driver of householder's industry reveals a deep income inequality between different industries.
7. As for the change in urban income inequality from 2002 to 2006, the variations in householder's education and age, and the number of state-owned employees in a family are the main drivers of income inequality, while regional economic development level, share of persons with income in household, householder's industry, householder's seniority, and sexuality play to the contrary effect.
8. In light of personal features of urban resident, his profession, education, and industry are the top three drivers of urban income inequality. If grouped by duty, the income inequality among differing duties contributes more than 20%; if grouped by education, the income inequality between different education contributes about 20%; if grouped by industry, the income inequality contributes around 18%, another evidence that for urban income inequality, that from industry can never be ignored.
9. Regarding the macroeconomic variables affecting urban income inequality, since the reform, the economic development plays a striking role in increasing income inequality. No inverted U relation between the two is spotted. In other words, no evidence in the change in urban income inequality has been found to substantiate the inverted U hypothesis. Next, foreign trade has obviously stepped up the urban income inequality, indicating that its development gives rise to income gap between

sectors inside and outside foreign trade and contributes to widening urban income inequality. Finally, inflation rate has a noted contribution to urban income inequality.

8.1.2 Conclusions for Income Inequality of Rural Resident

1. After 1978 Chinese rural income inequality has been increasing as demonstrated in the first half of inverted U curve. According to our measurement by officially published statistics, by 2008 the Gini of rural income inequality was 0.42616, beyond the cutoff Gini of 0.4, which is internationally reckoned as extreme income inequality, and approximates the cutoff point of Chinese polarization (Chen Zongsheng and Zhou Yunbo 2002). In the coming 7–8 years, the momentum of widening urban income inequality will continue.
2. Of the total rural income, agricultural income and non-agricultural income each take more than 40%. In relatively developed coastal cities like Tianjin, non-agricultural income has taken a share of more than 60%, while that of agricultural income is only about 30%. Concerning non-agricultural income, wage constitutes the major part, and non-agricultural household business income comes the next. Property income from interest rate, dividend, and rents, though having a small share, has a large potential for growth. It has doubled for the time under review.
3. Viewing the contribution to total income inequality, non-agricultural income takes the lead, and its marginal effect is kept negative over the time under review, or, the rise of its share in total income will reduce total income inequality. The conclusion is a bit different from previous studies (Knight and Song 1993; Rozell 1994; Zhang Ping 1996; Cheng 1996). Part of it is attributed to different sources of data, time period under review, levels of research samples, and range of non-agricultural income.
4. Of non-agricultural income, rural labor's wage from employment in local enterprises makes the largest contribution to total income inequality and its marginal effect changes from positive to negative for the time under review. In other words, this income raise plays a changing role from widening income inequality to its reduction. The contribution of rural household's income from non-agricultural household business to the income inequality comes the next and is on the rise. Its marginal effect is kept positive and growing. The third comes farmer's wage from employment in local non-enterprises whose marginal effect changes from positive to negative. Farmer's income from outside employment has a slight impact on total income inequality and its marginal effect remains negative as opposed to underdeveloped regions in mid-west China.
5. For the time under review, as a result of surging inequality in distribution, the contribution of agricultural income to total income inequality sees a comparatively large increase and its marginal effect changes from negative to positive.
6. The contribution rate of property income is slightly down for the time under review and its marginal effect changes from positive to negative. This is not like

that in developed and other developing countries, and also different from the change in urban income inequality in China.

7. Transfer income provided by government makes an increasing contribution to total income inequality, and its marginal effect is kept positive. That means, at present time, increasing subsidies on this income by government cannot reduce income inequality; instead, it works out to the contrary. Therefore, we need further investigation into rural transfer payment system in a bid to truly meet its target of relieving the poor and the low-income groups.
8. Decomposing the change in rural income inequality from 2000 to 2003 shows that the change in distribution pattern of each income component is mainly responsible for the enlarged total income inequality. That is to say, for the growing total income inequality from 2000 to 2003, distribution effect takes the predominant responsibility. The change in each income component's share in total income softens the income inequality, though to small effect. As to each income component, agricultural income contributes the most, and non-agricultural one comes the second, while income from friends and relatives as giveaway somehow countervails total income inequality.
9. In terms of macroeconomic factors that affected rural industrial structure, labor transfer from agricultural to non-agricultural industries is still at a phase of increasing rural income inequality. The regression coefficient of per capita GDP is positive, implying that economic development helps widen rural income inequality in some degree. Its square is negative, but it does not pass the significance test, which suggests that like the change in urban income inequality, by far, no evidence about the change in rural income inequality has been found to support the inverted U hypothesis. Foreign trade and inflation do not have a significant impact on rural income inequality.

8.1.3 Conclusions for Income Inequality of Total Resident

1. Since the system reform, China's income inequality of total resident has been rising as demonstrated in the first half of the inverted U curve typical of income inequality in public economy as a result of double transition. Influenced also by the phasic development of system reform, the enlargement of income inequality of total resident undergoes stage-like development. Calculated by urban/rural weighted method, by 2008 the Gini coefficient of income of total resident climbed to 0.46809, far ahead of the benchmark Gini coefficient 0.4 for internationally accepted extreme inequality, and also larger than 0.4262 which is reckoned as the benchmark Gini coefficient for Chinese polarization (Chen Zongsheng and Zhou Yunbo 2002). All told, it is certain that income inequality of China's total resident has come into the stage of polarization and in the coming 7–8 years will gain rising momentum.
2. Quantitative measurement shows that over the 30 years from 1978 to 2006, the urban–rural income inequality contributed to total income inequality by 56% on

average, ranging from 40 to 60%. It is because the urban–rural income inequality accounts for the most part of income inequality of total resident that the change of the two is basically in step. Of the added value of income inequality of total resident from 1978 to 2006, 60% was contributed by the urban–rural income inequality.

3. Urban income inequality has always been smaller than rural one. Presently, the population flow caused by urbanization is entering the stage of reducing income inequality of total resident. Empirical analysis shows that there arises an inverted U like relation between income inequality of total resident and the share of urban population. It is due to urbanization that the change in income inequality of total resident displays an inverted U relation to per capita GDP, or to put it another way, the inverted U hypothesis for income inequality under public economy is testified to be true. However, it does not have a strong showing.
4. The widening urban–rural gap and the priority transfer from rural areas to cities and town in system reform play a remarkable role in increasing income inequality of total resident, the policy of opening up to the world helps to certain extent enlarge income inequality of total resident, and the fluctuation of the macroeconomy influences income inequality of total resident only insignificantly.

8.1.4 Conclusions for the Impact of Rent-Seeking Activities on Income Inequality

1. By and large, in the new century, tax dodging and avoidance, smuggling, and corruption have shown varying scenarios. As for tax dodging and avoidance, that in underground economy witnesses a sharp decline, while personal income tax suffers a heavy loss. All told, tax dodging and avoidance is somehow curbed. As for smuggling, thanks to the reinforced strike on the part of the government, it is a bit held back. By contrast, the problem of corruption in form of bribery on the part of party and government officials and leaders of enterprises and institutions is running wild, with respect to either case values or the number and rank of officials involved.
2. Such rent-seeking activities as tax dodging and avoidance, smuggling, corruption, and group spending affect urban income inequality the most, multiplying the latter by 24% on average. They help widen rural income inequality by 17% on average, and income inequality of total resident by 13%, a conclusion in accordance with previous study (Chen Zongsheng and Zhou Yunbo 2002). In the long run, rent-seeking activities will see a shrinking impact on income inequality.
3. Two reasons may account for the birth and growth of rent-seeking activities since the system reform. First, the interim institutional arrangements in transitional economy gives rise to unequilibrium and instability, which in turn trigger

economic bodies' speculation motive. This is the subjective factor. Second, institutional defect in transitional economy creates space for rent-seeking activities. To root them out, we have to resort to the institutional reform.

8.2 Policy Suggestions

Given the fact that the income inequality of urban, rural, and total residents are constantly increasing, we make a point of "controlling the two ends and developing the medium" as the fundamental principle for regulating China's income distribution. In other words, by promoting the income of low-income and the poor groups, containing the rise of the income of high-income group, and developing the mid-income group, an olive-like or lozenge-like pattern of distribution is to be formed.

8.2.1 *Policies for Promoting the Income of Low-Income and the Poor Group*

1. *The central government and local governments need to increase fiscal spending on social security in a bid to improve the urban and rural social security systems.* Social security system, as part of income redistribution, is an important system and policy for a government to provide assistance to the low-income and the poor population. Since the system reform, China's social security system has been improved in that urban residents now get out of unit security system and are basically in social security or governmental security system. A social security system covering old age pension, medical care, unemployment, and the minimum living security has been established, though not without problems, such as the small coverage, the low security level, thin availability of medical treatment, and the exclusion of rural residents out of the system. The governments need to inject more money to social security, and the central government and provincial governments need to increase the fiscal spending on social security, especially on rural social security to solve the problems that the capital used for rural social security scarce and unstable.
2. *Targeted anti-poverty polices for the different low-income and the poor groups.* The current anti-poverty policies fall into two categories: one is development oriented, the other relief oriented. The former refers to the policies that are targeted at boosting economic development in poverty-struck areas, like petty loan and work relief. The latter purports to provide financial aids and material assistance for the poor population to guarantee a basic living. In fact, in order to improve the effect of poverty alleviation policies, the poor families and population must be differentiated. For those who are temporarily bankrupted because of bad management, development-oriented policies fit in, while for those who are

stuck in longstanding poverty because of serious disease and disability, relief-oriented policies come into rescue.

3. *The policies of increasing employment for the low-income group in urban and rural areas.* The leading reasons for urban and rural poverty are unemployment and inadequate employment. Obviously, to increase employment rate is the main way out. It may include improving the urban and rural labor markets, building unemployment insurance system, undertaking public projects aimed at improving employment and creating employment opportunities for the low-income and the poor population, developing self-employed and private economy, and developing labor-intensive industries to provide a variety of avenues for employment.
4. *Education policies for the low-income group.* Surveys on the low-income and the poor group show that children's schooling has been a great burden for these families. Considering the significance of education to urban and rural residents' income level, the government should warrant education for these children lest they should fall out of schools and bogged down in perpetual poverty. Besides, the government should ensure that they have easy access to technical education and training.

8.2.2 Policies for Regulating the Income of High-Income Group

1. *An all-around, normative, and efficient taxation regulation mechanism should be established particularly targeted at the high-income group.* Imposing personal income tax should be in more tightened control and under better surveillance. New avenues of tax need to be found in spending and property to regulate high income. For instance, special consumption tax may be imposed on fancy spending affordable only by the high-income group. Taxes on real estates, financial assets gains, donation, and inheritance should also be imposed. Some new taxes have just come out, like interest tax, but some are still in consideration.
2. *Normalize industry income distribution to eliminate high income in some monopoly industries.* Unreasonable income inequality exists across the different industries. In some industries like post and telecom, electricity, and communication, employees have extremely high income. As a matter of fact, in market economy, income inequality of one kind or another inevitably exists across different industry. The important thing is whether it is market behavior or governmental operation. Since China is now in a transitional economy, some industries are put under government's protection, forming irrational monopoly which should be rectified. To those industries under monopoly price protection and to some noncompetitive industries, monopoly income tax should be imposed. Although it is necessary to support and protect some industries, market access barriers must be cleared and additional personal income via industrial monopoly should never be permitted.

3. *Strike heavy blow on unreasonable and illegal income of high-income group.*[1] All statistics point to that rent-seeking activities are mainly committed by the high-income group. Apart from tax imposition on their normal income, efficient measures must be adopted to collect their abnormal and even illegal income. The government should divert their capitals originally aimed at rent-seeking to productive investment and thus increase employment opportunities.

8.2.3 Policies for Developing Mid-Income Group

The growth of mid-income group is of great importance to a country's healthy economy and social stability. But as to the coverage of mid-income group, there is not a clear definition. Chen Xinnian (2005), judging by China's urban and rural income levels, China's specific stage of economic development, and the reference to World Bank standard, defines that the mid-income group may cover individuals with yearly income from 30,000 to 100,000 yuan, families with per capita disposable yearly income from 18,000 to 54,000 yuan, and families with yearly income between 53,700 and 160,000 yuan. Given this standard, the mid-income group in contemporary China takes about 7% of its total population. A small group it is indeed and needs favorable policies for growth, which include:

1. *Increasing labor income's share in national income distribution.* Statistics show that the share of labor income in China's domestic income distribution is about 30–40% and is on the decline over the past few years, whereas in Europe and America it takes a share of up to 60–70%. We have to considerably raise the levels of labor income so as to promote its share in national income distribution.
2. *Developing modern service sectors.* Data of developed countries show that the majority of mid-income group are those intermediate and senior management engaged in banking, insurance and securities, information transmission, computer and software, scientific research, and technological service, or so-called "high-ranking white collars." At present time the added value of China's service sector take only about 40% of GDP, let alone modern services. In this sense, China's modern service sectors have huge potentials for development which will undoubtedly be advantageous to cultivating mid-income group.
3. *Creating healthy business environment and encouraging private business.* Data from Social Economic Survey Division of National Statistic Bureau (2006) show that in China's mid-income group, a large part of them are the employers of self-employed and private business. So, the government needs to create a healthy business environment and encourage private economy. The present enthusiasm of sitting for recruitment examinations for public service reveals that a fairly

[1] For policies concerning how to curb and eliminate rent-seeking activities, we will go into details in due course.

large number of college grads are eager to enter government departments and institutions, an indicator of a bad business environment. The government should lift all the irrational restraints on private business registration so as to cut off their transaction cost and spur the development of small and intermediate enterprises.

4. *Enhancing investment of human resource and cultivating a life-learning mechanism throughout the society.* In market economy, personal income is positively correlated to his education. Research on the population features of China's mid-income group indicates (Anhui Survey Team of National Statistic Bureau 2006) that in the mid-income group, most are from colleges and universities, scientific research unit, and sci-tech enterprises. Therefore, to enhance investment in human resource is the only policy in the long run for upgrading urban and rural income levels and making the mid-income group. In addition, the increasingly fast speed of technological progress and social change requires advanced vocational education and adult education and encourages continuous education, thus forming a life-learning mechanism throughout the whole society.
5. *Improving market system, opening more investment channels for residents, and cultivating sanitary investment habits.* Thirty years of market reform has seen an emerging socialist market economy in which residents' investment channels have been widened, though not without problems. The capital market, in particular, is far from mature regarding both channels and normalization. To improve the market system and open more investment channels for residents is to increase their income sources so that they have not only labor returns, but also capital gains.

8.2.4 Policies for Reducing Urban–Rural Income Inequality

Too large urban–rural income inequality has long been the biggest headache in China's income distribution, but unfortunately, also a long-neglected issue. What underpins the too large urban–rural inequality is the discriminative dual administration system of urban–rural divide. Consequently, the key to reducing urban–rural income inequality is to end the dual administration system, on the one hand, and boost rural economy and upgrade rural income level, on the other hand. Detailed polices include:

1. *Lifting barriers of urban–rural divide.* The separate household registration system underpins China's dual administration system of urban–rural divide. The system prevents rural labors from transferring to cities and towns, produces multitudinous surplus labors in rural areas, and restricts the improvement of farming productivity. Obviously barriers of urban–rural divide must be lifted so that all production factors and labor forces should enjoy free flow between the urban areas and the rural areas, urbanization progress should be quickened, and the dual economic framework should be broken.

2. *Speeding up urbanization in rural areas and transferring surplus rural labors.* Since China is a great farming country, alongside transferring rural surplus labors to cities and towns, another important way out is to speed up urbanization in rural areas where some sparsely scattered small villages may be administratively canceled so as to develop other sizable ones into towns. However, considering the vast rural territory and the complication involved, developing small towns should be motivated by a sustainable urbanization movement.
3. *Quicken the pace of industrialized and modernized agriculture.* A key factor behind the overlarge urban–rural inequality is the relatively low level of farming productivity. So an important policy for reducing urban–rural income inequality is to step up agricultural industrialization and modernization to improve farming productivity. Policies are: first, to encourage farmers to develop businesses like household ranch and fishery alongside traditional planting; second, to further improve rural land market so that the land may be concentrated on the more specialized and land scale operation may be realized; to give priority to publicizing and developing farming sci-tech, enhance farmers' sci-tech awareness, and cultivate the agriculture scientifically; continue the training of agricultural technicians and build up a group of farmers and technicians qualified with scientific technology.
4. *Developing non-agricultural industry in rural areas.* Statistics show that in farmers' net income in 2006, 49.75% came from non-agriculture. It goes without saying that to develop non-agricultural economy is of great significance to increasing rural households' income. Measures need to be taken as follows. First, great efforts should be taken to develop township, self-employed, and private enterprises in conjunction with privileged policies in credit, taxation, and talent flow. Second, the countries may set up a variety of fair trade markets, specialized wholesale markets, and technical markets with a view to improving rural market system.
5. *Developing rural education.* Backward education in rural areas underpins the underdeveloped rural economy. The only way to reduce the gap between the rich and the poor is to upgrade the human capital reserve, and increase investment in fundamental education in particular in rural areas, especially in the poorest provinces. Otherwise, the publicity of agricultural sci-tech will be held back, and the development of non-agricultural industry and diversified operations will prove an abortion. Moreover, to develop rural education is to help farmers get rid of ignorance and embrace new concepts of market economy, so that they could try all means to improve their income level. To that effect, the government should waive the tuition and fees for primary and secondary schooling in rural areas, completely lifting the educational burden for rural residents.
6. *Making vigorous effort to promote the construction of socialist new countryside and put more funds into rural infrastructural construction.* It is up to all levels of governments to formulate favorable fiscal and taxation policies to promote the construction of socialist new countryside and increase investment in rural infrastructural construction in road, bridge, railway, electricity, and water power. Lessons in developed countries demonstrate that more investment in

rural infrastructural construction proves fruitful in helping farmers getting rid of poverty. The practice of active fiscal policy in China tells the same story, only that it is a longstanding process and cannot be achieved at one stroke.

8.2.5 Policies for Eliminating Rent-Seeking Activities

1. *Severely punish those who undertake various rent-seeking activities.* China has a folksay, "to administrate the troubled times with severe punishment," severe punishment must be imposed on those engaged in tax dodging and avoidance, corruption, and smuggling. In a China with relatively low level of economic growth and overall quality of the people, severe punishment is necessary to massively cut down and even eliminate various abnormal and illegal rent-seeking activities.
2. *Cut the number of government-controlled resources and diminish government's intervention in economic life.* Due to the lingering impact of planning economy, the government's intervention in economy remains a serious problem. Modern rent-seeking theory holds that government's intervention gives birth to corruption, as demonstrated by lessons in developing and emerging industrialized countries. A transformation of the government's function from intervening economy to service economy is necessary. The government should withdraw its distribution of resources and reform the approval procedures by simplifying the procedures so that corruption on the part of government officials should be stopped.
3. *Establish efficient social credit system.* A successful market economy relies on the good credit of economic bodies, but rent-seeking as a form of speculation in itself falls short of good credit. So a good credit system must be established as soon as possible. For this purpose, we need to set up personal and corporate credit accounts which record violation of laws of the concerned parties which should be made public if there is any. In addition, government's behavior should be standardized, transparent, and legalized. Finally, policies concerned should be stable for certain time. Policies subject to changes signal bad credit and become a vital drive for economic bodies to seek after short-term speculation activities.
4. *Make full use of the public and the media's role of monitoring to ensure transparent government's operations.* A mechanism should be established in which the general public and the media play a role in monitoring the government's operations. The public's right to know should be respected. Competitive bidding and public auction in government's procurement and some engineering projects should be adopted. A system of declaration and auditing on government officials' property should be set up. The party and government's fiscal budget and actual spending must be made public or be based on hearing system. More journalistic freedom should be endowed to mass media.

5. *Improve legal system.* Modern rent-seeking theory tells us that only when a healthy legal system supportive of market economy is constituted can various rent-seeking activities in a transit economy be rooted out. A healthy legal system creates an institutional environment for efficient resource allotment and transaction cost reduction, protects social equity, and boosts economic growth. Some scholars consider the construction of healthy legal system is the top issue on China's coming reform agenda since it runs through the whole process of legislation, jurisdiction, and law-abiding awareness and it is an indispensable requisite for guaranteeing a highly efficient and orderly market mechanism and a sustainable economic growth. In one sense, we may say legislation construction is easier, but jurisdiction and law-abiding awareness is more time assuming, since the latter is concerned with casting off traditional cultural mentality incompatible with legal society, as well as with changing the vested interest pattern. That is the difference between law and rule by law. Hence, jurisdiction construction and improving law-abiding awareness should come as the predominant task on China's current agenda of building a healthy market economy.

Appendix A

Table A.1 Employment in self-employed and private business 2000–2006 (100,000 people)

Year	Number of township enterprises	Urban			Rural		
		Employment in self-employed	Private business		Employment in self-employed	Private business	
			Employment	Investors		Employment	Investors
2000	2,085	2,136	1,268	246.9	2,934	1,139	148.5
2001	2,116	2,131	1,527	298.8	2,629	1,187	162.1
2002	2,133	2,269	1,999	419.4	2,474	1,411	203.5
2003	2,185	2,377	2,545	520.0	2,260	1,754	252.9
2004	2,213	2,421	2,994	610.4	2,066	2,024	338.2
2005	2,250	2,778	3,458	721.0	2,123	2,366	389.0
2006	2,314	3,012	3,954	852.9	2,147	2,632	418.7

Source: *China Yearbook of Statistics 2001–2007*

Table A.2 Per capita illegal gains from tax dodging and avoidance in self-employed and private business 2000–2006

Year	Per capita illegal gains (yuan)
2000	18,000
2001	17,000
2002	19,000
2003	16,000
2004	15,000
2005	7,000
2006	15,000

Source: Authors' estimation from data and cases provided by tax inspection Departments of some districts and counties in Tianjin

Y. Zhou and Y. Qin, *Empirical Analysis on Income Inequality of Chinese Residents*, Gu Shutang Acad Fund Econ, DOI 10.1007/978-3-642-24952-5,

Table A.3 Aggregate number of urban and rural party and government officials (2000–2006)

Year	Urban party and government officials (10,000)	Rural PGO			
		Number of towns	Number of leaders	Number of villagers committees	Number of leaders
2000	1,419.45	43,735	524,820	734,715	3,673,575
2001	1,421.32	40,161	481,932	709,257	3,546,285
2002	1,424.84	39,054	468,648	694,515	3,472,575
2003	1,422.26	38,028	456,336	678,589	3,362,945
2004	1,420.59	36,952	443,424	652,718	3,263,590
2005	1,421.37	35,509	426,108	640,139	3,200,695
2006	1,418.62	34,756	417,072	637,011	3,185,055

Source: Urban party and government officials is the authors' estimation from data provided by Tianjin Bureau of Personnel, rural party and government officials are the authors' own estimation. Based on our survey on some towns and villagers committees, there are in general 10 to 15 leaders in a town (we take 12 here) and five leaders in a villagers committee. Then according to the numbers of towns and villagers committees in *China Yearbook of Statistics*, the number of rural party and government officials can be roughly estimated

Table A.4 Cases of corruption accepted by procuratorial organs 2000–2005

Year	Number of cases put on record	Number of people involved	Case value (100 m yuan)	Per capita money involved (10,000)
2000	37,183	41,377	44.2	10.68
2001	36,447	–	41	–
2002	34,716	38,022	41	10.78
2003	31,953	34,922	41	11.74
2004	30,548	35,031	42.9	12.25
2005	28,322	33,366	64	19.18

Source: *China Yearbook of Laws 2001–2006*

Table A.5 Estimated per capita illegal income of corrupted officials 2000–2005

Year	Per capita illegal income (yuan)
2000	26,700
2001	26,825
2002	26,950
2003	29,350
2004	30,625
2005	47,950
2006	43,500

Source: Data about 2000–2005 are converted in proportion to that in Table A.4. Table 6.1.4 gives per capita money involved, but they cannot be taken as per capita illegal income of corrupted officials, for most corruptions are not committed in a single year. Zongsheng and Zhou Yunbo (2002) suggested 2.5 as the conversion coefficient. But here, considering the cost of corrupted officials, we take 4. To divide the per capita money involved in Table A.5 with 4 and round it up, we have the per capita illegal income. Data of 2006 are estimated from cases provided by procuratorial organs in Tianjin

Table A.6 Personal income transferred from group spending 2000–2006

Year	Administrative fees (100 m yuan)	Added personal income of PGO on 15% conversion rate (yuan)
2000	2,768.22	2,925
2001	3,512.49	3,707
2002	4,101.32	4,318
2003	4,691.26	4,948
2004	5,521.98	5,831
2005	6,512.34	6,873
2006	7,571.05	8,005

Source: *China Yearbook of Statistics 2001–2007*

Table A.7 Forecast value of Gini coefficient of urban resident's income 2009–2015

Year	Double exponential smoothing	Holt–Winters-No Seasonal	Holt–Winters-Additive	Holt–Winters-Multiplicative
2009	0.38022	0.38792	0.39191	0.39287
2010	0.37921	0.39527	0.39667	0.39687
2011	0.37820	0.40263	0.40507	0.40806
2012	0.37719	0.40998	0.40903	0.40944
2013	0.37618	0.41733	0.42151	0.42184
2014	0.37517	0.42469	0.43282	0.43414
2015	0.37416	0.43204	0.43758	0.43769

Source: Authors' estimation from data in Table 5.1.1

Table A.8 Forecast value of Gini coefficient of rural resident's income 2009–2015

Year	Double exponential smoothing	Holt–Winters-No Seasonal	Holt–Winters-Additive	Holt–Winters-Multiplicative
2009	0.43547	0.43359	0.44088	0.44497
2010	0.44305	0.44065	0.44569	0.44834
2011	0.45063	0.44772	0.44539	0.44404
2012	0.45820	0.45478	0.45034	0.44749
2013	0.46578	0.46184	0.46439	0.46532
2014	0.47336	0.46890	0.47687	0.48173
2015	0.48094	0.47596	0.48169	0.48477

Source: Authors' estimation from data in Table 5.1.1

Table A.9 Forecast value of Gini coefficient of total resident's income 2009–2015

Year	Double exponential smoothing	Holt–Winters-No Seasonal	Holt–Winters-Additive	Holt–Winters-Multiplicative
2009	0.46785	0.46787	0.47950	0.48145
2010	0.46760	0.46764	0.48221	0.48311
2011	0.46736	0.46742	0.48532	0.48530
2012	0.46712	0.46719	0.48793	0.48492
2013	0.46687	0.46696	0.50228	0.50236
2014	0.46663	0.46674	0.51369	0.51619
2015	0.46639	0.46651	0.51639	0.51747

Source: Authors' estimation from data in Table 5.1.1

Table A.10 Forecast value of urban–rural income ratio (2009–2015)

Year	Double exponential smoothing	Holt–Winters-No Seasonal	Holt–Winters-Additive	Holt–Winters-Multiplicative
2009	3.30	3.29	3.26	3.26
2010	3.30	3.27	3.17	3.16
2011	3.29	3.25	3.09	3.10
2012	3.28	3.23	3.02	3.02
2013	3.27	3.21	3.01	3.01
2014	3.26	3.19	2.97	2.96
2015	3.26	3.17	2.87	2.87

Source: Authors' estimation from data in Table 5.1.1

References

Aaberge R (2001) Axiomatic characterization of the Gini coefficient and Lorenz curve orderings. J Econ Theory 101:115–132

Adams RH (1994) Non-farm income and inequality in rural Pakistan. J Dev Stud 31(1):110–133

Adams RH (1996) Remittances, inequality and asset accumulation: the case of rural Pakistan. In: O'Connor D, Farsakh L (eds) Development strategy, employment and migration. OECD, Paris, pp 149–170

Adams RH Jr, He JJ (1995) Sources of income inequality and poverty in rural Pakistan. International Food Policy Research Institute, Washington, DC

Adelmen Irma, David Sunding (1987) Economic policy and income distribution in China. J Comp Econ 11:444–461

Anand Sudhir (1983) Inequality and Poverty in Malaysia: Measurement and Decomposition, Oxford University Press, London

Anand Sudhir, Kanbur SMR (1993) The Kuznets process and the inequality—development relationship. J Dev Econ 40(1):25–52

Anhui Survey Team of National Statistic Bureau (2006) "The Research of the Urban Middle", in China's Social & Economic Focus Report, China Statistics Press, 2006, Oct.

Aronson JR, Lambert PJ (1994) Decomposing the Gini coefficient to reveal the vertical, horizontal, and reranking effects of income taxation. Natl Tax J 47(2):273–294

Arrow KJ (1970) Public investment, the rate of return and optimal fiscal policy. John Hopkins University Press, Baltimore, MD

Athar Hussain, Peter Lanjouw, Nicholas Stern (1994) Income inequalities in China: evidence from household survey data. World Dev 22(12):1947–1957

Atkinson AB (1969) Poverty in Britain and the reform of social security. Cambridge University Press, London

Atkinson AB (1970) On the measurement of inequality. J Econ Theory 2:244–263

Atkinson AB (1987) On the measurement of poverty. Econometrica 55(4):749–764

Bai Nansheng, Song Hongyuan (2002) Return to the countryside or move to the city? A study on the backflow of China's rural labors. Chinese Fiscal Economic Publisher, Beijing

Barro RJ (1990) Government spending in a simple model of endogeneous growth. J Polit Econ 98(5), Part 2: The problem of development: a conference of the institute for the study of free enterprise system: S103–S125

Basu K (1985) Poverty measurement: a decomposition of the normalization axiom. Econometrica 53(6):1439–1444

Bhagwati Jagdish (1982) Directly unproductive profit-seeking (DUP) activities. J Polit Econ 90:988–1002

Bhattacharyya A, Parker E (1999) Labor productivity and migration in Chinese agriculture: a stochastic frontier approach. China Econ Rev 10:59–74

Y. Zhou and Y. Qin, *Empirical Analysis on Income Inequality of Chinese Residents*, Gu Shutang Acad Fund Econ, DOI 10.1007/978-3-642-24952-5,

Bin Jiancheng (2000) Studies on Chinese residents' income inequality. Chinese Cultural Association Publisher, Beijing

Bourguignon F, Chakravarty SR (2003) The measurement of multidimensional poverty. J Econ Inequal 1:25–49

Bowerman BL, O'Connell, RT (1979) "Forecasting and time series", Duxbury, Massachusetts, North Scituate

Bowlus AJ, Sicular T (2003) Moving toward markets? Labor allocation in rural China. J Dev Econ 73:561–583

Cai Renhua (ed) (1998) Practical encyclopaedia of Chinese medical security system reform. Chinese Personnel Press, Beijing

Cai Fang (2002) Report of population and labor force—the solution for rural and urban employment. Social Science Academic Press, Beijing

Cai Fang (2005) Why doesn't labor flow reduce urban–rural income inequality? Theor Front 20:18–20

Cai Fang, Wang Dewen (2002) Comparative advantages difference, variation and their impact on regional gap. Chin Soc Sci 5

Cai Fang, Chen Fan, Zhang Chewei (2001) Government's funding policy based on development-oriented poverty relief and investment efficiency. Chin Youth Polit J 3

Cameron LA (2000) Poverty and inequality in java: examining the impact of the changing age, educational and industrial structure. J Dev Econ 62:149–180

Cantó O (2003) Finding out the routes to escape poverty: the relevance of demographic vs. labor market events in Spain. Rev Income Wealth 49(4):569–588

Cashin P, Sahay R (1996) Internal migration, center-state grants and economic growth in the states of India. IMF Staff Papers 43(1)

Catin M et al (2005) Openness, Industrialization and geographic concentration of activities in China. World Bank Policy Research Working Paper 3706, 01 Sep 2005

Chakravarty SR (1997) On Shorrock's reinvestigation of the Sen's poverty index. Econometrica 65(5):1241–1242

Champernowne DJ (1953) A model of income distribution. Econ J 63(250):318–350

Chen Chi (2000) Review of small loan in China. Agric Econ 6

Chen Zongsheng (1991) Income distribution in economic development under public ownership. Shanghai Sanlian Bookshop and Shanghai People Press, Shanghai

Chen Zongsheng (1994) Income distribution in economic growth. Shanghai & Sanlian Press, Shanghai

Chen Zongsheng (1997) Differences in the distribution of income of Chinese urban residents status, trends and influencing factors. Econ Res J (3):21–31

Chen Zongsheng (1997) The urban China's income gap: actual condition, trend and influences—a case form Tianjin. Econ Res J (3):21–39

Chen Zongsheng (1999) Reform, development and income distribution. Shanghai Fudan University Press, Shanghai

Chen Zongsheng (2000a) Further studies on Chinese residents' income inequality. Econ Res 7

Chen Zongsheng (2000c) Income inequality, poverty and unemployment. Nankai University Press, Tianjin

Chen Zongsheng (2002) On several methods in the study of inverted U curve of income inequality and polarization. Chin Soc Sci 5

Chen Xinnian (2005) On mid-income group. Chinese Planning Press, Beijing

Chen Zongsheng, Cao Guiquan (2000) Research on Chinese regional gap and the great exploration of the west. Prospect of the Bohai Rim Economy 2

Chen Zongsheng, Li Defu (2007) Has there been rapid productivity growth in China during its reform period? China Econ Q 1–24

Chen Zongsheng, Li Ming (2000) Study on the impact of illegal and abnormal income on income inequality. Hebei J 4

Chen Zongsheng, Wu Zhe, Xie Siquan (1999) Study on the progress of Chinese economic system marketization. Shanghai People's Publisher, Shanghai
Chen Langnan, Xie Qinghe (2002) Studies on Chinese small loan. Agric Econ Issue 3
Chen Zongsheng, Zhou Yunbo (2001a) Contribution of population features like education to urban resident's income and income inequality. Nankai Econ Stud 4:38–42
Chen Zongsheng, Zhou Yunbo (2001b) Impact of illegal and abnormal income on residents' income inequality and its economic explanation. Econ Res 4
Chen Zongsheng, Zhou Yunbo (2001c) The Impact of system reform on urban income inequality. Chin Soc Sci 6:54–62
Chen Zongsheng, Zhou Yunbo (2002) More remarks on income distribution during China's reform and development—is there polarization in China? Economy and Science Press, Beijing
Chen Zongsheng, Zhou Yunbo (2004) Income distribution during system reform and economic development in China—the status and trend of income inequality of Chinese residents. Nova Science Publisher, New York
Chen Zongsheng, Zhou Yunbo, Ren Guoqiang (2006) Main factors influencing the three non-agricultural employment avenues in rural areas Beijing. Fin Econ Res 5
Cheng YS (1996) A decomposition analysis of income inequality of Chinese rural household. China Econ Rev 7(2):155–167
Collier P, Dollar D (2002) Aid allocation and poverty reduction. Eur Econ Rev 46:1475–1500
Cook S (1999) Surplus labor and productivity in Chinese agriculture: evidence from household survey data. J Dev Stud 35:16–44
Cramer JS (1978) A function for size distribution of incomes: comment. Econometrica 46 (2):459–460
Cronin DC (1979) A function for size distribution of incomes: a further comment. Econometrica 47(3):773–774
Datt G (1998) Computational tools for poverty measurement and analysis. Discussion paper of Food Consumption and Nutrition Division of International Food Policy Research Institute, October
Datt G, Ravallion M (1992) Growth and redistribution components of changes in poverty measures: a decomposition with application to Brazil and India in the 1980s. J Dev Econ 38:275–295
Davies J, Hoy M (1995) Making inequality comparisons when Lorenz curves intersect. Am Econ Rev 85(4):980–987
De Brauw A, Rozelle S (2002) Reconciling the returns to education in rural China. Department of economics, Williams College, Working Paper, August 27
De Brauw A et al (2002) The evolution of China's rural labor markets during the reforms. J Comp Econ 30(2):329–353
De Haan A (1997) Rural–urban migration and poverty: the case of India. LDS Bull 28:35–47
Deininger K, Okidi J (2001) Growth and poverty reduction in Uganda, 1992–2000: panel data evidence. The World Bank, Washington DC and Economic Research Council, Kampala, Unpublished mimeo
Deng Xiang (2002) Decomposing Chinese regional inequality and enlightenment. Sichuan Univ J (Humanities) 2
Ding Renzhong, Chen Zhizhou, Gu Wenjun (2003) The inverted-U hypothesis and income inequality during the transformation period. Economist (6):43–49
Dollar D, Kraay A (2000) Growth is good for the poor. The World Bank, Washington, DC, Mimeo
Dong Xiaoyuan (1998) Employment and wage determination in China's rural industry: investigation using 1984–1990 panel data. J Comp Econ 28:485–501
Duan Qinglin (1999) The basic character of rural residents' income gap. Stat Decis (4):22–24
Du Xiaoshan (2004) Experiments of petty credits in rural areas. Rural Econ 8
Du Yang, Piao Zhishui (2003) Income transfer from labor transfer and change of poverty. Observation of Chinese Countryside 5

Du Yang, Piao Zhishui (2003) Migration and poverty relief—empirical proof from rural household survey. Chin Popul Sci 4
Du Zhixiong, Tang Jianhua (2001) Review of discussions on several issues about small loan. Observation of Chinese Countryside 2
Du Yang, Wang Meiyan (2004) Human capital investment and its impact on Chinese regional inequality. In: Wang Xiaolu, Fan Gang (eds) Chinese regional gap: dynamics and drivers over 20 years. Economy and Science Press, Beijing
Éltetö Ö, Frigyes E (1968) New income inequality measures as efficient tools for causal analysis and planning. Econometrica 36(2):383–396
Esteban JM, Ray D (1994) On the measurement of polarization. Econometrica 62(4):819–851
Fan Xiaoyu (2002) Analysis on China's rural labor transfer. Research Reference Documents 37
Fan Gang, Wang Xiaolu, Zhang Liwen (2003) Report on marketization relative progress in Chinese regions. Econ Res 3
Fan Shenggen, Zhang Linxiu, Zhang Xiaobo (2002) Growth, inequality and poverty in rural China: the role of public investments. International Food Policy Research Institute, Washington, DC
Fan Shenggen, Zhang Xiaobo, Robinson S (2003b) Structural change and economic growth in China. Rev Dev Econ 7(3):360–377
Fang Cheng, Zhang Xiaobo, Fan Shenggen (2002) Emergence of urban poverty and inequality in China: evidence from household survey. China Econ Rev 13(4):430–443
Fei, Ranis, Shirley (1979) Growth and the family distribution of income by factor components. Q J Econ 92:17–53
Fei JCH, Ranis G, Kuo SWY (1978) Growth and the family distribution of income by factor components. Q J Econ 92(1):17–53
Fellman J (1976) The effect of transformation on Lorenz curves. Econometrica 44(4):823–824
Finan F, Sadoulet E, de Janvry A (2005) Measuring the poverty reduction potential of land in rural Mexico. J Dev Econ 77:27–51
Fosters J, Greer J, Thorbecke E (1984) A class of decomposable poverty measures. Econometrica 52(3):761–766
Fu Daozhong (2004) Urban–rural inequality and its cause of dual fiscal policy. Fin Trade Res 2
Fu Xiaolan (2004b) Limited linkages from growth engines and regional disparities in China. J Comp Econ 32:148–164
Gastwirth JL (1971) A general definition of the Lorenz curve. Econometrica 39(6):1037–1039
Gastwirth JL (1972) The estimation of the Lorenz curve and Gini index. Rev Econ Stat 54 (3):306–316
Gastwirth JL, Glauberman M (1976) The interpolation of the Lorenz curve and Gini index from grouped data. Econometrica 44(3):479–483
Ghatak S, Levine P, Price SW (1996) Migration theories and evidence: an assessment. J Econ Surv 10(2):159–198
Ghosh B (1992) Migration-development linkages: some specific issues and practical policy measures. Int Migr 30(4):423–452
Gibson J (2001) Measuring chronic poverty without a panel. J Dev Econ 65:243–266
Gibson J, Huang J, Rozelle S (1999) Measuring inequality and poverty in urban China: can we do it as accurately, but more cheaply? A technical report of the World Bank
Gibson J, Huang J, Rozelle S (2001) Why is income inequality so low in China compared to other countries? The effect of household survey methods. Econ Lett 71:329–333
Glomm Gerhard, Ravikumar B (1992) Public versus private investment in human capital: endogenous growth and income inequality. J Polit Econ 100(4):818–834
Gordon Tullock (1967) The calculus of consent: logical foundations of constitutional democracy. University of Michigan Press, Michigan
Guo Wei (2003) Demonstration and causes of enlarged urban–rural inequality and policy adjustment. Agric Econ Issue 5
Gustafsson Björn, Li Shi (2000) Economic transformation and the gender earnings gap in urban China. J Popul Econ 13(2):305–329

Gustafsson Björn, Li Shi (2001) The anatomy of rising earnings inequality in urban China. J Comp Econ 29(1):118–135
Han Jijiang (2003) Analysis on the surplus labor force in rural China. Chin Rural Econ (5):18–22
Hare D (1999) Push versus pull factors in migration outflows and returns: determinants of migration status and spell duration among china's rural population. J Dev Stud 35(3):45–72
Harris TF, Harriman BB, Loannides YM (2000) History versus expectations: an empirical investigation. Working paper 2000–14
Hendel I, Shapira J, Willen P (2005) Education opportunity and income inequality. Public Policy Discussion Papers of Federal Reserve Bank of Boston, 04–5
Hong Xingjian, Li Jinchang (2007) Review of methods for measuring polarization and polarized Chinese residents' income. Econ Res 11
Hou Shi'an (2000) Study on give-and-take relation between farmers and the state. Agric Econ Issue 6
Hu Heli (1989) Estimating Chinese rent value in 1988. Economic and Social Systems Comparison 5
Hu Yongtai (1998) Chinese TFP: important role of labor redistribution in farming sectors. Econ Res 3
Hu Zuguang (2004) Study on the optimal value of Gini coefficient and its simplified computation formula. Econ Res 9
Huang Taiyan, Wang Jiangui (1999) Viewing policy option of expanding domestic demand from the perspective of urban–rural inequality. Macro-Econ Res 6
Irfan M (1986) Migration and development in Pakistan: some selected issues. Pakistan Dev Rev 25 (4):743–753
Jalan J, Ravallion M (1998) Transient poverty in postreform rural China. J Comp Econ 26:338–357
Jalan J, Ravallion M (2001) Behavioral responses to risk in rural China. J Dev Econ 66:23–49
Jenkins S (1988) Calculating income distribution indices from micro-data. Natl Tax J 41 (1):139–142
Jha R (2004) Modern Public Economics (trans. By Wang Pu et al). China Youth Press, Beijing
Jia Shaohua (2002) Analysis of Chinese tax loss measurement and policy response. Fin Trade Econ 4
Jiang Aiqun (2005) Research on small loan performance. Chin Agron Bull 21(11)
Johnson W, Kitamura Y, Neal D (2000) Evaluating a simple method for estimating black–white gaps in median wages. Am Econ Rev 90(2):339–343
Jolliffe D (2004) The Impact of education in rural Ghana: examining household labor allocation and returns on and off the farm. J Dev Econ 73:287–314
Kabra KN (1997) Urbanization, migration and poverty: some recent debates and their policy implications. Asia-Pacific J Rural Dev 7(2):81–95
Kakwani NC (1974) A note on the efficient estimation of the new measures of income inequality. Econometrica 42(3):597–600
Kakwani NC (1977) Application of Lorenz curve in economic analysis. Econometrica 45(3): 719–727
Kakwani NC (1980a) Income inequality and poverty methods of estimation and policy applications. Oxford University Press, London
Kakwani NC (1980b) Functional forms for estimating the Lorenz curve: a reply. Econometrica 48(4):1063–1064
Kakwani NC (1993) Poverty and economic growth with application to côte d'ivoire. Rev Income Wealth Series 39(2):121–139
Kakwani NC, Podder N (1973) On the estimation of Lorenz curves from grouped observations. Int Econ Rev 14(2):278–292
Kakwani NC, Podder N (1976) Efficient estimation of the Lorenz curve and associated inequality measures from grouped observations. Econometrica 44(1):137–148

Kanbur R, Zhang Xiaobo (2003) Fifty years of regional inequality in china: a journey through central planning, reform and openness. Paper prepared for the UNU/WIDER project conference on spatial inequality in Asia

Keith B. Griffin (1984) Institutional reform and economic development in the Chinese countryside, M.E. Sharpe.

Khan AR (1993) Sources of income inequality in post-reform China. China Econ Rev 4(1):19–35

Khan, Azizur Rahman (1999) The analysis of Chinese poverty during reform and development. In: Zhao Renwei, Li Shi, Riskin Carl (1999) Re-research on income distribution of Chinese residents. Chinese Financial and Economic Press, Beijing

Khan, Riskin (1998) Income and inequality in China: composition, distribution and growth of household income, 1988 to 1995. China Q 154:221–253

Khan A, Riskin C (2001) Inequality and poverty in China in the age of globalization. Oxford University Press, New York

Knight J, Song Lina (1993) The spatial contribution to income inequality in rural China. Camb J Econ 17(2):195–213

Knight John, Song Lina (1996) Migration, rural industry, or farming: Chinese peasant choices. Paper presented at the international conference on the flow of rural labor in China, Beijing, June

Kondor Y (1971) An old-new measure of income inequality. Econometrica 39(6):1041–1042

Kung JK (2002) Off-farm labor markets and emergence of rental markets in rural China. J Comp Econ 30:395–414

Kuznets (1995) Economic growth and income inequality. Am Econ Rev 45(1):1–28

Lerman RI, Yitzhaki S (1985) Income inequality effects by income source: a new approach and applications to the United States. Rev Econ Stat 67:151–156

Levine DB, Singer NM (1970) The mathematical relation of between the income density function and the measurement of income inequality. Econometrica 38(2):324–330

Levy MB, Wadycki WJ (1974) Education and the decision to migrate: an econometric analysis of migration in Venezuela. Econometrica 42(2):377–387

Lewis WA (1954) Economic development with unlimited supplies of labour. Manch Sch Econ Soc 22:139–191

Li Shi (1999) Chinese rural labor flow and income rise and distribution. Chin Soc Sci 2

Li Shi (2001) Female labor force behavior study in rural China. Shanghai Econ Rev 38–46

Li Chaolin (2000) Upgrading the quality of rural human resource is fundamental to increase rural residents' income. Contemp Econ Stud 11

Li Chengrui (1986) The statistic report about recent economic policy and situation of residents' consumption and income. Stat Res (1):1–11

Li Qiang (2003) Analysis on push-and-pull force of Chinese population flow. Chin Soc Sci 1

Li Shi (2004) Survey on urban–rural inequality. Towns and Villages Tribune 4

Li Chungen (2006) Fiscal, farmer's burden and government legitimacy—an explanation for rural taxes and charges reform. Shanxi Fin Econ Univ J 3

Li Defu, Huang Jiuli (2006) Influence of structural impact and transformation on Chinese regional inequality dynamics. Nankai Econ Res 1

Li Xueqin, Li Xuehui (1999) Record of anti-corruption in New China. Nankai University Press, Tianjin

Li Yifu, Cai Fang, Li Zhou (1998) Analysis on Chinese regional gap in a transit economy. Econ Res 6

Li Shantong et al (2004) Chinese regional gap: history, current position and future. Reform 5

Li Ruifen, He Meili, Guo Aiyun (2006) Rural labor transfer: scenario and policy. Chinese Agriculture Press, Beijing

Liberati P (2003) Poverty reducing reforms and subgroup consumption dominance curves. Rev Income Wealth 49(4):589–601

Lin Yuhong, Sun Zhijun (2003) Education, income and labor market experience in underdeveloped regions—a study based on urban Chifang in Innermongolia. Manage World 9
Lin Yifu et al (1998) The analysis of regional inequality during the period of economy transition. Econ Res J (6):3–10
Lin Yifu, Cai Fang, Li Zhou (1994) China's miracle: development strategy and economy reform. Shanghai Sanlian Bookshop and Shanghai People Press, Shanghai
Lin Yifu, Cai Fang, Li Zhou (1999) Chinese miracle: development strategy and economic reform. Shanghai & Sanlian Press, Shanghai
Lipton M (1982) Migration from rural areas of poor countries: the impact on rural productivity and income distribution. In: Sabot RH (ed) Migration and the labor market in developing countries. Westview press, Boulder, CO, pp 191–228
Li Shi, Wei Zhong, Gustafsson (1999) Distribution of wealth among urban and township households in China. Econ Res J (3):16–23
Li Shi, Yue Ximing (2004) The investigation of income gap between urban and rural China. China Commer (6):9–10
Li Shi, Zhao Renwei (1999) Re-research on income distribution of Chinese residents. Econ Res J (4):3–17
Li Yonghui, Xiu Zerui (2005) How did the housing reform in urban China impact the income distribution. Contemp Econ Res (5):45–48
Liu Jianjin (1997) An empirical study on farmers equation and agricultural surplus labors. Chin Rural Econ 6
Liu Jiping (2000) Poverty relief on small loan in China: accomplishment, problems and countermeasure. Econ Issue 5
Liu Jianjin (2001) Position of Chinese rural labors' employment and flow 1997–1998 (Chinese rural development report 2). Social Sciences Documents Press, Beijing
Liu Jinquan, Zhang Ailian (2003) The stage of economic growth and implementation the overall well-off society. Soc Sci Front (2):169–173
Liu Naiquan (2005a) Influence of labor flow on regional economic growth. Shanghai Finance and Economy Press, Shanghai
Liu Zhiqiang (2005b) Institution and inequality: the *hukou* system in China. J Comp Econ 33:133–157
Liu Lanhuan, Tian Pingfeng, Wei Zhimin (2004) Issues of fiscal investment policy in rural fundamental education and countermeasure. Econ Manage 2
Liu Xiaming, Wei Yingqi, Li Guoping (2004) Centralization or decentralization?—literature review of Chinese regional economic growth debate. Econ Res 7
Lu Ding (2002) Sectoral factor reallocation and productivity growth: recent trends in the Chinese economy. J Econ Dev 27(2):95–111
Luo Chuliang (2004) The development factors and reform factors for income gaps of urban resident. Shanghai Econ Rev (1):20–27
Ma Jiujie (2001) Agricultural and rural industrial structure adjustment and change of farmers' income inequality. Reform 6
Ma Guoqiang, Su ming, Shi Aihu (1994) A study on Chinese farmers' income. Guizhou People's Press, Guiyang
Martić L (1970) A geometrical note on new income inequality measures. Econometrica 38(6):936–937
Martin Ravallion, Chen Shaohua (2004) How have the world's poorest fared since the early 1980s? World Bank Res Obs 19(2):141–170
Matsuyama K (1992) A simple model of sectoral adjustment. Rev Econ Stud 59(2):375–387
Maurer-Fazio M (1999) Earnings and education in China's transition to market economy: evidence from 1989 to 1992. China Econ Rev 10:17–40
Metcalf CE (1969) The size distribution of personal income during the business cycle. Am Econ Rev 59(4):657–668

Mo Ziping, Wu Wenliang (2004) Farmers' income rise and rural labor transfer. Heilingjiang Agricultural Information Website, May 11

Moody C (2006) Migration and economic growth: a 21st century perspective. New Zealand Treasury Working Paper, 06/02

Morduch Jonathan, Sicular Terry (2000) Politics, growth, and inequality in rural China: does it pay to join the party? J Public Econ 77(1):331–356

Morrison CJ, Schwartz AE (1996a) State infrastructure and productive performance. Am Econ Rev 86(5):1095–1111

Morrison CJ, Schwartz AE (1996b) Public infrastructure, private input demand, and economic performance in New England manufacturing. J Bus Econ Stat 14(1):91–101

Nong Zhu, Xubei Luo (2006) Nonfarm activity and rural income inequality: a case study of two provinces in China. World Bank policy research working paper, January

Pan Wenqing (1999) Efficient measurement on Chinese rural surplus labor transfer. Stat Study 4

Park A, Wang Sangui (2001) China's poverty statistics. China Econ Rev 12:384–398

Podder N (1993) The disaggregation of the Gini coefficient by factor components and its application to Australia. Rev Income Wealth 39(1):51–61

Podder, Tran-Nam (1991) Use and abuse of the decomposition of Gini index by factor components. The University of New South Wales, Mimeo

Podder Nripesh, Mukhopadhaya Pundarik (2001) The changing pattern of sources of income and its impact on inequality: the method and its application to Australia, 1975–94. Econ Rec 77 (238):242–251

Poirson H (2000) Factor reallocation and growth in developing countries. IMF Working Paper 0094

Poirson H (2001) The impact of intersectoral labour reallocation on economic growth. J Afr Econ 10(1):37–63

Human Resources Institute National Planning Commission (1995) Changes in personal income of urban residents and adjustment policies in recent years. Manage World 2:163–172

Pyatt G (1976) On the interpretation and disaggregation of Gini coefficients. Econ J 86(342):243–255

Pyatt G, Round JI (1979) Accounting and fixed price multipliers in a social accounting matrix framework. Econ J 89:850–873, December

Pyatt G, Chen C-n, Fei J (1980) The distribution of income by factor components. Q J Econ 95 (3):451–473

Qian Huakun (2005) Forgotten area by social security—brief analysis on rural social security. Social Observation 9

Qin Hailin (2006) Spending structural difference between rural households and their income distribution. Fin Econ Sci 11

Ranis G, Fei JCH (1961) A theory of economic development. Am Econ Rev LI 4:533–565

Rao VM (1969) Two decomposition of concentration ratio. J R Stat Soc Series A 132(3):418–425

Rasche RH (1980) Functional forms for estimating the Lorenz curve. Econometrica 48(4):1061–1062

Ravallion M (2001) Growth, inequality and poverty: looking beyond average. World Dev 29:1803–1815

Ren Caifag, Cheng Xuetin (1996) Distribution of revenues from the gap between urban residents. Rev Econ Res F7:2–9

Ren Caifang, Cheng Xuebin (1996) Urban residents' income distribution and income gap. Rev Econ Res (7):2–9

Rizov M, Swinnen JFM (2004) Human capital, market imperfection, and labor reallocation in transition. J Comp Econ 32:745–774

Robertson PE (1998) Growth accounting, growth theory and the East Asian miracle. Working Paper, University of New South Wales

Robinson Sherman (1976) A note on the U hypothesis relating income inequality and economic development. Am Econ Rev 66(3):437–440

Rozelle S (1994) Rural industrialization and inequality: emerging patterns in china's reforming economy. J Comp Econ 19(3):362–391
Rozelle S (1996) Stagnation without equity: patterns of growth and inequality in China's rural economy. China Journal 35:63–96
Ru Xin (2003) Analysis on Chinese social situation and forecast. Chinese Social Sciences Documents Press, Beijing
Salem ABZ, Mount TD (1974) A convenient descriptive model of income distribution: the gamma density. Econometrica 42(6):1115–1127
Satya Paul (2004) Income sources effects on inequality. J Dev Econ 73(1):435–451
Sen A (1976) Poverty: an ordinal approach to measurement. Econometrica 44(2):219–231
Sha Zhifang, Sun Jingliang (2004) The promotion industrialization of special agriculture of Yang Zhou. Macroeconomics (2):30–33
Shen Baifu, Wang Hong (2003) Completion rate of Chinese compulsory education and funding problem. Educ Dev Res 11
Shorrock AF (1984) Inequality decomposition by population subgroups. Econometrica 52(6):1369–1385
Shorrock AF (1995) Revisiting the sen poverty index. Econometrica 63(5):1225–1230
Shorrocks AF (1982) Inequality decomposition by factor component. Econometrica 50(1):193–211
Shorrocks AF (1983) The impact of income components on the distribution of family incomes. Q J Econ 98(2):311–326
Shujie Yao (1999) Economic growth, income inequality and poverty in China under economic reforms. J Dev Stud 35(6):104–130
Simon HA (1955) On a class of skew distribution functions. Biometrika 42(3/4):425–440
Simon HA, Bonini CP (1958) The size distribution firms. Am Econ Rev 48(4):607–617
Singh SK, Maddala GS (1976) A function for size distribution of incomes. Econometrica 44(5):963–969
Singh SK, Maddala GS (1978) A function for size distribution of incomes: reply. Econometrica 46(2):461
Skeldon R (1997) Rural–urban migration and its implication for poverty alleviation. Asia-Pac Popul J 12(1):3–16
Son HH (2003) A new poverty decomposition. J Econ Inequality, August:181–187
Stark O (1984) Rural to urban migration in LDCs: a relative deprivation approach. Econ Dev Cult Change 32(3):475–486
Sundrum RM (1990) Income distribution in less developed countries. Routledge, London
Su Ming (2002) Research on fiscal backup policy for Chinese rural fundamental education. Econ Res Ref 25
Sun Wenxiang, Zhang Zhichao (2004) Impact of fiscal expense on economic growth and social equity. Shanghai Fin Econ Univ J 6
Sun Tanzhen, Zhou Gang (1993) Fiscal analysis outside Chinese towns and villages. Econ Res 9
Tan Chongtai (1999) New development of development economics. Wuhan University Press, Wuhan
Tang Zhong (1999) Comparative study on rural land system. Chinese Agricultural Technology Press, Beijing
Tang Ping (2006) The analysis of rural residents' income inequality change and its factors. Manage World (5):69–75
Tang Ping, Lai Weining (2001) Impact of township enterprises development on farmers' income rise. Investig Res World 2
Temple J, Wößmann L (2004) Dualism and cross-country growth regressions. Discussion Paper, No 04/560
Thorbecke E, Jung H-S (1996) A multiplier decomposition method to analyze poverty alleviation. J Dev Econ 48:279–300
Tsui KY (1993) Decomposition of China's regional inequality. J Comp Econ 17:600–627

Tsui KY (1996) Economic reform and interprovincial inequality. J Dev Econ 50:353–368
Tsui KY (1998a) Factor decomposition of Chinese rural income inequality: new methodology, empirical findings and policy implication. J Comp Econ 26:502–528
Tsui KY (1998b) Trends and inequalities of rural welfare in China: evidence from rural households in Guangdong and Sichuan. J Comp Econ 26:783–804
Urban Social Economic Survey Division of SBS (2006) Hot issues of Chinese urban social economy. Chinese Statistics Press, Beijing
van de Ven J, Greedy J, Lambert PJ (2001) Close equals and calculation of the vertical horizontal and reranking effects of taxation. Oxford B Econ Stat 63(3):381–394
Walder AG (2002) Income determination and market opportunity in rural China, 1978–1996. J Comp Econ 30(3):54–375
Wan Anpei (1995) Investigation into dynamics of rent size. Econ Res 2
Wan Anpei (1998) Another investigation into dynamics of rent size. Econ Res 7
Wang Zhuo (1997) Practice and thinking of poverty relief on petty credits. Rural Econ 11
Wang Xiyu (2000) China's flow of rural labor force under dual structure and policymaking. Manage World 5
Wang Jiangui, Ding Shouhai (2005) How many rural surplus labors in China? Chin Soc Sci 5
Wang Xiaolu, Fan Gang (2004) Chinese regional gap: trend of change and drivers for 20 years. Economic Science Press, Beijing
Wang Hongchun, Luan Yisheng (2004) Economic analysis on Chinese migrant workers boom. Chinese Business Press, Beijing
Wang Feng, Zuo Xuejin (1999) History's largest labor flow: understanding China's rural migration inside China's cities: institutional barriers and opportunities for urban migrants. Am Econ Rev 89(2):276–280
Wang Zhigang, Gong Liutang, Chen Yuyu (2006) Decomposing productivity across regions and TFP Rise Rate 1978–2003. Chin Soc Sci 2
Wei Houkai (1996) Regional income difference in rural areas. Econ Res 8
Wei Zhong, Gustafsson B (1999) Analysis on dynamics of poverty in transitional China. In: Zhao Renwei, Li Shi, Riskin K (eds) Income distribution in economic reform and growth: a second study on china's income distribution. Chinese Fiscal and Economic Press, Beijing
Wei Houkai, Liu Kai (1994) Analysis on Chinese regional difference dynamics and forecast. Chin Ind Econ Res 3
Wei Jei, Tan Wei (2003) Seeing insufficient effectual demand from income inequality. Fin Trade Econ 6
Williamson JG (1991) Inequality, poverty, and history: the Kuznets memorial lectures of the economic growth center, Yale University. Basil Blackwell, Cambridge
World Bank (1992) China: strategies for reducing poverty in the 1990s. World Bank, Washington, DC
World Bank (1993) The East Asian miracle: economic growth and public policy. Oxford University Press, London
World Bank (1997) Sharing rising income: disparities in China, China 2020 Series. World Bank, Washington, DC
Wu Xiaohua (2002) Reform land regime to increase farmers' income. Reform 2
Wu Xinglu, Yuan Mingjie (2005) Probe into social and cultural factors of migrant workers transfer policy. Chin Rural Econ 1
Xiang Shujian (1998a) Calculation and regression of the Gini index in China. Theory Pract Finance Econ 1:75–80
Xiang Shujian, Lili (1998b) Dynamics research of China urban–rural income gap. J Hebei Univ Econ Trade (6):30–34
Ximing Wu, Jeffrey M. Perloff (2005) China income distribution, 1985–2001. Rev Econ Stat 87 (4):763–775
Xin Meng (2004) Economic restructuring and income distribution, 1985–2001. Rev Econ Stat 87 (4):763–775
Xiong Siyuan (2001) A study on Yunnan rural labor flow and human resource exploit. Econ Issues 1

Xiong Deping (2005) Petty loans in countryside: mode, practice and enlightenment. Fin Econ Theory Pract 3
Xue Junmin (2003) Rural labor transfer and equity and efficiency of rural economy. Fin Econ Res 4
Xue Shougang, Zhou Yunbo (2005) The major factors which cause the income inequality of in China's urban residents-a case analysis of the population characters in Tianjin. Nankai Econ Stud (3):42–47
Yang DT (1997a) China's land arrangements and rural labor mobility. China Econ Rev 8(2):101–106
Yang Jun et al (2006) The analysis of the level of financial development and income distribution, Econ Sci 2:23–33
Yang DT (1997b) Education and off-farm work. Econ Dev Cult Change 45(3):613–632
Yao Yang (2000) China's land regime and rural social security. Chin Soc Sci Q (Hong Kong), for Autumn
Yao Yang (2000) China's land regime: an analytical framework. Chin Soc Sci 2
Yao Zhizhong, Zhou Sufang (2003) Labor flow and regional gap. World Econ 4
Yao Shujie, Zhang Zongyi, Hanmer L (2004) Growing inequality and poverty in China. China Econ Rev 15:145–163
You Hongbing (1998) The research of China's income distribution. China Economics Press
Yue Ximeng (1999) Income transfer and regional income inequality. Manage World 6
Yu Zuyao (1998) Political economics analysis of upstarts groups in transition period. Econ Res J 2:70–79
Zeng Yinchu (2005) Rural surplus labor transfer and dual economy transformation. In: Ji Baocheng (ed) Economic growth report by Chinese people's university: the "three farming" issues in urban–rural coordinated development. Chinese People's University Press, Beijing
Zhang Ping (1992) Chinese rural income inequality across regions. Econ Res 2
Zhang Ping (1996) Poverty reduction and development of border farms. China Soft Sci (7):53–58
Zhang Ping (1998) China's rural residents inter-regional income inequality and non-agricultural employment. Econ Res J (8):59–66
Zhang Weidong (1994) Drivers of farmers' income rise. Economist 6
Zhang Ping (1999) Chinese rural income inequality across regions and non-farming employment. In: Zhao Renwei, Li Shi, Riskin K (eds) Income distribution in economic reform and growth: a second study on china's income distribution. Chinese Fiscal and Economic Press, Beijing
Zhang Gongping (2003) Not a petty problem—farmers' small loan in China. Bankers 2
Zhang Yulin (2004) A decade's education investment and current educational crisis in countryside, http://www.ccrs.org.cn/, 18th March 2004
Zhang Lijun, Zhan Yong (2006) China rural financial development influence on urban–rural income gap. Finance Econ (4):53–60
Zhang Zongyi, Zou Chang (2006) Chinese regional inequality across time and space. Contemp Econ Sci 1
Zhang Linxiu, Huang Jikun, Rozelle S (2001a) Off-farm jobs and on farm work in periods of boom and bust in rural China. J Comp Econ 29:505–526
Zhang Linxiu, Rozelle S, Huang Jinkun (2001b) Off-farm jobs and on-farm work in periods of boom and bust in rural China. J Comp Econ 29:505–526
Zhang Zhongfa et al (2001) Rural labor transfer: progress, features and new challenge. Econ Res Ref 3
Zhang Linxiu, Huang Jikun, Rozelle S (2002) Employment, emerging labor markets, and the role of education in rural China. China Econ Rev 13:313–328
Zhang Qi, He Fan, Liu Mingxing (2003) Financial liberalization, policy consistent and the financial frangibility: theoretical frames and empirical evidence. World Econ (12):3–13
Zhao Renwei (1999) Re-research on income distribution of Chinese residents. Chinese Public Finance and Economy press, Beijing
Zhao Renwei, Griffin K (1994) The research on income distribution of Chinese residents. Chinese Social Science Press, Beijing

Zhao Renwei, Li Shi, Carl Riskin (1999) Re-research on income distribution of Chinese residents. Chinese Financial and Economic Press, Beijing

Zhao Yaohui (1999a) Leaving the countryside: rural-to-urban migration decision in China. Am Econ Rev 89(2):281–286

Zhao Y (1999b) Labor migration and earnings differences: the case of rural China. Econ Dev Cult Change 47(4):767–82

Zhao Yaohui (2002) Causes and consequences of return migration: recent evidence from China. J Comp Econ 30(2):376–394

Zhao Limei (2004) Comparative study on petty loan in China and Bangladesh. Rural Econ 12

Zhao Xiaobiao (2004) Viewing unbalanced growth of non-public economy in Eastern and Western China in light of social capital. Prod Res 11

Zhao Zong (2006) Analysis on rural emigrant and economy. In: Cai Fang, Bai Nansheng (eds) Labor flow in transitional economy. Social Sciences Documents Press, Beijing

Zhao Renwei, Li Shi, Riskin K (eds) (1999) Income distribution in economic reform and growth: a second study on China's income distribution. Chinese Fiscal and Economic Press, Beijing

Zheng Buhong (1994) Can a poverty index be both relative and absolute? Econometrica 62(6):1453–1458

Zhou Yunbo (2004) China's rural dual economy transformation and its impact on residents' income inequality. Economist 1

Zhou Wenxing (2002) Empirical analysis on the relationship of urban income inequality and economic growth. Econ Sci (1):40–47

Zhu Ling (1992) The influence of the non-farm activity to the rural residents' income distribution. Econ Res J (3):23–30

Zhu Ling (2000) Government and its adoption of rural basic medical and health security system. Chin Soc Sci 4

Zhu Ling (2003) To create employment opportunities for farmers by welfare-to-work in combination with grain-for-green. Forestry and Society 4

Zhu Nong, Luo Xubei (2006) Nonfarm activity and rural income inequality: a case study of two provinces in China, World Bank Policy Research Working Paper, January

Zhuang Longde (2002) Basic features of rural surplus labor transfer in Shanghai and follow-up policy. Shanghai Stat 2

Zou Xiaojuan, Zhang Zhi (2004) On the function of welfare-to-work in current rural poverty relief. Inf Fin Econ Polit Law 2

MIX
Papier aus verantwortungsvollen Quellen
Paper from responsible sources
FSC® C105338

If you have any concerns about our products,
you can contact us on
ProductSafety@springernature.com

In case Publisher is established outside the EU,
the EU authorized representative is:
Springer Nature Customer Service Center GmbH
Europaplatz 3, 69115 Heidelberg, Germany

Printed by Libri Plureos GmbH
in Hamburg, Germany